THE AUTHENTIC WRITER

ENGLISH RHETORIC
AND COMPOSITION

THE AUTHENTIC WRITER

ENGLISH RHETORIC AND COMPOSITION

JAMES M. MELLARD
Northern Illinois University

JAMES C. WILCOX
Boston University

D. C. HEATH AND COMPANY
LEXINGTON, MASSACHUSETTS   TORONTO

ACKNOWLEDGMENTS

A. ALVAREZ, from "A Visit with Ingmar Bergman." *New York Times Magazine*, December 7, 1975. © 1975 by The New York Times Company. Reprinted by permission.

AL CALLOWAY, from "An Introduction to Soul." *Esquire*, April 1968. Reprinted by permission.

WILLIAM FAULKNER, from "The Bear." *Three Famous Short Novels*. New York: Random House, Inc., 1958. Reprinted by permission.

PETER KLAPPERT, from "Let Them Eat Wonderbread." *The Saturday Review*, October 7, 1972. Reprinted by permission.

STEPHEN KOCH, from "The Guilty Sex."*Esquire*, July 1975. Reprinted by permission.

MELVIN MADDOCKS, from "The Limitations of Language" (March 8, 1971), and from "The Message of History's Biggest Happening" (August 29, 1969). Reprinted by permission from TIME, The Weekly Newsmagazine; Copyright Time Inc.

MARSHALL McLUHAN, from "Classroom Without Walls" and "Five Sovereign Fingers Taxed The Breath." *Explorations in Communication*, edited by Edmund Carpenter and Marshall McLuhan. Boston: Beacon Press, 1960. Reprinted by permission.

ROBERT M. PIRSIG, from *Zen and the Art of Motorcycle Maintenance*. Abridged by permission of William Morrow & Co., Inc., from *Zen and the Art of Motorcycle Maintenance* by Robert M. Pirsig. Copyright © 1974 by Robert M. Pirsig.

ADRIENNE RICH, from "When We Dead Awaken: Writing as Re-Vision." *Adrienne Rich's Poetry* edited by Barbara Gelpi and Albert Gelpi. New York: W.W. Norton, 1975. Reprinted by permission of the National Council of Teachers of English. Originally appeared in *College English* in 1971.

CAROL SALINE, from "Blame It on Your Biorhythms." *Boston Magazine*, June 1974. Reprinted by permission.

PAUL SIMON, from "The Sounds of Silence." © 1964 Paul Simon. Used with the permission of the publisher.

JEAN STAFFORD, from "The Plight of the American Language." *Saturday Review/World*, December 4, 1973. Reprinted by permission.

WALLACE STEVENS, from "Peter Quince at the Clavier." *The Collected Poems of Wallace Stevens*. New York: Alfred A. Knopf, 1954. Reprinted by permission.

WILLIAM STYRON, from *The Confessions of Nat Turner*. New York: Random House, Inc., 1967. Reprinted by permission.

ROBERT WUTHNOW and CHARLES Y. GLOCK, from "God In The Gut." *psychology today*, November 1974. Reprinted by permission.

We also wish to thank the following students for allowing us to reprint their material: Sally Baldwin, Robert Murphy, William Shields, and Kimberly V. Weeks.

For
Tandy, Cynthia, and *Catherine*
Gary, Bret, and *Karin*

↪ PREFACE ↩

Every teacher of rhetoric and composition holds to some theory of how writing should be taught. Our feeling is that, although it should be taught systematically, the *system* should make the writer aware not only of the practical aspects of writing but also of the cultural and philosophical milieu in which he or she lives. This means that the discipline called *rhetoric,* or the principles surrounding effective composition and speech, should effect a balance between the commitment we have for others and for ourselves. The balance to be struck, in short, is between an objective, pragmatic concern for our audience and a subjective, expressive concern for ourselves. When these two responsibilities—audience and self—are realized and fulfilled, we can say the writer is being "authentic." *The Authentic Writer* attempts to show students how they can effectively balance these two concerns.

We have thus thought of the book as being divided into three parts. Chapter 1 introduces our basic conceptual framework and concerns itself with a general understanding of language and its relation to us in our daily lives. Our concerns in this chapter are essentially with the forms of writing identified with self-expression, and we focus upon the largely self-oriented activity of journal-keeping. We believe that, if students or anyone else keep a journal for any length of time, their writing will improve and they will become better able to adjust to the continuing, often contradictory, demands of the self and the world outside. In this portion of the book—as well as throughout—we have included excerpts from writers who effectively have employed modes of self-expression in prose and, occasionally, poetry.

Chapters 2, 3, and 4 introduce our theory of rhetoric and consider how writers can move from self-expression to the discursive forms of communication that permit us to fulfill our obligations to others. Herein we concern ourselves with matters of *audience, substance, structure,* and *style*. Our discussions and illustrations—and often the excerpts—attempt to make clear what the available choices are in these rhetorical areas. In these chapters, as throughout the entire book, we try to make clear that we all make rhetorical decisions in every form of our communication—written, spoken, or gestural.

Chapter 5 provides a conclusion showing some of the implications for the writer who stresses the oral dimensions of language. Moreover, since Marshall McLuhan, Walter Ong, and others have made us aware of the impact of other communications media on perception and reality, we have tried to extend the student's understanding of rhetoric into media such as television and film.

Throughout the text we have suggested writing assignments to help students with particular aspects of rhetoric. But we also feel that one of the obligations we have as teachers of *writing* is to acknowledge that students do all sorts of writing, usually under assignments from others, in disciplines other than literature and the arts. We have thus offered suggestions for writing assignments that touch on many different fields of study. We want the student to understand full well that the principles of rhetoric apply to all forms of communication—in essay examinations, research papers, journal entries, letters home, or whatever.

Finally, we insist that rhetoric is a subject that can make the student aware of the interdisciplinary nature of all learning. The study of the principles of rhetoric will aid the student in all studies, for rhetoric is not a narrow discipline. It is a subject incorporating philosophy, psychology, history, linguistics, literature, and the arts. Whenever possible, therefore, we have tried to establish the interrelatedness of the various subjects and to dramatize the interdisciplinary quality of rhetoric by inserting into the text excerpted quotations from various sources. Many of these excerpts establish a counterpoint to our own stated position, but most provide parallel or substantiating statements. In all cases, however, the excerpted quotations can be used as examples employing a variety of rhetorical principles. Above all, they represent our attempt to make rhetoric the focus of an interdisciplinary approach to composition and communication.

✎ CONTENTS ✎

LANGUAGE:
AN INTRODUCTION

*No matter how carelessly or how viciously man
abuses the language he has inherited, he simply cannot
live without it. Even Woodstock Nation cannot survive
on an oral diet of grunts and expletives. Mankind
craves definition as he craves lost innocence. He simply does
not know what his life means until he says it.
Until the day he dies he will grapple with
mystery by trying to find the word for it.
"The limits of my language," Ludwig Wittgenstein observed,
"are the limits of my world." Man's purifying
motive is that he cannot let go
of the Adam urge to name things — and
finally, out of his unbearable solitude, to
pronounce to others his own identity.*

MELVIN MADDOCKS
"The Limitations of Language"
(1971)

LANGUAGE AND THE AUTHENTIC WRITER

We are choking on a cloud of verbal pollution that envelops us every day of our lives. It affects us perhaps most dramatically where it hits our pocketbooks and our governance: in the slick jargon of Madison Avenue advertising agencies and the carefully screened oblique language of public officials. To examine these sources of language pollution carefully is to realize that our sense of reality is being manipulated. We must all manipulate words, but we are apparently at the mercy of those con men who deliberately misuse words in order to hide or corrupt the essential truth about experience. All too often we fall in with their plans, and by our acquiescence we seem to approve the motives that lie behind them. Why? Russell Baker, a columnist for the *New York Times*, would suggest that the reason lies in a wedding of language and public morality: "Americans don't like plain talk anymore. Nowadays they like fat talk. Show them a lean, plain word that cuts to the bone and watch them lard it with thick greasy syllables front and back until it wheezes and gasps for breath as it comes lumbering down upon some poor threadbare sentence like a sack of iron on a swayback horse." This attitude toward language, Baker suggests, may well be at the center of our national values, for it represents an attempt "to conceal a thinness of the spirit" from which the words originate. We don't lie anymore, but we do make statements that become "inoperative."

One of the most obvious sources of "fat" or polluted language in recent years has been the government. During the Vietnam War, for example, the American public was issued communiques that deliberately created a smokescreen to obscure the cruel facts of the war. Activities such as bombing missions or air raids became "limited duration protective reaction strikes"; defoliation became "resources control program"; refugee camps became "new life hamlets"; napalm became "selective ordinance"; and even the withdrawal of troops became hidden in the process called "Vietnamization." This kind of language, according to George Orwell in his essay "Politics and the English Language," ". . . is designed to make lies sound truthful and murder respectable, and to give an appearance of solidity to pure wind." The results, Orwell suggests, are "imaginary solutions to imaginary problems of imaginary

What do existential writers mean when they speak of inauthenticity? What do Zen authors refer to with terms such as "the dual mode"? In my opinion, they are referring to the tendency to treat oneself as an object, a tool to be manipulated in ways thought necessary to bring about popularity, vocational success, power, and similar goals. When one treats oneself as a tool or as a thing, one treats others in the same way. This objectifying of the self is accompanied by self-concealment, or the repression of one's being and experiencing. This, in turn, results in what has been called self-alienation. A self-alienated person, among other things, does not know what he needs to sustain the wellness of his organism. He is desensitized to his experiencing, and hence will not recognize early warning signals that all is not well.

— Sidney M. Jourard, *The Transparent Self* (1964)

people." The method of those who use such language is simply to remove the human dimension inherent in the acts described. Inevitably, language that deliberately conceals the fact that human beings are involved has a dehumanizing effect.

The general effect on us of the widespread pollution of language is a desensitization to the very meaning and significance of communication. In *The Flood*, a novel by J. M. G. Le Clezio, the protagonist suffers from an overexposure to words. Even when he is walking down the street, his mind reels under the deluge of newsprint (PLANE CRASH AT TEL AVIV), instructions (WALK — DON'T WALK), and threats (TRESPASSERS WILL BE PROSECUTED). Eventually, he becomes numb, and neither written nor oral language has any effect on him: his verbal catatonia is his last resistance to the cacophony of language. Paul Simon in his lyrics from "The Sound of Silence" describes the end result:

> And in the naked light I saw
> Ten thousand people maybe more,
> People talking without speaking,
> People hearing without listening,
> People writing songs that voices never share
> And no one dares disturb the sound of silence.

What Le Clezio's hero feels and Paul Simon's lyrics reveal is what we are experiencing as a culture. The breakdown of communication, our realization that words are masking rather than revealing reality, and our flight from words, all suggest how limited a view we now have of language. Yet it is *language* that virtually all thinkers regard as our most human characteristic.

The pervasive abuse of language in our society creates a problem for all of us in our attempts to understand experience and self. The limitations imposed on language — to use an ancient metaphor revived by James Joyce — form a labyrinth from which most of us instinctively desire to escape. To escape the maze, Joyce shows us, is to gain a perspective both of self and the world. Our "escape" from the misuses of language is made possible by knowledge of how language functions in the processes by which self and the outer self are created. It is primarily through language that we are united with family, community, country, and even the universe at large. That is the theme of Joyce's Stephen Dedalus, who in *A Portrait of the Artist as a Young Man* writes in his geography book:

> Stephen Dedalus
> Class of Elements
> Clongowes Wood College
> Sallins
> County Kildare
> Ireland
> Europe
> The World
> The Universe

As a young man, Stephen is fascinated by words, phrases, and language rhythms, and, like Joyce, he is convinced he will find his place (a self) in the scheme of existence if he can find the right words. Thus, the impetus of the novel's first chapter is toward Stephen's gaining mastery of language and, consequently, self and reality. The relationships he lists in his book may encompass our external reality, the reality that gives experiential contexts to our lives, but our understanding of them comes less through experience than through language. In a very broad sense, as Joyce's Dedalus learns, our discovery of the relationships of language to reality and to self is the one *essential* discovery of the authentic person — and the authentic writer.

As in the writings of Joyce, modern science and modern philosophy reveal to us a universe that is personal for each of us because we are incapable of an *im*personal, truly objective response to it, one that is not a product of our language and our perspectives. Consequently, the authentic writer is one who begins with the assumption that he is a person speaking/writing to other persons about experiences that are also personal. He will then reveal attitudes and feelings to an audience that may, in turn, respond personally. Though *rhetoric* (as we shall explain it in

It was a long evolutionary course which the human mind had to traverse, to pass from the belief in a physico-magical power comprised in the Word to a realization of its spiritual power. Indeed, it is the Word, it is language, that really reveals to man that world which is closer to him than any world of natural objects and touches his weal and woe more directly than physical nature. For it is language that makes his existence in a community possible; and only in society, in relation to a "Thee," can his subjectivity assert itself as a "Me."

— Ernst Cassirer, *Language and Myth* (1946)

Chapter 2) cannot be avoided, the authentic writer is aware that he or she can choose a rhetorical stance that will communicate in good faith to people who truly wish to grow. Ideally, authentic writing enlarges ourselves, too, as it openly addresses itself to people who themselves are willing to be enlarged. The authentic writer wants to enrich, rather than impoverish, experience for all of us.

Authentic writing entails risk. We must be willing to reveal the experiences, the events, prejudices, and feelings that make up life. Public actions are often radically different from what we actually feel and believe. The problem of the divided self, according to the noted psychotherapist Rollo May, is the result of the loss of "the sense of self," which in turn generates a feeling of insecurity. What we tend to do as individuals and as a society is to mask our authentic selves to the point where we convince ourselves that the mask itself is reality. An extension of this dilemma, May says in *Man's Search for Himself,* is the general breakdown of personal communication in our society: "When it comes to meaningful interpersonal relations, our language is lost: we stumble, and are practically as isolated as deaf and dumb people who can only communicate in sign language."

Another psychologist, R. D. Laing, suggests that we can remedy the fragmentation of self and eliminate limitations of language by peeling off layers of social and communicative conditioning. The outer self that people present to the world, Laing says, is but an image of the role-definitions that teachers, parents, politicians, television announcers, peers, and the like have laid on them. The inner or authentic self lies somewhere beneath that image. At a symposium on contemporary magazines, an example of how absurd this conditioning process can be was offered by one of the participants: "In India, when you ask a student to describe autumn, he doesn't look out the window; instead, he describes an English autumn." The problem of conditioning that kept the

5

Indian students from describing what *they* saw is like the language problem we are experiencing in our culture. It is as if our minds have been colonized by imperial jargons.

When we are asked to communicate something about a particular subject, we try to express ourselves in vocabularies that are not really ours any more than the experiences they denote are ours. We do so because, even when we know better, we act as if *our* reality will not be acknowledged unless we use a cliché or a stereotyped notion. We know that language comes to us from others, but that is all the more reason to free ourselves from the bondage of unexamined words. We must probe into the vocabularies of racial or ethnic or religious slurs, of partisan politics, of advertising, of national, regional, or local institutional group or family "myths." You *do* have choices, which you can exercise only through knowledge, so you *can* discover who you really are, speak/write with your own voice, and become an authentic person/writer.

After discovering the *real* self, the next step for the authentic writer is to consider audience — the individual or individuals to whom we are trying to communicate. The knowledge of audience does not mean that we manipulate that audience; it *does* mean that we take into consideration rhetorical options associated with structure and style. If we are authentic and address our audience as authentic people, then the communication process becomes a way to reveal rather than conceal; in short, it becomes a humanistic process. All this can be effectively achieved through the study of rhetoric, for it is rhetoric that gives us choices of form and style that can authentically relate the self to audience.

Most artists fulfill our concept of an authentic writer, for one difference between an artist and a hack is authentic self-awareness. Poets such

---

Only when something has become problematic do we start to ask questions. Disagreement shakes us out of our slumbers and forces us to see our own point of view through contrast with another person who does not share it. But we resist such confrontations. The history of heresies of all kinds testifies to more than the tendency to break off communication (excommunication) with those who hold different dogmas or opinions; it bears witness to our intolerance of different fundamental structures of experience. We seem to need to share a communal meaning to human existence, to give with others a common sense to the world, to maintain a consensus.

— R. D. Laing, *The Politics of Experience* (1967)

as Robert Frost, William Carlos Williams, and Adrienne Rich, unlike most politicians and advertising writers, use language to reveal personal truths beneath the clichés that so often swaddle human experience. Each poet's "truth" may not be a scientific "fact"; instead, it may be a truth of feeling, such as that revealed in the lines of Frost's "Stopping by Woods on a Snowy Evening," or Rich's "Aunt Jennifer's Tigers." In these poems, the poets use all the resources of language, from its oral-aural qualities to the etymologies of words, in order to suggest that words are more than a means or a commodity on the marketplace; in their feel, shape, and sound they are part of the end in themselves. This attitude toward words, however, does not and should not rest with the poet. It will be an attitude of all writers who aspire to authenticity in their relations to self and audience.

We have tried so far to suggest that writing we would call *authentic* involves ourselves in a sensitive way with our audience (that is, by our choice of structure and style). Perhaps no dimension of our experience involves us more than our sexual roles, and in recent years much of the most searchingly honest — as well as dishonest — writing to appear in print has been by men and women trying to come to terms with old and new norms, roles, and identities. It would be possible to offer examples of open expression by those writing from the perspectives of fathers, mothers, children, husbands and wives, heterosexuals and homosexuals, as well as simply *man* and *woman*, the perspectives assumed by Adrienne Rich and Stephen Koch below. In these passages, one can see how fully and openly and at what *risk* each writer has revealed him/ herself with a particular audience in mind. Both are writing *analytical* essays, to be sure, and yet each is willing to include personal elements — details that suggest they have "paid their dues" — that bring critical analysis alive. We may or may not find it necessary or desirable to risk as

---

Poets . . . are idealists, or Edenists — or, as someone has put it, disillusioned Edenists. They are notoriously impractical, since "poetry makes nothing happen." Like politicians, poets deal in specifics, but they do so in order to shed light on the human condition in general. That is, whereas the politician is expected to use generalities to talk about specific events, poets use specific events to discover and express larger truths. Poetry talks about the inner man in the outer world and, doing so, helps us to see what is — what might be.

— Peter Klappert, "Let Them Eat Wonderbread,"
Saturday Review, October 7, 1972

much as Rich and Koch, but if we are going to become truly effective writers we must recognize that the risk is always present.

I wanted then, more than anything, the one thing of which there was never enough: time to think, time to write. The fifties and early sixties were years of rapid revelations: the sit-ins and marches in the South, the Bay of Pigs, the early anti-war movement raised large questions — questions for which the masculine world of the academy around me seemed to have expert and fluent answers. But I needed desperately to think for myself — about pacifism and dissent and violence, about poetry and society and about my own relationship to all these things. For about ten years I was reading in fierce snatches, scribbling in notebooks, writing poetry in fragments; I was looking desperately for clues, because if there were no clues then I thought I might be insane. I wrote in a notebook about this time: "Paralyzed by the sense that there exists a mesh of relationships — e.g. between my anger at the children, my sensual life, pacifism, sex (I mean sex in its broadest significance, not merely sexual desire) — an interconnectedness which, if I could see it, make it valid, would give me back myself, make it possible to function lucidly and passionately. Yet I grope in and out among these dark webs." I think I began at this point to feel that politics was not something "out there" but something "in here" and of the essence of my condition.

— Adrienne Rich, "When We Dead Awaken:
Writing as Re-vision" (1971)

Perhaps I should say that, like how many hundred thousand — how many million? — others, I too have lived in some considerable pain with every aspect (except fatherhood) of the masculine dilemma Feigen Fasteau discusses [in *The Male Machine*, 1974] — and several he does not. Like them, I too have felt mutilated, baffled and enraged by plenty of the prevalent middleclass notions of manhood. It is indeed difficult to either surrender or fulfill the desire to be recognized, loved and admired as a man; difficult to surrender or fulfill the absurd sexualized fantasy of wisdom, self-confidence, attractiveness, focus of identity, fulsomeness of love, totality of competence, personal power and success one is supposed to want. Like a million others, I have found the mystery of sexual identity baffling indeed. Like them I have known fear and pain over sexual humiliation, guilt over humiliation. I have sometimes confused and betrayed myself trying to "be a man," and likewise trying not to be. I have indeed craved, despised, and been refused entry into the great magic circle of mutual masculine approval. I have known a certain amount of self-recognition, not all of it totally false, I hope. During childhood, an all-loved, all-feared father dies young; on the baseball diamond — "he swings like a girl!" Growing up, love. Marriage. Deep dependence. Divorce. Confused and not so confused affairs ending badly or at least ending. Homosexuality. Heterosexuality. No sexuality. Some very rough romps with the muscular demons of self-destruction. Some surges of strength, some growth, some collapses in weakness. Discovery of some strength in weakness, and vice versa. Some numb cynicism. Some faith. Some failure. Some success. Some love. Some being loved. A life, in a word.

— Stephen Koch, "The Guilty Sex" (1975)

EXERCISES

In both of the above passages, the authors are searching for a meaningful pattern to their experiences. These "patterns" often have to do with finding a sexual identity. Traditionally our self-image or sexual role has been shaped by such attributes as are schematized in the following list of "male" and "female" characteristics:

Feminine	*Masculine*
passive	active
soft	hard
patient	insistent
welcoming	penetrating
private (home, family, children)	public (politics, war, work)
Yin (darkness, moon, left hand)	Yang (light, sun, right hand)
submissive	dominant
inferior	superior
emotional	logical
mystical	mythic

Circle those qualities that seem to best represent what you are as a person. Write a series of short paragraphs explaining as concretely as possible (using examples, illustrations, anecdotes, a narrative, description, and so on) how you came to recognize each of the particular qualities at a given time in your life. Obviously, the stereotypes do not always hold, so consider both lists carefully. *Or* write an essay explaining some of the roles (daughter/son, sister/brother, student, team member) you have to play. Be sure to explore both the obvious and subtle differences among the roles.

LANGUAGE AND THE INDIVIDUAL VOICE

Amidst language and external reality, where are *we*? Self and language are for the most part indistinguishable. It is through language that we establish our identity, our individuality as a person. As blacks, women, and other racial, sexual, or ethnic minorities have learned, language becomes the very fabric of our reality. If that reality is oppressive of ourselves and others, we may begin our nonviolent revolutions by altering the aspects of language we use that perpetuate such a reality. The reason is simple enough, for it relates to the ways we learn language as children. To a child, the *word* for a thing fixes the chaotic visual field and helps him or her to focus on a particular object. As the child's facility for language grows, he or she is able to group, identify, and correlate experiences, giving a sense of participation and communion that ultimately leads to a definition of self and world. The child's needs, then, remain primarily conservative and imperative. Our early perceptions of the world are a disorganized flux of sensory impressions. We feel, however, an instinctive urge to organize this flux. To regulate the flux of experience, we discover, one has only to name it. Ernst Cassirer describes the process in *An Essay on Man*:

> The first names of which a child makes conscious use may be compared to a stick by the aid of which a blind man gropes his way. And language, taken as a whole, becomes the gateway to a new world. All progress here opens a new perspective and widens and enriches our concrete experience. Eagerness and enthusiasm to talk do not originate in a mere desire for learning or using names; they mark the desire for the detection and conquest of an objective world.

Cassirer makes it plain that language becomes a tool and a weapon: it shows a new territory to the child, but it also allows him to *conquer* it. There is something both liberating and enslaving in language, but that is perhaps the last thing a child — or any of us — learns. It is the potential that language has for locking us into particular beliefs, attitudes, identities, roles, and the like which so many contemporary thinkers would have us understand fully. Blacks, women, and others have discovered that language is reality, but language *can* be changed. Ralph Ellison says, "change the joke and slip the yoke"; the feminists say, remove the sexist bias of everyday speech and open up a new reality for women. And they are right. Consequently, at the same time that we understand the freedom language gives us, we must also understand the limitations it sets on us.

Every person is composed of at least three nations — one public, one private, and one unknown. Each nation has its own boundaries, customs, laws, language, and traditions. Some boundaries are guarded and may be crossed only by trusted friends. The frontier between the known and the unknown self is always heavily guarded. No one of us can travel freely in the hidden places of his consciousness but, fortunately, messengers slip past the border guards and bring us dreams and images from the unknown. Ideally the highways that connect the nations should be well marked so that we can travel anywhere. But ignorance or fear keeps us from exploring the outer limits of ourselves.

— Sam Keen and Anne Valley Fox, *Telling Your Story* (1973)

There are conflicting opinions as to how children acquire and first learn to use language. One group of observers — those called empiricists and, more recently, behavioralists, such as B. F. Skinner — says that a child learns language as a habit: words are repeated by the parents, and eventually the child begins to imitate them. Anthropologist Claude Lévi-Strauss suggests that the environment is so influential in the shaping of language that there is even a relationship between food resources and linguistic forms. He has found that certain primitive cultures with meager food resources have very complex grammars, as if the complexity of the linguistic form makes up for the absence of resources. Other, resource-rich, cultures use words sparingly; they rely on understatement and grammatical simplicity. Americans, for example, like to think of themselves as a laconic, tight-lipped nation of Gary Cooper–Clint Eastwood types. Indeed, at one time travelers to this country *were* struck by our silences as much as by our speeches. But nowadays, at least in the view of Russell Baker, whom we quoted at the opening of this chapter, some Americans have adopted a fat, heavy, larded speech because of a poverty not of physical resources but of ethical and spiritual resources. Consequently, we might suggest that, though Lévi-Strauss's theory may well be appropriate for relatively simple cultures (regardless of how rich or poor), one must modify it to account for other kinds of resources and the ways they are reflected in languages.

On the other hand, prominent MIT linguist Noam Chomsky argues that the principles of language are present in the mind at birth, and that the four to five thousand known languages all rest on the same principles. Chomsky identifies these principles as "linguistic universals" that are determined by our chromosomes at birth and are simply "biological properties of the human mind." Chomsky believes a child "knows" — not consciously, but instinctually — the principles of language before he says his first word, largely because the categories of perception become grammatical categories as well. The interplay of these pre-existing, embedded structures with the child's environment ultimately allows him or her to acquire knowledge of a specific language. Regardless of how we learn it — by imitation or by filling in imprinted channels in the human brain cortex — language gives us a reciprocal relationship with our environment. It is our way of understanding and ordering the world around us, but it also *shapes* our way of looking at the world. As our language alters, our perception of the world alters, and our selves, our identities, alter as well.

Clearly, a two-way street links self and world/environment. That is a happy situation, for the multiplicity of human environments permits a fortuitous diversity of peoples. An individual who develops in the linguistic environment of Boston's Roxbury is going to have a different language personality from someone who develops in DeKalb, Illinois. Much more goes into our linguistic inheritance than place alone, but regional speech illustrates how much our individual "voices" depend on very specific circumstances. That voice which constitutes our authenticity as a speaker and writer comes from family, peers, ethnic, and other social contexts that are usually contained by an identifiable space/time. Virtually every literary revolution in history has been ignited by this recognition. The forces Twain, Hemingway, Faulkner, and others saw acting on them and their "voices" have also been acting on you as students. They found their voices — and their freedom from a conservative literary tradition — by resorting to regional vocabularies, structures, and rhythms. Their triumphs suggest that improved strains of language come about by blending fading conventions with more vivid dialectal and colloquial elements. They found their voices and their selves by not denying the power and authority of either source of language. Clearly, we may do the same thing. Jean Stafford, in a style recognizably affected by several diverse sets of conventions, makes our point in a colorful way:

> If everyone is to have a radio or a television set and is to be subliminally infused with the homogeneous palaver of the announcers and commentators and your friendly Chase Manhattan banker and the purveyors of mouthwash, eyewash, and hogwash, what is going to become of regional speech? Who will carry on the rich oral traditions of New England and the South and the West? I reckon that convicts and children, who have the most time on their hands, will go on contriving slang and jokes, and God willing, the wellspring will not be polluted and will not go dry, and

hillbillies and pickpockets and able-bodied seamen and timber-cruisers and southern politicians will go on sweetening the pot.

— Jean Stafford, "The Plight of the American Language" (1973)

If one values diversity — as we do — then a serious problem of any culture is the implosive impact of a powerful *mass, standardized* language. Our uniqueness is always threatened by those elements that give us conventional roles and identities.

The forces for standardization of language, both in the schools and mass media, cause some observers to project that before too long all of us will speak and write in one uniform way. We should avoid such verbal uniformity as much as Al Calloway would have us avoid walking alike:

> When I walk on Eighth Avenue, man, I see rhythms I don't see downtown. Polyrhythms. You look at one cat, he may be goin' bop, bop-bop, bop-bop, and another one goin' bop-de-bop, de-bop. Beautiful, man. Those are beautiful people. Yeah. But when I go downtown to Thirty-fourth Street, everybody's walkin' the same, you dig? They don't put themselves into it. Their walk tells you nothing about who they are. Polyrhythms. That's what it is. Like a flower garden in a breeze. The roses swing a little bit from side to side, kind of stiff, not too much. The lilacs swing wide, slow, lazy, not in a hurry. A blade of grass wiggles. It's cause they're all different and they're bein' themselves. Polyrhythms, like on Eighth Avenue. That's soul.
>
> — Al Calloway, "An Introduction to Soul" (1968)

Like the gaits of those people on Eighth Avenue, language and the way we use it ought to reflect the essence of our selves. Language that does not authentically reveal our "voices" eventually depersonalizes us: it becomes the language of a Thirty-fourth Street where "they don't put themselves into it," one that "tells you nothing about who they are." Each of us can have a unique language rhythm, however, and this rhythm, once discovered, can be used as the basis for our communication. Writer Frank O'Connor explains it in *his* way:

> And in fact, in real life, when you meet somebody in the street you don't start recording that she had this sort of nose — at least a man doesn't. I mean, if you're the sort of person that meets a girl in the street and instantly notices the color of her eyes and of her hair and the sort of dress she's wearing, then you're not in the least like me. I just notice a feeling from people. I notice particularly the cadence of their voices, the sort of

phrases they'll use, and that's what I'm all the time trying to hear in my head, how people word things — because everybody speaks an entirely different language, that's really what it amounts to.

— Frank O'Connor, *Writers at Work: The Paris Review Interviews* (1958)

Some linguists have suggested that our sense of language rhythm begins before birth through tactile communication. As the fetus floats in the fluids of the womb, it is bathed by the continuously rhythmic impact of the maternal heartbeat. After the birth of the child, its rhythmic tactile communication continues through bodily contact with the mother and her caressing and stroking. Within a short period of time, the baby explores the shape and texture of his/her own body and thereby establishes a body image. Eventually, the child begins to accept the rhythm of the mother's voice — humming, talking, singing — as an extension of tactile communication. It is possible that the child's later propensity for the highly rhythmic forms of poetry and music can be traced to the intensity and length of these early tactile and speech communication rhythms. A child deprived of these early forms of communication, psychologists have found, is particularly inhibited in later speech development and in communication with others. Each culture defines the boundaries of these experiences, and, interestingly, in our culture the male is more quickly separated from his mother than the female, a fact that perhaps explains the general slowness of language development for boys in the early grades. Their "deficiency," however, is quickly made up when they develop their capacity for visual communication through reading and writing.

Only recently has any great awareness developed about the language of the body. Hunches may frequently be traced to its territory. "Instinctive" reaction. "Gut" feelings. Listen to your body, the modern therapist says. Listen to the *sound* of your voice, for the vocal cord is only partially under the control of the mind. Consider it a disputed territory, for muscular responses will control its foreign policies. Actual words will be selected according to the bias of the mind, but they will be delivered by an organ whose work, whether quick or plodding, harried, exhausted, elated, angry or frightened, will be done in accordance to instruction from the body.

— Robert Hunter, *The Storming of the Mind* (1972)

There is no doubt that *all* of our communication experiences have contributed to our language "voice," and as an authentic writer it is important that we identify and use this voice. Like that fetus in the womb, we too are enveloped in an environment of which we are largely unconscious. We are bathed in language every day of our lives through television, radio, newspapers, lectures, discussions, idle conversations. Wherever it is from and however we imagine it, this language is outside ourselves. But there is also an inner realm of language we can and must explore. Our minds offer just as vast a world to explore and organize as the oceans or outer space, and the only way to chart its combinations of words and nonverbal images is through language itself. To explore this rich inner dimension, twentieth-century novelists have experimented with new techniques of association, montage, discontinuity, and the like. One special technique is known as stream-of-consciousness. Many writers have plumbed the depths of the mind, but perhaps none as effectively as James Joyce in his novel *Ulysses*. *Ulysses* explores the relationship between external reality and internal awareness and attempts to give form to this very fluid conjunction. As Leopold Bloom, the novel's protagonist, sips a glass of wine with his lunch, he observes two flies buzzing, "stuck." The catalyst of the wine and "stuck" flies opens the floodgate of the memory stream associated with Molly and their first sexual experience, which leads to his marriage proposal:

> Hidden under wild ferns on Howth. Below us bay sleeping sky. No sound. The sky. The bay purple by the Lion's head. Green by Drumleck. Yellow-green towards Sutton. Fields of undersea, the lines faint brown in grass, buried cities. Pillowed on my coat she had her hair, earwigs in the heather scrub my hand under her nape, you'll toss me all. O wonder! Coolsoft with ointments her hand touched me, caressed: her eyes upon me did not turn away. Ravished over her I lay, full lips full open, kissed her mouth. Yum. Softly she gave me in my mouth the seedcake warm and chewed. Mawkish pulp her mouth had mumbled sweet and sour with spittle. Joy: I ate it: joy. Young life, her lips that gave me pouting. Soft, warm, sticky gumjelly lips. Flowers her eyes were, take me, willing eyes.
>
> — James Joyce, *Ulysses* (1914)

As Bloom's inner world of images is shaped by Joyce in language and as it penetrates the outer world (in the form of the spoken or written word), a process of selection has begun that reflects the mind's constant attempt to order itself. Before Joyce, Virginia Woolf, William Faulkner, and other such modern experimental writers, the main concern of much of our literature was to present an external world about which we could all agree. After Joyce *et al.* our literature has become less concerned with what is to be known than with the ways we can know it. In philosophy, it is the contrast between *ontology* and *epistemology*. More consciously than any past generation of writers, the moderns have been concerned with the philosophical bases of language and its reciprocal relations to self and world. But the endeavor of the modern writer remains a humanistic one.

According to I. A. Richards, this need, this "rage for order," is the reason we have language, for language is the "instrument of all our distinctively human development." Our capacity for language permits us to order our experience in ways beyond the capacity of other animals. The essential forms in language used by humanity to order (comprehend) experience fall into the two classifications of logic and myth. On the one hand, we reduce, through logical patterns such as deduction, induction, classification, definition, and analysis, an infinite number of sensory, intellectual, and psychic experiences to manageable classes. On the other hand, we order experience imaginatively through narrative, symbolic, and mythic patterns reflecting the individual's relationship with his or her social and natural world. In essence, the functions of language work in two distinct ways to help us cope with existence. In one, it limits the totality of experience so that we can comprehend it, while, in another way, it extends the boundaries of our world. Commands of both ways are vital to our personal and interpersonal identities.

Our dilemma is a serious one. Cut off by the currents of the age both from my own inner story and from the story of my people, I listen for another story to hear and to tell myself. I listen because I have no real choice. As a homo sapien I am an incorrigibly storytelling animal. Literally I cannot live without a story. But I do not have to search long. A substitute is readily supplied. The most powerful technologies ever devised churn out signals to keep me pliable, immature and weak. They hit at my most vulnerable spot. There is still time for us to learn again to tell stories — mine, yours, ours. If we do not, the signals will sweep all before them. Their gentle bleeps and reassuring winks will lull us into a trance from which there is no awakening. If there is any hell where souls are lost forever, that would be it.

— Harvey Cox, *The Seduction of the Spirit* (1973)

SELF-DISCOVERY THROUGH WRITING:
"SAYS I TO MYSELF"*

Emil Sinclair, a character in Herman Hesse's novel *Demian*, suggests that we are always in the process of becoming, that "each man's life represents a road toward himself," and that it is our destiny to follow and study that road. We contend that the first step taken on that "road" is the first step toward becoming an authentic writer. The process of writing is itself one of the few ways that we have to explore self. According to Eldridge Cleaver in *Soul on Ice*, writing became his only way to salvation, and salvation could be achieved only after finding out who he was and what he wanted to do. One way to explore the road toward self — to try to do what Joyce and Hesse do for their characters and Cleaver and Rich for themselves — is to keep a journal. As Thoreau suggests, ". . . a writer must first speak to himself."

The keeping of a journal can enhance the exciting and exacting process of self-discovery through a careful detailing of daily experiences. Unlike a diary, which is usually a log of daily events, a journal ideally represents a record of one's experiments to find language to cope with perceptions, feelings, attitudes, and ideas. What is more, as Thoreau says in one of his journal entries (January 24, 1856), ". . . a journal is a record of experience and growth." It is therefore both practical and expressive, and he goes on to explain:

> I am occasionally reminded of a statement which I have made in conversation and immediately forgotten, which would read much better than what I put in my journal. It is a ripe, dry fruit of long-past experience which falls from me easily, without giving pain or pleasure. The charm of the journal must consist in a certain greenness, though freshness, and not in maturity. Here I cannot afford to be remembering what I said or did, my scurf cast off, but what I am and aspire to become.
>
> — Henry David Thoreau, *Journals*

The people we talk with, then, the ways we use language, the things we see, hear, smell, touch, and taste, and our intellectual experiences — all combine to help shape the essential self, what we are and aspire to become.

We suggest that in developing a journal you faithfully record material daily. Break experiences down into specific categories — by subject or theme — so that patterns of recurrence and preoccupation may

* Motto to Thoreau's *Journals*.

> Journals are places to create, experiment, write, jot, make mistakes and revise. They'll help you bring what is inside and outside of you together in a way that makes sense.
>
> — Joyce Carroll, "The Written Word Is Not Dead," *Media and Methods*, November 1972

emerge more clearly. Those clusters of experiences, thoughts, and images are the materials that will develop into formal writing assignments. Write as often as possible. Though it should not be a chore, journal-keeping is a disciplined activity. Discipline yourself at the beginning, and later the journal will become a significant part of your total experience.

EXERCISES

Some topics around which you might order your experiences include the following:

1. Write about *relationships with people*, how you react to them and how they react to you.
2. Record *sensory experiences* in a descriptive paragraph. For example, observe and describe a natural object at different times of the day and in different weather conditions.
3. Put down your *dreams* in narrative (story) form. If you are interested in dreams, you might read *Dream Power* by Dr. Ann Faraday.
4. Write a *description of yourself as you think others perceive you.*
5. Record the *effects a news event has on you.*
6. Record a *profile of yourself for one day* using specific details.
7. Record *the stream of your inner language* relating to a specific experience during the day.
8. Write about *intellectual experiences* such as ideas encountered in lectures, books read, and films seen and your feelings concerning them.

Following are some exercises in self-discovery:

1. Sam Keen and Anne Valley Fox in their book *Telling Your Story* suggest that "one way to identify your public self is to locate the words

you most often use to describe yourself to others." For example, compile a list of eight to ten words or phrases that describe you best (consider such factors as feelings, activities, an organization you belong to). Then rank the words in order of those least important to those most important, eliminating each until you have the single word or phrase that best describes you.

2. Researchers for the army have found that the old saying "you are what you eat" has more truth in it than we may have suspected. For example, if you would rather eat a massive piece of sirloin steak than a piece of fish, you are probably sociable, enthusiastic, and active, and you would probably make a good politician, businessman, salesman, or career army officer. If you would rather have the fish, you are more likely to be reserved, noncompetitive, and not altogether comfortable in social situations. Some other findings include: (a) big dessert eaters have an even stronger personality than the big meat eaters (also, the big dessert eater usually has a good sense of humor and tends to be overweight); (b) those who consistently opt for meals of fish, fruits, and vegetables (besides being noncompetitive) tend to be bookish, preferring the aesthetic values of art; (c) heavy salad eaters are full of energy and good listeners who are sympathetic to the problems of others; and (d) those who consistently reach for starches are generally complacent and almost constitutionally incapable of making decisions and solving problems.

   Using the findings of the army researchers as a guide, make a list of your favorite foods and try to determine how closely your personality coincides with the foods you eat. Write a paragraph arguing for or against the findings.

3. One way to help discover self is to examine one's heroes and heroines. Make a list of your heroes from childhood to the present time. Be sure to consider the heroes of books, films, and those in real life. Make a list of the villains. Write a few paragraphs explaining the significance of these two lists as they relate to you today. Explain what "hero" you seem to be most like today.

4. Write a paragraph exploring each of the following areas (when applicable) of self-knowledge. You might have to do some reading in order to answer some of the questions. While explaining the various questions, try to be as concrete as possible; offer specific examples and appeals to the senses whenever possible. You might title these pages of your journal "Walking on Eighth Avenue."

   a. What is your astrological sign? Are there characteristics of the sign that relate to your personality? How deeply do you believe in horoscopes? Why do you read them (if you do)?

b. What geographical location seems to reflect your inner emotions and feelings? In other words, if you had to choose a metaphor of place to describe you, what would it be (for example, the heart of a dark forest, sailing on the middle of a lake)? Describe the setting in detail.

c. If you had to choose one sense (sight, taste, etc.) with which to perceive the world, which one would it be? Which sense gives you the most pleasure? Use an illustration.

d. Do you remember your dreams? How important are they to you? Write a paragraph presenting the details of a dream you have had and then try an interpretation of it.

e. Have you ever had an experience you think is an example of telepathy (awareness of others' thoughts)? Explain and describe. Have you ever had an experience you think is an example of clairvoyance (awareness of distant events)? Explain and describe.

f. Do you consider yourself a rhythmic person? What do you do that is particularly rhythmic? Describe a situation or experience in which the awareness of rhythm became very important to you (for example, rock climbing, running in a race, swimming, dancing).

g. What is your favorite shape (circle, flower, leaf, triangle)? Are you sensitive to balance, proportion, and symmetry when you observe things around you? Describe a scene, painting, building, or the like that strikes you as being particularly well proportioned.

h. Which tells you more about life, songs and stories or science? Give an example.

i. Do you consider yourself a logical person? Imaginative? Illustrate.

j. In what kind of clothes do you feel most comfortable? What do your clothes communicate about you?

k. What is your reaction to the following story:

Pat told of spying a small green beetle on the porch steps one day. Pat said:

"I began to think about the beetle, where it was going, what it thought of me. Suddenly I felt very close to the beetle. It was just as important as I was. It overwhelmed me to be in the world with this beetle.

"Then the beetle smiled and said to me, 'How are you doing? It's such a nice day.' And the beetle began to glow and I felt warm all over. Never before have I felt so at peace with everything."

— From *Psychology Today*, December 1973

l. Can you describe some unique features of your "voice"? Explain some of the linguistic qualities in your speech as they relate to the geographical area you are from. Whose speech patterns did you imitate when you were young? Whose do you imitate now?

m. Write an evaluation of the experiences and personality definitions you have discussed above as they relate to your astrological sign.

In addition to being a source for self-discovery, a journal, faithfully compiled, in a very practical way becomes a rich mine of ideas and materials for writing assignments. The spontaneous flow of words on paper is a stage much like the prewriting state of thinking about the subject that helps to define the form and scope of formal writing selections. You can supplement the journal-writing exercise with outside reading and research: pepper your journal with those interesting quotes, those entries toward a more picturesque speech, you run across in daily reading and listening. In addition, the journal can be and perhaps should be used as a place in which to practice ways of observation and to experiment with structures, styles, tones, "voices." Mess around with it. Play. Have fun, and it will work for you.

The following are journal entries among which you may discover models. The first three entries are from Thoreau's *Journals*; the remaining are selections from various student journals.

August 1827.

It is so cool a morning that for the first time I move into the entry to sit in the sun. But in this cooler weather I feel as if the fruit of my summer were hardening and maturing a little, acquiring color and flavor like the corn and other fruits in the field. When the very earliest ripe grapes begin to be scented in the cool nights, then, too, the first cooler airs of autumn begin to waft my sweetness on the desert airs of summer. Now, too, poets nib their pens afresh. I scent their first-fruits in the cool evening air of the year. By the coolness the experience of the summer is condensed and matured, whether our fruits be pumpkins or grapes. Man, too, ripens with the grapes and apples.

March 1853.

Man cannot afford to be a naturalist, to look at Nature directly, but only with the side of his eye. He must look through and beyond her. To look at her is as fatal as to look at the head of Medusa. It turns the man of science to stone. I feel that I am dissipated by so many observations. I should be the magnet in the midst of all this dust and filings. I knock the back of my hand against a rock, and as I smooth back the skin, I find myself prepared to study lichens there. I look upon man but as a fungus. I have almost a slight, dry headache as the result of all this observing. How to observe is how to behave. O for a little Lethe! To crown all, lichens, which are so thin, are described in the *dry* state, as they are most commonly, not most truly, seen.

June 1852.

Moon half full. Fields dusky; the evening star and one other bright one near the moon. It is a cool but pretty still night. Methinks I am less thoughtful than I was last year at this time. The flute I now hear from the Depot Field does not find such caverns to echo and resound in in my mind, — no such answering depths. Our minds should echo at least as many times as a Mammoth Cave to every musical sound. It should awaken reflections in us. I hear not many crickets. Some children calling their kitten home by some endearing name. Now his day's work is done, the laborer plays his flute, — only possible at this hour. Contrasted with his work, what an accomplishment! Some drink and gamble. He plays some well-known march. But the music is not in the tune; it is in the sound. It does not proceed from the trading nor political world. He practices his ancient art. There are light, vaporous clouds overhead; dark, fuscous ones in the north. The trees are turned black. As candles are lit on earth, stars are lit in the heavens. I hear the bullfrog's trump from afar.

Student entry: on visiting a brother in jail.

It is the most silent and somber room one could enter with the atmosphere of a morgue. Each person there is bleeding inside, crying to no one, begging for nonexistent answers. Their eyes stare aimlessly at the gray cinderblock wall. Years of unfelt emotions are clogged within their tired souls, stopped and stifled by a solitary glance. Their tears remain uncried longing to flow through the iron bars while creative thoughts bleed from the pores of their minds.

Student entry: after viewing the Japanese film Woman in the Dunes.

Men may lead their lives according to their perception of that which surrounds them — seeing only those things that please, satisfy and endure in their minds. Yet, if man will allow himself to transcend the physical, place himself in an abstract metaphysical world he will find himself with the knowledge of the apparent in harmony with the wisdom of the intended. By seeing more than is present, the imagination runs free, new images are created and man can ultimately gain the wisdom to incorporate himself with the spirits of nature and the universe.

Student entry: after reading e. e. cummings' poetry.

```
-happy                    s
people cling             no
t                        w
o   the.  r                   f
        i                      a  ll
         r  e                     i
            a                     n
            l                     g
k                        on the ground
no                       me
wledge of                    l
t                             l  t
rut                              s un
h                        der
       un-                   t
                            he
                         feet
                         of  t
                            he   still
                         born
                                    children
```

Student entry: philosophical reflection.

i awoke this morning to find myself. to find myself. and i wondered what i was doing here on this earth, this rounded planet, amid the stars. i looked at people and discovered Man and thought how funny this creature. two arms, two legs, a brain, a mind, and yet, and yet, devoid of Heart. i learned History — man's sweet diary — and gathered to myself certain pre-suppositions which grew in time into a philosophy of Life. no longer linear or flat, man's life appeared to me just as cyclical and un-progressive, just as repetitious and enchaining as the cycle of the seasons and the turn of the earth. karma, bad karma . . . but why? Why? man's self-fulfilling prophecy? and if so, why could he not have chosen to believe, to fulfill some other prophecy — less selfish, less limited — less destructive.

Student entry: on grandmother's funeral.

Grandma's coffin was placed about five feet away from where the minister was standing and though I was at least twenty feet away, I could feel each of his words, like flannel, touching and crowding around me. He kept glancing at the coffin and toward us and repeating in many different ways how sad it was and how we would all miss her. But after a while his dry tone changed and took on an authoritative sound. He didn't come right out and say it, but what he meant was that grandma had been mentally ill and had been a burden on all of us. I looked around to see if anyone would object to what this stranger was saying, but from the looks on their faces I couldn't even tell what they were thinking. Trying to think of grandma in these terms was impossible for me. All I could think of was the way she always wore an apron and those two silver bracelets, clinking that she always had on.

Student entry: identifying a state of mind.

As I lay here in the grass, with the sun beating down upon my body and the gusty wind chilling not only me, but also my thoughts, I begin to wonder, to ponder the idea of loneliness. For to be lonely is to be one grain of sand on the beach; one budding leaf on a tree; one stalk of wheat in a field of thousands. It has no meaning, no importance, no necessity. Being alone. The thought itself depresses me. Here I am. One thousand miles away from security — my family. One thousand miles away from love and affection and warmth. Amid a mass of unknown and perplexing people I cry out. But no one hears the echo of my voice. I need someone, something, I need security. I am not a loner, nor do I claim to be one now. I am not a rock, for I cannot be thrown and tossed or pushed aside; I do feel pain. Nor am I an island, for I cannot stand alone, surrounded by a sense of nothingness; I do cry. I am just a human being. And if being human means the same to you as it does to me, then you can understand my feelings.

᪻ RHETORIC ᪻

Rhetoric at its truest seeks to perfect men
by showing them better visions of themselves, links
in that chain extending up toward the ideal
which only the intellect can apprehend and
only the soul have affection for.

RICHARD WEAVER

Ethics of Rhetoric

(1953)

BEYOND SELF: THE AUTHENTIC ATTITUDE

Journal writing is personal by its very nature, largely because the entries are meant primarily for one's eyes alone. As a student, however, a good deal of "public" writing and speaking is expected of you. Essay exams, book reviews, abstracts, term papers, research essays, and the like all require you to write with an audience, often a *particular* audience, in mind. You are no longer writing only for yourself but for a specific person or persons. These assignments require some understanding on your part of the nature of your audience. As soon as you — the *sender* of a message — communicate, not by some spontaneous outburst but by sentences and paragraphs, keeping in mind an audience — the *receiver* of a message — you are in the province of rhetoric, the study of effective methods of communication.

The term *rhetoric* is derived from the Greek word "to say." Rhetoric was originally associated with the spoken word and must be understood in the context of oral communication. Rhetoric is not usually taught like subjects such as math, the sciences, or literature. Achieving effective methods of communication comes more from our experience than from formal study. In this respect, rhetoric is like grammar; we may learn either unconsciously, but we may also *study* them. In oral cultures such as the Greek, in which rhetoric first was formalized and studied, sharp differences in rhetorical manner and method are rare, for a high degree of homogeneity is one of the primary characteristics of an oral culture. Between one person and another, the virtually automatic, unconscious grasp of rhetorical principles will be similar because of the homogeneity of experiences *in* communication. The development of the alphabet, offset printing, and other visual means of communication, however, has led to a diversification of experience and a loss of the rhetorical unity possible in oral cultures of limited media. It is no longer a matter of learning a few oral patterns or formulas almost as we learn grammar and language itself. Formulas, clichés, and stereotyped language still exist, of course, and, as we pointed out in Chapter 1, a *mass* language and rhetoric are available to us. But such language and rhetoric are *threats* to the very sense of identity, individuality, and uniqueness the explosion of the media seems to have created. If you are going to achieve an authentic rhetoric today, you must do so working from — not *against* — a clear definition of your self. Your authentic, unique *rhetorical stance* will derive from and be in harmony with that perception of self when you have solved the riddle of identity.

Aristotle's approach to rhetoric, which forms the basis of rhetoric in Western culture, focuses on the study of persuasive techniques that were to be used in public ceremonies, political debates, and courts of law. The modern concept of rhetoric expands Aristotle's to include virtually all forms of communication. Why? Because most communication has persuasion as its basic motive force. Whether consciously or not, we attempt to make our audience "see," believe, or understand as we do, though our objective in doing so may be totally without ulterior motive. Though *all* forms of communication, all forms of advertising, even the clothes we wear, the car we drive, the house we own or rent, and the way we walk and sit, *can* have a "grammar" or a "rhetoric," it is to *language*, primarily the written *word*, that we shall restrict our study of rhetorical principles. If through keeping a journal (and in other ways) you have begun to get at who you *really* are, then your study of rhetoric will permit you *consciously* to master the most effective ways to communicate — to commune, in short, as one authentic person to another, regardless of external circumstances or occasions.

It is easier to communicate with a person or a group when we can relate to them through more than one kind of "language" or "rhetoric." Speaking to another person in one-to-one conversation permits facial expressions and physical gestures ("body language") to supplement spoken words. Our most effective rhetoric is based on combinations of devices addressed to more than one sense of perception such as are found in a colorfully illustrated magazine advertisement or in a dramati-

---

Rhetoric may be defined as the faculty of observing in any given case the available means of persuasion. This is not a function of any other subject. Every other subject can instruct or persuade about its own substance; for instance, medicine about what is healthy and unhealthy, geometry about the properties of magnitudes, and the same is true of the other arts and sciences. But rhetoric we look upon as the power of observing the means of persuasion on almost any subject presented to us; and that is why we say that, in its technical character, it is not concerned with any special or definite class of subjects.

— Aristotle, *Rhetoric*

> If it were possible to commission some omnipotent scientist to develop a pill that would make us all great writers, it would have three powers. It would give us the significant ideas that are at the core of all great writing. It would give us the ability to analyze those ideas and make them clear, interesting, and convincing. And it would provide us with the writing ability to fulfill that obligation. Fortunately or unfortunately, scientists have not yet provided us with pills for instant genius, and we must look elsewhere for all three powers. This is the purpose of studying rhetoric.
>
> — Harry H. Crosby and George F. Estey,
> *College Writing* (1968)

zation on television. When we write, however, we must communicate through the ostensibly monosensory medium of the visible word, and that medium imposes certain limitations. We must be aware of the many available methods for addressing an audience to allow us to go beyond a single medium or a two-dimensional relation.

A rhetoric — any rhetoric, regardless of the medium — involves an attitude toward another person or other persons. A rhetoric involves a set of presuppositions about human nature — including one's own nature or self. For Plato, man was an ethical being who was striving for perfection, so his rhetoric evolved in order to express the moral and ethical person; for Aristotle, man was a rational being, so his rhetoric was designed to express his primary logical and rational dimension: Aristotle's model person approached self and the other — including the "world" — as empirical objects, not as ideal constructs. For Pavlovian behavioralists, man is an animal who can be manipulated by means of reflex conditioning repetitions. For the Skinnerian behavioralists, man remains a manipulable being, but Skinner returns an ethical dimension to the rhetorical stance he takes toward man by saying that our knowledge of man ought to be used for more beneficial results in order to cure his anxieties, his alcoholism, his sexual dysfunctions, or whatever.

We must not ignore the truths of all these philosophies and their implicit rhetorical stances toward man, particularly the findings of the behavioralists. But we believe that Skinner, while he is correct in admitting that we all *can* be conditioned, is wrong in not emphasizing that man's continually expanding *knowledge* of self still permits him to remain a free being. Indeed, we can choose to act in one way or another on the information the behavioralists themselves give us about humanity in general. The attitude of an authentic rhetoric toward any other being —

> When two men inform one another of their basically different views about an object, each aiming to convince the other of the rightness of his own way of looking at the matter, everything depends so far as human life is concerned, on whether each thinks of the other as the one he is, whether each, that is, with all his desire to influence the other, nevertheless unreservedly accepts and confirms him in his being this man and in his being made in this particular way. . . . The desire to influence the other then does not mean the effort to change the other, to inject one's "rightness" into him; but it means the effort to let that which is recognized as right, as just, as true . . . through one's influence take seed and grow in the form suited to individuation.
>
> — Martin Buber, *The Knowledge of Man* (1965)

and thus toward humanity — must insist on our freedom and the freedoms of that other, upon the authenticity of *my*-self and *your*-self at the same time. I *can* manipulate you; you *can* manipulate me. But as authentic writers/speakers/persons, we choose not to.

The authentic rhetorical stance evolves from our concern for an existence based on the freedom and responsibility of the individual for his decisions. Our concern is for the end terms — the sender and the receiver — in the rhetorical triad in which *message* becomes the middle term. The traditional rhetoric, assuming as a given the rational construction of the world and man as a rational being who searches for truth over falsehood, develops techniques to discover truth, examines both sides of arguments, and stresses the form of the message. Our rhetoric is concerned primarily, then, with the form called *dialogue*, for dialogue stresses the dynamic relationships among individuals when each recognizes the individuality of the other.

The philosophical position of what we shall call the "rhetoric of dialogue" is seen in the studies of Martin Buber. Trying to find a model for ideal human behavior, Buber developed the I-Message-Thou paradigm. In Buber's model formula, the relationship of *I* (individual, group, society, nation) and *Thou* (the receiver) involves a message that presupposes individuals who acknowledge the free identity of other individuals. The very basis of the sender's authenticity depends on bringing into focus the personal presence of the receiver's being, to acknowledge him or her *as a person*. This rhetorical approach requires the careful consideration of attitude, meaning both how I *stand* in relation to you and what I *think* about you, and vice versa. What are those attitudes?

Richard Johannesen has identified them as "mutuality, openhearted-ness, directness, honesty, spontaneity, frankness, lack of pretense, non-manipulative intent, communion, intensity, and love," one human being taking responsibility for another. In the rhetoric of dialogue, there is no "I" independent of another in whose presence we stand. There is only the "I" existing and known in the "other" as encompassed and encoun-tered by the "Thou." "I" do not exist in a relationship to a stone, nor do I exist if my relationship turns a person into an object. In the actual or imagined presence of another, I can have an *authentic* existence only by positing a relationship to a real person whom I accept as a *Thou*.

If we believe that "reality" and value are shown in the relationships between us and others, then allowing those relationships to achieve genuine understanding is vital. The relationships we pursue are often shaped by the roles we play in the social system and by the role require-ments of that system. These limitations are not easily controlled. But does that mean we have no freedom or that we will employ no rhetoric? The answers, we believe, are *no* to both questions. As individuals in a society, we cannot exist without choosing a rhetoric or rhetorics, for rhetorics convey in their assumptions how we define the factors that link us to one another: Are they power or love, authority or mutuality? *Your* stance will tell us, in any case. As long as we remember to emphasize the necessary attitude toward ourselves and our audience, we can do much to achieve a rhetorical *stance* that establishes an authentic, clearly com-prehensible relationship conveyed through an *exchange* of attitudes ex-pressed in the act of communication. In essence, our objective for communication is a kind of awakening, a setting aside of "laid on" ideas in favor of an achieved, authentic form of life. The values associated with the rhetoric of dialogue are more and more reflected in changes in the values of our culture as a whole. A resurgent communal interest in

---

Rhetoric as persuasion, some argue, has the persuader manipulate and exploit the audience to achieve his specific ends; the persuader utilizes audience feedback only to gain more control over them. Dialogue, in contrast, is seen as involving mutual understanding, suspension of judg-ment, respect for the other person, and a receptive attitude in the sender. In dialogue the communication attitude of the participants is one of equality, honesty, genuineness, concern, and nonexploitation.

— Richard L. Johannesen, *Contemporary Theories*
of Rhetoric (1971)

the sixties and seventies has made us reorient our priorities, and many today are putting people ahead of jobs, things, careers, wealth, at a time when economic forces make these elements take on powerful significance. But even if, because of those forces, positive changes cease, the rhetorical *stance* we choose ought to gain a wide acceptance in the seventies in America.

THE AUTHENTIC METHOD

We have given you our operating assumptions. So, you ask, what are the practical solutions, what does the authentic rhetorical method involve? Our reply is this: The specific techniques we employ and the considerations we engage in are not substantially different from those of traditional rhetorics. We must possess a particular attitude when we approach *self* and *audience* through the *message,* but the shaping of the content of our message must proceed along well-worn paths. Like any other rhetoric, an authentic rhetoric must blend *substance, structure,* and *style.*

Our prescription is for a modification of a traditional Aristotelian method of rhetoric, which identified five different concerns in the ana-

---

As a process, rhetoric clearly begins with a person's impulse to communicate, to share some experience with others — although this is a somewhat arbitrary starting point since he often has explored his experiences and formulated ordering principles before he feels a desire to communicate. At some stage in the process he must identify his audience and decide what strategy he can use to present his ideas. If he chooses to write rather than speak, he must at some stage begin to write and rewrite what he wants to say. However, the process is not strictly linear, with clearly defined stages; they often overlap — the writing stage, for example, frequently serves as an opportunity to explore and clarify the experience in his own mind. But in spite of this blurring and merging of stages, the writer does at various times shift his attention from his experience and his own resources to his audience and to the written work itself; these shifts of attention and activity constitute the rhetorical process for the writer.

— R. Young, A. Becker, K. Pike, *Rhetoric: Discovery and Change* (1970)

---

lytic process: *invention, arrangement, style, memory,* and *delivery.* We must be concerned with the two basic divisions of *arrangement* (the study of structure) and *style* only. Invention has to do with having something to communicate, but we grant that; memory and delivery have to do with speeches, not texts, so we simply disregard them. What's left are structure and style, and the ways they relate to *substance* ultimately determine the success of any writing. The complex relationships between structure and style come out of the *sender's* understanding of his subject matter and audience. Though choice of subject matter may arise out of a set of circumstances, the manner (style) and the form (structure) in which we present a subject matter must be selected in light of our relationship to the audience. The application of an authentic method can be demonstrated through written versions of speeches by Abraham Lincoln and John F. Kennedy.

THE METHOD APPLIED

"THE GETTYSBURG ADDRESS"

Your first step toward acquiring an understanding of our rhetorical method is learning how to recognize its possibilities. You do this best by studying models as they appear in the writings of others, in much the same way you learned language by conscious and unconscious imitation of models. In the best models, you will discover that the basic considerations of rhetoric are almost inevitably present. The *sender* of the message will demonstrate concern for his or her audience, an understanding of *substance,* care taken in the *ordering or arrangement* of the substance, and selection of a suitable *style* in which to present it. The total effect of the best rhetorical models will suggest just how cohesive these elements must be. The best models suggest that their forms are organic, a living body, in which *structure* becomes a skeletal framework, *style* becomes the visible external surface, the two together becoming a whole body, the completed, fulfilled *message.* In the best models, we see that structure and style are aspects of our messages that we can analyze, but they are not the message itself. Structure and style are in harmony with substance. Such a sense of total, organic unity can be observed in Lincoln's "Gettysburg Address."

Fourscore and seven years ago our fathers brought forth on this continent a new nation, conceived in liberty, and dedicated to the proposition that all men are created equal.

Now we are engaged in a great civil war, testing whether that nation, or any nation so conceived or so dedicated, can long endure. We are met on a great battle-field of that war. We have come to dedicate a portion of that field, as a final resting place for those who here gave their lives that that nation might live. It is altogether fitting and proper that we should do this.

But, in a larger sense, we cannot dedicate — we cannot consecrate, we cannot hallow — this ground. The brave men, living and dead, who struggled here, have consecrated it, far above our poor power to add or detract. The world will little note, nor long remember, what we say here, but it can never forget what they did here. It is for us the living, rather, to be dedicated here to the unfinished work which they who fought here have thus far so nobly advanced. It is rather for us to be here dedicated to the great task remaining before us — that from these honored dead we take increased devotion to that cause for which they gave the last full measure of devotion — that we here highly resolve that these dead shall not have died in vain — that this nation, under God, shall have a new birth of freedom — and that government of the people, by the people, for the people, shall not perish from the earth.

The occasion for the speech on November 19, 1863, was the dedication of the battlefield at Gettysburg where General Meade had defeated General Lee on July 4, 1863. Since it curbed Lee's invasion of Pennsylvania and the North, the battle was even then recognizable as a turning point in the Civil War. The *message-substance* of the speech, in keeping with the significance of the battle, has its center in a potential for a cycle of life, death, and rebirth. Lincoln suggests that, if the sacrifices are clearly understood and their significance heeded, then out of the destruction of war and death could come a rebirth of the nation. This informing theme (the ultimate *message*) is announced in the initial sentence of the speech in a metaphor of conception ("conceived in liberty"), and it concludes in the last sentence with a metaphor of birth ("a new birth of freedom").

The cycle of life-death-rebirth becomes part and parcel of the *structure* of the speech which, schematized, looks like this:

Paragraph 1: describes the occasion (past)

Paragraph 2: dedicates the ground (present)

Paragraph 3: asks the audience to dedicate themselves to the union (future)

Lincoln's structural emphasis on the rhythm of time is in harmony with the message — the potential for rebirth after destruction. This structure gives Lincoln an opportunity to explore each phase of the cycle while simultaneously emphasizing what he considered the most important single idea present — opportunity for renewal. A public ceremony of mourning has no place for unrelieved despair, so the theme of rebirth well enables Lincoln to achieve another goal of his speech — a renewal of commitment, a willingness to suffer sacrifice, on the part of the living for the new life to come. "It is for us, the living, rather, to be dedicated here to the unfinished work which they who fought here have thus far so nobly advanced." This correlative and the primary theme are further strengthened by the rhythmic development of the paragraphs. The rather thin first paragraph's building toward climax in the fully developed third paragraph reveals Lincoln's attempt to stress the future and the possibility for rebirth toward which the nation's commitment must be directed.

Lincoln's *style* also harmonizes with the thematic substance and organizing structure. One stylistic device is the use of three-part repetitions ("We cannot dedicate — we cannot consecrate — we cannot hallow"). These three-part repetitions of sound echo the three-part theme and structure. Often, together with repetitive sounds, Lincoln chooses to employ frequent balance and parallelism of idea and grammatical structure. These stylistic features climax in Lincoln's last sentence: ". . . and that government of the people, by the people, for the people shall not perish from the earth." These are not all the stylistic features of the speech, but discussion of them may suggest how Lincoln has formed an organic unity through substance, structure, and style. This organic unity

---

Rhetoric exists . . . because a world of certainty is not the world of human affairs. It exists because the world of human affairs is a world where there must be an alternative to certain knowledge on the one hand and pure chance or whimsey on the other. The alternative is informed opinion, the nearest approach to knowledge which the circumstances of decision in any given case will permit. The art, or science, or method whose realm this is, is rhetoric. Rhetoric, therefore, is the method, the strategy, the organon of the principles for deciding best the undecidable questions, for arriving at solutions of the unsolvable problems, for instituting method in those vital phases of human activity where no method is inherent in the total subject-matter of decision.

— Donald Bryant, "Rhetoric: Its Functions
and Its Scope" (1953)

is the goal we want to set as the basis of our rhetorical method. Study such models; from them you can learn how to use a variety of structural and stylistic devices.

The harmony of style and structure with theme just examined would probably not exist if Lincoln had not considered his audience. Since Lincoln's address came last in the day's activities and he knew the audience would be tired from listening to all the other speeches, he deliberately kept the length short and made his appeal primarily on the emotional level. Such an appeal was in keeping with his attempt to get the audience to continue the war effort, for reason alone would not be enough to keep a weary nation fighting. After listening to the featured speaker, Edward Everett (a Harvard historian), analyze at length the strategy and historical significance of the battle, the audience must have found Lincoln's short speech powerful and emotionally stimulating. But Lincoln also imitated models. His success stems in part from his fusing a momentous occasion with rhetorical methods (including stylistic and structural choices) from the King James Bible and the works of Shakespeare. His notebooks are filled with rhetorical exercises, and many of his contemporaries testified to his penchant for memorizing and reciting poetry. His ability to combine rhetoric and a sense of poetry makes Lincoln's speech melodic, rhythmic, organic. By combining the three basic rhetorical elements — substance, structure, and style — in complete harmony, he achieved one of the most moving works in the English language. A more recent but similarly impressive achievement, though in a context less momentous, is found in John F. Kennedy's speech "Poetry and Power."

"POETRY AND POWER"

As part of the preparation for your understanding and use of the rhetorical method, it is helpful to read closely not only for ideas but also for specific structural and stylistic devices. For most of us, the experience of reading for *what* is being communicated (content, theme, ideas) is commonplace; the experience of reading for *how* (style and structure) the what is communicated may be less familiar. Students, as well as rhetoricians, must study the techniques used by orators and writers to help them understand the processes being used and to give them the opportunity to use or experiment with different techniques in their own communication. Following is John F. Kennedy's address titled "Poetry and Power" dedicating the Robert Frost Library at Amherst College on October 26, 1963.

[1] This day, devoted to the memory of Robert Frost, offers an opportunity for reflection which is prized by politicians as well as by others and even by poets. For Robert Frost was one of the granite figures of our time in America. He was supremely two things: an artist and an American. A nation reveals itself not only by the men it produces but also by the men it honors, the men it remembers.

[2] In America our heroes have customarily run to men of large accomplishments. But today this college and country honor a man whose contribution was not to our size but to our spirit; not to our political beliefs but to our insight; not to our self-esteem but to our self-comprehension.

[3] In honoring Robert Frost we therefore can pay honor to the deepest sources of our national strength. That strength takes many forms, and the most obvious forms are not always the most significant.

[4] The men who create power make an indispensable contribution to the nation's greatness, but the men who question power make a contribution just as indispensable, especially when that questioning is disinterested, for they determine whether we use power or power uses us. Our national strength matters; but the spirit which informs and controls our strength matters just as much. This was the special significance of Robert Frost.

[5] He brought an unsparing instinct for reality to bear on the platitudes and pieties of society. His sense of the human tragedy fortified him against self-deception and easy consolation.

[6] "I have been," he wrote, "one acquainted with the night." And because he knew the midnight as well as the high noon, because he understood the ordeal as well as the triumph of the human spirit, he gave the age strength with which to overcome despair.

[7] At bottom he held a deep faith in the spirit of man. And it is hardly an accident that Robert Frost coupled poetry and power, for he saw poetry as the means of saving power from itself.

[8] When power leads man toward arrogance, poetry reminds him of his limitations. When power narrows the areas of man's concern, poetry reminds him of the richness and diversity of his existence. When power corrupts, poetry cleanses, for art establishes the basic human truths which must serve as the touchstones of our judgment. The artist, however faithful to his personal vision of reality, becomes the last champion of the individual mind and sensibility against an intrusive society and an officious state. The great artist is thus a solitary figure. He has, as Frost said, "a lover's quarrel with the world." In pursuing his perceptions of reality he must often sail against the currents of his time. This is not a popular role.

If Robert Frost was much honored during his lifetime, it was because a good many preferred to ignore his darker truths. Yet, in retrospect, we see how the artist's fidelity has strengthened the fiber of our national life.

[9] If sometimes our great artists have been the most critical of our society, it is because their sensitivity and their concern for justice, which must motivate any true artist, make them aware that our nation falls short of its highest potential.

[10] I see little of more importance to the future of our country and our civilization than full recognition of the place of the artist. If art is to nourish the roots of our culture, society must set the artist free to follow his vision wherever it takes him.

[11] We must never forget that art is not a form of propaganda; it is a form of truth. And as Mr. MacLeish once remarked of poets, "There is nothing worse for our trade than to be in style."

[12] In a free society art is not a weapon, and it does not belong to the sphere of polemics and ideology. Artists are not engineers of the soul. It may be different elsewhere. But in a democratic society the highest duty to the writer, the composer, the artist, is to remain true to himself and to let the chips fall where they may. In serving his vision of the truth, the artist best serves his nation. And the nation which disdains the mission of art invites the fate of Robert Frost's hired man — the fate of having "nothing to look backward to with pride, and nothing to look forward to with hope."

[13] I look forward to a great future for America — a future in which our country will match its military strength with our moral strength, its wealth with our wisdom, its power with our purpose.

[14] I look forward to an America which will not be afraid of grace and beauty, which will protect the beauty of our natural environment, which will preserve the great old American houses and squares and parks of our national past, and which will build handsome and balanced cities for our future.

[15] I look forward to an America which will reward achievement in the arts as we reward achievement in business or statecraft.

[16] I look forward to an America which will steadily raise the standards of artistic accomplishment and which will steadily enlarge cultural opportunities for all of our citizens.

[17] And I look forward to an America which commands respect throughout the world, not only for its strength but for its civilization as well.

[18] And I look forward to a world which will be safe, not only for democracy and diversity but also for personal distinction.

One of the most effective approaches to the study of rhetorical method is the outline. Properly constructed, the outline gives a picture of the essay's overall structure and of the interaction of various thought patterns within it. For example, an outline of Kennedy's address demonstrates the structure of the address and suggests many of the rhetorical elements associated with the Kennedy style. The outline, properly constructed, represents a visual picture of the essay's overall structure as well as the interaction of various thought patterns.

Outline of "Poetry and Power"

I. Tribute to Robert Frost (Past)
  A. An artist and an American (1)
  B. His contributions (2)
  C. His strengths
    1. A deep source of national strength (3)
    2. An informing and controlling spirit of nation's power (4)
    3. An instinct for reality and a sense of tragedy (5)
    4. An understanding of ordeal (6)
    5. A deep faith in the spirit of man (7)

II. Tribute to Poetry (Present)
  A. Its saving qualities (8)
  B. Its critical value (9)

III. Tribute to the Arts (Future)
  A. As free expression
    1. Nourishes our culture (10)
    2. A form of truth (11)
    3. A service to the nation (12)
  B. As inspiration
    1. Integration of our best qualities (13)
    2. Pride in our past and beauty (14)
    3. Equal achievement and reward (15)
    4. Enhancement of itself and our citizens (16)
    5. Creator of prestige (17)
    6. Guardian of the democratic aspiration (18)

As this outline shows, the structural movement of Kennedy's essay is from specific to general and past to future. This type of pattern extends the significance of the occasion; it gives the President an opportunity to talk about more than Robert Frost. But Kennedy does not lose coherence, because Parts II and III are made to grow out of the personal dedicatory tribute. Concerned with the relationship of power to poetry, Kennedy develops his theme by going through Robert Frost toward art and on to power. He creates this rhythm by building the essay toward its center, found in its most fully developed paragraph (8) and the one related to a pivotal present that leads a concerned, thoughtful man of power to think of his country's future. What Kennedy does here is similar to what Lincoln had done: He uses a ceremonial occasion to express what we believe are authentic sympathies and worthwhile objectives. Few American men of power have better explained the role of the arts in a democratic society.

The use of an outline is a good learning device. It not only allows us to visualize a total structure, but it also enables us to consider the potential structural significance of each idea, sentence, and paragraph. An outline need not be elaborate, but it should signify the intended relationships among the paragraphs in the essay, whether the ordering principle is temporal, spatial, logical, or climactic. A good example of a climactic relationship among paragraphs is demonstrated in Kennedy's essay in I-C (paragraphs 3–7). There, the order of Robert Frost's strengths is based on the sequential movement from the least to the most important — from nation to mankind. In contrast, the last six paragraphs are ordered on a principle of equality, rather than climax, and the sentence structure in each is balanced and parallel. As represented in the outline, Kennedy's essay, built on the three-part form of the temporal movement from past to present to future, and within a logical rhythm of specific to general, reveals a structure that has an organic unity concerning Robert Frost, poetry, art, and power.

We think and write largely by free association, following the drift of thought as it comes, picking up some of our best ideas from below the logical surface. But to explain these thoughts fully to your reader, and to yourself, you need to discover and outline their logical pattern. Once you get the logic down on paper and out of the way, you can let yourself go, writing from heading to heading, sure of your direction, and sure of your order of ascending interest. You can push aside without worry the good ideas constantly crowding in for your notice: your outline has already scheduled them up ahead, each in its most logical and effective place.

— Sheridan Baker, *The Complete Stylist* (1966)

The style, like the structure, is also in harmony with the theme. Perhaps to suggest the balance of power and poetry in a democratic society, the style of the essay is replete with balanced and parallel forms. Beginning with the balance in the first paragraph ("A nation reveals itself *not only by the men it produces* but *also by the men it honors, the men it remembers.*") and ending with the parallel sentence forms in the last six paragraphs, the essay presents an excellent example of the uses of harmony and rhythm to support theme. Both Lincoln's "Gettysburg Address" and Kennedy's "Poetry and Power" provide good illustrations of the organic workings of substance, structure, and style.

A POSTSCRIPT

The recognition and acceptance of rhetoric in the communication process is essentially the acceptance of a social act. For it is through our writing, our speech, and the "statements" made by our behavior that our authenticity and existence become visible. Henry James expressed his understanding of this relationship in the following statement about speech, though it may well apply to all our expressions of self:

> All life . . . comes back to the question of our speech, the medium through which we communicate with each other; for all life comes back to the question of our relations with each other. These relations are made possible, are registered, are verily constituted, by our speech, and are successful . . . in proportion as our speech is worthy of its great human and social function: is developed, delicate, flexible, rich — an adequate accomplished fact. The more it suggests and expresses the more we live by it — the more it promotes and enhances life. Its quality, its authenticity, its security, are hence supremely important for the general multifold opportunity, for the dignity and integrity, of our existence.
>
> — Henry James, *The Question of Our Speech*

There is little we can add to what James suggests of the social significance of our acts of communication, whether spoken or written. What he says may also encourage us to a greater use of language that appeals to the ear as well as the eye. We selected "The Gettysburg Address" and "Poetry and Power" as models because originally they were oral presentations, and as such have made more use of the properties of sound than most of us do when we write. In a later section we will argue that we as a society are in the midst of the growing influence of oral language on our communications forms, but relatively little of that influence is permitted to affect the way we write. We emphasize that our approach makes no arbitrary distinction between oral and written communications. You may achieve an authentic rhetoric in either form, and each will affect the other in your personal style. Therefore, when we get to the study of structure and style, we will be concerned with techniques for both oral and written language.

EXERCISES

1. *Exercise in outlining.* Although the following selection is not formally paragraphed, establish the major structural divisions in the selection in outline form. Be prepared to explain the basis or rationale for such divisions.

   Studies serve for delight, for ornament, and for ability. Their chief use for delight is in privateness and retiring; for ornament, is in discourse; and for ability, is in the judgment and disposition of business. For expert men can execute, and perhaps judge of particulars, one by one; but the general counsels and the plots and marshalling of affairs come best from those that are learned. To spend too much time in studies is sloth; to use them too much for ornament is affectation; to make judgment wholly by their rules is the humour of a scholar. They perfect nature and are perfected by experience: for natural abilities are like natural plants that need pruning by study; and studies themselves do give forth directions too much at large, except they be bounded in by experience. Crafty men contemn studies, simple men admire them, and wise men use them: for they teach not their own use; but that is a wisdom without them and above them, won by observation. Read not to contradict and confute, nor to believe and take for granted, nor to find talk and discourse, but to weigh and consider. Some books are to be tasted, others to be swallowed, and some few to be chewed and digested; that is, some books are to be read only in parts; others to be read, but not curiously; and some few to be read wholly, and with diligence and attention. Some books also may be read by deputy, and extracts made of them by others; but that would be only in the less important arguments and the meaner sort of books; else distilled books are, like common distilled waters, flashy things. Reading maketh a full man; conference a ready man; and writing an exact man. And, therefore, if a man write little, he had need have a great memory; if he confer little, he had need have a present wit; and if he read little, he had need have much cunning, to seem to know that he doth not. Histories make men wise; poets, witty; the mathematics, subtile; natural philosophy, deep; moral, grave; logic and rhetoric, able to contend. Nay, there is no stond or impediment in the wit but may be wrought out by fit studies, like as diseases of the body may have appropriate exercises. Bowling is good for the stone and reins, shooting for the lungs and breast, gentle walking for the stomach, riding for the head and the like. So if a man's wit be wandering, let him study the mathematics; for in demonstrations, if his wit be called away never so little, he must begin again. If his wit be not apt to distinguish or find differences, let him study the school men; for they are *cymini sectores.* If he be not apt to beat over matters and to call up one thing to prove and illustrate another, let him study the lawyers' cases. So every defect of the mind may have a special receipt.

— Francis Bacon, *Of Studies*

2. *Exercise in style.* Read carefully through each of the paragraphs in Kennedy's "Poetry and Power" and underline the balanced words, phrases, clauses, and sentences. Also analyze Kennedy's use of language in the speech. How, for example, does he choose words in order to convey the idea that poetry is a form or source of power? If Kennedy does attribute power to poetry, why is it necessary to do so? Does poetry *have to be* a power? If the situation were reversed and Frost had dedicated a building named for Kennedy, would the poet have used language suggesting power or might he have turned in another direction? This is not an analysis of Kennedy's language, but your consideration of these questions will help you see how important the connotations of words can be in addition to their usual denotations.

3. *The logical order of sentences.* The order of the following six sentences has been altered. Determine what you think is a logical sequence.

   a. If we polish the rough truth that is here being grasped, we come to the distinction between knowledge and action as the two ends a writer may have in mind.

   b. There is an element of truth in this.

   c. Everyone uses the words "theoretical" and "practical," but not everyone knows what they mean, perhaps least of all the hardheaded practical man who distrusts all theorists, especially if they are in the government.

   d. The theoretical concerns something to be seen or understood.

   e. For such persons, "theoretical" means visionary or even mystical;

"practical" means something that works, something that has an immediate cash return.

f.   The practical has to do with what works in some way, at once or in the long run.

— From M. Adler and C. Van Doren, How to Read a Book

4. *I-Message-Thou writing assignment.* Using the rhetorical stance based on an I-Message-Thou relationship, write an essay in which you reveal some authentic aspect of yourself. The "message" might be an experience you have had, a philosophical or political position you believe in, or a psychological state you are in or have been in. Above all be as honest as you can.

5. *The concern for audience.* One of the best sources for the study of audience is the newspaper. Select a newspaper familiar to you and write an article for it. The article can be any regular feature of the paper: an editorial, a letter to the editor, a film review, a sports presentation, an Ann Landers-like column, or whatever. What you should not do is a reporter's news story, which would tend to mask the personality of the writer. Even though you are probably writing for a large audience, it does not mean that you cannot be an authentic writer — reveal experience as honestly as you can. In order to do the assignment you must accept the following responsibilities:

   a.   Analyze the audience to which the newspaper is directed generally and, depending on the article, the audience in particular (for example, most of the writing in the "household" pages of a newspaper is geared toward women).

   b.   Each section of the newspaper has its own stylistic and structural requirements. Be sure to analyze the section you choose to do before you begin to write.

   c.   Since this is an article for a public audience, you have also to be a good proofreader and editor. You are responsible for the mechanical and grammatical quality of the article.

   d.   Take into careful consideration the structure and style of your piece: work toward an organic relationship among substance, style, and structure — that is, use the rhetorical method.

   e.   Hand in a note attached to the piece that has the name of the newspaper and an evaluation of the audience for which the article is intended.

   f.   The length will be determined by the subject and the kind of article you choose to write.

6. *The study of audience.* One of the characteristics of today's successful magazines is their ability to identify a select audience. This audience is often very visible. Choose a magazine and analyze it for evidence about the nature of its audience. Try to infer the age, sex, income, education, sophistication, special interests, and lifestyle of its ideal reader. Base your analysis on the advertisements, cover, layout, artwork, and cartoons as well as on the articles, fiction, and poetry. Be as specific as possible — use examples and illustrations.

7. *Revision for audience.* Choose a short article (about 500 words) from a newspaper or magazine. Without changing the facts given, rewrite it so that it appeals to a different audience — your peers, for example. Be sure to hand in the original article with the rewritten version.

8. *The relationship of form and audience.* One of the best sources for writing assignments is the short news items found in newspapers. The following is such a news item (some of the details have been altered):

A UNIVERSITY STUDENT'S CAR BROKE DOWN ALONG HIGHWAY 50. AFTER TRYING TO HITCH A RIDE FOR SIX HOURS AND AFTER WATCHING HUNDREDS OF CARS GO BY WITHOUT STOPPING, DENNIS ROGERS RETURNED TO HIS CAR, WROTE A NOTE, AND SHOT HIMSELF. THE SUICIDE NOTE SIMPLY READ, "I CAN NO LONGER LIVE IN AN INDIFFERENT WORLD. PERHAPS MY DEATH WILL MEAN MORE THAN MY LIFE."

Using the above experience, communicate its essential meaning in one of the following situations. Remember that each has its particular characteristics and audience. Be sure you define both the structure and audience in your mind or on a piece of paper before you begin to write:

a. an editorial for a large newspaper

b. a social scientist such as Margaret Mead using the incident as a comment on our civilization

c. a short story writer's "fictionalized" account of the incident

d. the position of an existential philosopher (Camus, Sartre, Tillich) concerning Dennis Roger's act

e. a psychologist's interpretation of the act using a specific frame or frames of reference, such as Freud's, Skinner's, Rollo May's, or Carl Rogers' (of course, you will have to invent the details of Dennis Rogers' life)

f. a student writing an open letter to the victim's parents that is to be published in the school newspaper

3

✒ STRUCTURE ✑

Order, arrangement, structure —
these concepts seem to be a necessary
precondition in order for the mind to be able to
understand anything. Without order the world of
experience becomes a shapeless mass. Music
becomes mere noise; a painting becomes a blob of
paint; a play becomes a happening. The human mind, the
order of nature, social organizations, art, the solar system —
all dissolve in a chaos of particles. The idea of order seems to be
deeply rooted in the human condition. It would be difficult,
perhaps impossible, to find objects and events which do not reflect
some signs of an underlying order. The houses that we live in display
some sort of spatial order. The streets of our cities reveal
planning of some kind. The displays of food in
our supermarkets exhibit a pattern of arrangement.
The cycle of the seasons and the movement
of planets clearly proclaim that
nature is orderly.

FRANK J. D'ANGELO
A Conceptual Theory of Rhetoric
(1975)

THE ROLE OF STRUCTURE

The structuring process of speech or writing begins with private understandings and feelings an individual wishes translated into public forms and statements. At the point at which you want to go beyond self to communicate with another, your sense of rhetoric must take over and guide your search for suitable methods. You believe you have something to say (substance, a *what* to be said), but you need a way or combinations of ways to say it (rhetorical skills, techniques, a *how*). Immediately, you discover an important feature of any communication: there is no such thing as a substance by itself, no way in which content can be separated from its form. *How* something is presented, the form it takes, will always affect *what* the receiver manages to get. *Structure* and *style* are different aspects of *how*.

Structure, as part of the rhetorical method, is linked with your awareness of audience and the kind of impact you want to make on it. Varied subjects, audiences, and situations force you to recognize that many structural patterns exist and that you should be able to use them consciously. Structure is a quality best and most consistently achieved through planning; it is something that can be thought out before you actually begin to write. An outline can be used as a visual picture of the internal skeleton of your essay. In the previous chapter, we saw in an outline how the structure of Kennedy's speech was built on a pattern relating smaller parts to a larger whole. Before you begin to write, an outline can give you an idea of the placement of major units in your presentation — units usually in the form of paragraphs. The outline normally will be composed from your notes and your thoughts related to your understanding of the content and your audience, but it should not eliminate free choices that occur in the writing which may result in improved communication.

Whatever specific form they take, outline arrangements are based on patterns in your experience; two patterns you know, for example, are the *logical* and the *chronological*. Each whole paragraph in its relationship with other paragraphs in your essay normally is governed by a structural principle: If logic directs your order, then your paragraphs should explain inductions, deductions, premises; if chronology directs it, then paragraphs must explain how events and ideas are related to each other in a unified sequence in time. *Within* the paragraph, however, you will find that you may also use structural patterns not governed by the overall pattern. Your main structural decisions work to tie the essay together by creating an overall pattern, but one decision — to use a chronological order, for example — does not remove the possible need to employ a logical pattern such as analysis within the framework of chronological narrative. For this reason, each paragraph can be considered a "mini" essay; neither as a whole nor in its parts, however, can it be totally independent. What your outline shows is that each paragraph is part of, and functions to fulfill, a larger structural pattern. The ways in which paragraphs are built will be developed in relation to the various principles of structure (definition, analysis, comparison and contrast, and so on).

The degree to which you permit one or another kind of structure to govern your writing — or your life, for that matter — has to be worked out on an individual basis. Novelist Jack Kerouac once suggested that the infatuation with conscious, rational, logical form leads to the denial of spontaneity and personal expression, and consequently, he said, the creative writer must avoid that type of form. In the same vein, political activist Abbie Hoffman, during the riots in Chicago at the 1968 Democratic Convention, told his followers to be aware of the "structure freak." But we cannot get along without form or structure in our communications. Kerouac and Hoffman merely opt for structures that run counter to the structures we expect. No matter what you decide to

---

One of the most characteristic traits of human beings is their ability to conceive systems of arrangement and to impose these systems on different objects. Though you and I as individuals may have to struggle to maintain such superficial manifestations of order as tidy rooms and neatly combed hair, nevertheless, as human beings with rational intellects we constantly conceive mental relationships and *perceive* these relationships in stars or atoms, or we *arrange* things — from silverware to steel girders — in orderly patterns. It is scarcely inaccurate to say that all order is manmade, since whatever the absolute nature of non-human objects, all we as human beings can know about them is determined by our sensory and intellectual perceptions.

— James W. Johnson, *Logic and Rhetoric* (1962)

communicate, you must give some attention to form. Only the type is an individual choice, but it should be determined, as Hoffman's was, by a personal rhetorical stance, embracing both a concept of self and an understanding of human nature.

There is nothing intrinsically evil about logic any more than there is about free association; you merely need to know how and when to use one or the other. Syllogistic reasoning allows us to approach a problem through a careful series of steps, however concealed the steps may be. And nonlogical, discontinuous, seemingly chaotic structures such as you find in stream-of-consciousness allow us to surround a problem with images from which readers can infer solutions. This is only to point out what modern psychology tells us — that dreams, as well as logic, can teach. Dream structures are open to analysis, but they happen not to be the ones most useful for conventional dialogue, the traditional essay you most frequently have to write and read. This chapter will be concerned, then, with studying a variety of structural patterns. All are seen in our culture and are likely to occur in your experience. Practice using them. Find those that are suitable to you and that fit your needs on different occasions. Eventually, you will discover that you have begun to use many different patterns effectively, but almost unconsciously, just as you have in your use of spoken language.

BEGINNINGS AND ENDINGS

As a form, the essay can be divided into three distinct parts — beginning, middle, and end, or introduction, body, and conclusion. Almost any object or unit of time we experience sequentially can be so divided, but the divisions here are arrived at less on the basis of logic than on the history of rhetoric. They come from the organization of the classical oration. The original seven parts of the oration have been reduced, but they still exist in some manner in most essays. The seven parts consisted of *exordium, narration, exposition, proposition, confirmation, refutation,* and *peroration.* The *exordium* established the speaker's relationship with the audience; the *narration* explained the reason for the subject; the *exposition* defined terms and demonstrated the significance of the topic; the *proposition* directly and clearly stated the thesis; the *confirmation* developed the various arguments; the *refutation* answered opposing arguments; and the *peroration* established an emotional appeal and a summary of key points. In the ancient Greek educational system this pattern was taught to everyone. One advantage for the Greek orator in using the seven-part structure was the audience's familiarity with the form. Obviously, when your listeners know the conventions of your argument, it is easier for them to follow your line of thinking, and, hence, your chances of success are just that much greater.

In our culture, in which there is no such standard form, speakers or writers cannot easily find a culturally familiar way to communicate their ideas. By using this fundamentally sound three-part formula (either in whole structures or in parts of the whole), you can be sure that most of the audiences for which you write in college will be able to follow you. But you may need to modify this formula — expand it or reduce it — in order to achieve your specific goals on a given occasion. You may need to curtail introductions or conclusions, or to expand the pattern of middles. A suggestion for accomplishing this latter is our modification, appropriate for the modern student, of the classical form.

A Classical Form for a Modern Student

Introduction: (usually one paragraph)	Contains material/language that: (1) captures interest of and relates to audience (*exordium*) (2) gives background, history, or reminds the audience of what they already know (*narration*) (3) states the relevance or validity of the subject matter and defines terms where necessary (*exposition*) (4) establishes tone (5) states the main idea (thesis, proposition) and suggests the method of development (*proposition*)
Body: Confirmation (an adequate number of paragraphs to fully develop the thesis)	Contains material that develops, illustrates, and proves the main idea (thesis) by appealing to the intellect of the audience. Each paragraph of the body may follow this pattern: (1) topical material (topic sentence that supports the main thesis)

49

	(2) development (material that supports and explains by use of definition, examples, analysis, etc.)
	(3) concluding sentence that acts as a transition to the next paragraph
Refutation: (The length and force of a refutation are governed by the writer's estimation of the audience's interest in and sympathy for his thesis. In some cases, a refutation need only be implied. In all cases, a writer should be alert to the breadth of the audience's knowledge and the depth of their prejudices.)	Contains material that: 1) states opposing view in an honest but concise form (2) quickly indicates the opposition's inadequacy if possible
Conclusion: Peroration (usually one paragraph)	Contains material that: (1) gives a summary or restatement of thesis, usually marked by an appeal to the emotions of the audience (2) relates the subject back to the audience in the same way as the introduction related to the audience

You are not obliged to use this pattern. We merely want you to see — in a visual scheme — what often goes into an essay. The pattern, instead, might be used as a checklist of your responsibilities as a *sender* of an extensive message. *We* have not felt bound to such a pattern in this book. Like you, we have often made decisions to modify our patterns in order to achieve specific results. But in order to give a fuller discussion of structure, we will consider most of the parts of the classical essay in some detail in the following sections.

INTRODUCTORY PARAGRAPHS

The purpose of your introductory paragraph is to prepare your audience for what is to follow. As a writer, you must direct your material to your audience; you must make it interesting, significant, and relevant. The stance you take in your opening can make the difference between a

> Where does the writer actually begin? He does not necessarily begin at the beginning of the piece of writing. Some authors like to get a jump-off sentence, but if one does not come, a writer cannot afford to wait for it. The likelihood is that whatever he puts down at the head of a rough draft will have to be changed anyway. Indeed, the first paragraph is often better written last. Neither does he normally begin with the title, although that will stand at the head of the finished work. A catchy title can be the inspiration for an essay; but the danger is that the essay will not fit the preselected label and the writer will not be able to bring himself to abandon it — condemning the paper to a fate like that of a girl bearing a masculine name because her parents expected a boy. Children are better named after they are born, and essays after they are written. At any rate, a writer does not wait until he gets the perfect title before he starts.
>
> — John Jordon, *Using Rhetoric* (1965)

successful attempt at communication and one that fails. What stances can you take? Carl Rogers, the noted therapist, suggests that effective communication can take place only when an audience is made to feel secure. Although we would prefer our model of writing to be based on this assumption, we recognize that a posture of affection or humility is not always possible or even (in extreme circumstances) desirable — in your life experiences or in your writing. An authentic person tries to communicate with other authentic persons, but there are occasions when you know — as Julius Lester knows in the excerpt on p. 54 — that those others are or have been engaged in denying your authentic being. So, *at the same time* that we argue for an authentic writer and an authentic rhetoric, we realize that a rhetoric of hostility exists and may be a necessity for you occasionally. Your first duty, regardless, is to take a stance in your introduction that will most effectively connect you with the personality of your reader. There is no single formula to achieve this: it must be accomplished out of an informed sensitivity to your audience. Many different methods by which you can approach your audience are available, and as a student-writer you will need to practice them in writing exercises that will strengthen your hold on certain rhetorical principles.

The following examples of introductory paragraphs are ways by which you might approach the responsibility of audience appeal. The particular tack you take should not always remain the same, but it should be altered to meet the needs of the material and the audience with which you want to communicate. You may begin:

51

(1) with a straightforward statement of opinion:

> Ian Fleming's James Bond is the most famous spy since Mata Hari. The indomitable secret agent reaches every level of literacy: Presidents to popcorn chewers. Not only has the author become a kind of subliterary lion in *Time, The New Yorker,* and the *Saturday Review,* which have devoted interviews and articles to his work, but his opinion was solicited on a major network show about the U-2 affair, the producers seeming to consider Mr. Fleming something like the Walter Lippmann of espionage.
>
> — George Grella, "James Bond: Culture Hero"

An opening like this will be most effective with a literate, well-read audience. Not every student knows of Mata Hari, U-2s, Walter Lippmann, or even James Bond. But most college-educated readers will recognize these and perhaps be amused by the attention given to a fictional hero and his author-creator.

(2) with an anecdote:

> I had a job interview several weeks ago. Friends warned me not to be too aggressive. During the interview, I tried to present myself as a competent candidate, able to "think like a man" and yet not to be a "masculine" female. After fielding several questions relevant to the job, I suddenly heard, "Miss Stern, are you in love?"
>
> — Paula Stern, "The Womanly Image"

Unlike the previous introduction, this opening, though once likely to have aroused only a sophisticated audience with an intellectual interest in women's liberation, would appeal to a massive audience of women and men today. Writing the article for *The Atlantic Monthly,* the author may go on to treat her subject quite abstractly, but for her beginning she resorts to an anecdotal approach. Such a quick little story can effectively suggest the dimensions of a topic as well as gain an audience's attention, whether the latter is comprised of schoolgirls or of adults who have read weighty books on the plight of women in our culture.

(3) with an historical perspective:

> The baffling history of mankind is full of obvious turning points and significant events: battles won, treaties signed, rulers elected or deposed, and now, seemingly, planets conquered. Equally important are the great

groundswells of popular movements that affect the minds and values of a generation or more, not all of which can be neatly tied to a time and place. Looking back upon the America of the '60s future historians may well search for the meaning of one such movement. It drew the public's notice on the days and nights of August 15 through 17, 1969, on the 600-acre farm of Max Yasgur in Bethel, N.Y.

— *Time* Essay, "The Message of History's Biggest Happening"

(4) with a play on familiar words or rhythms:

Television is something by our times, out of our times, for our times. It reflects the virtues and faults of our times.

— Aubrey Singer, "Television: Window on Culture or
Reflection in the Glass?"

(5) with a relevant quotation:

"When we try to pick out anything by itself," wrote wilderness wanderer John Muir, "we find it hitched to everything else in the universe." Thus did Muir, who founded the Sierra Club in 1892, become one of the first to define in 25 words or less what ecology is all about. At the time, perhaps, his simple eloquence was wasted on a generation that had devoted itself to the unhitching of North American species, including the Indian, and was now hell-bent on stoking the new fires of technology.

— John G. Mitchell, "Environment and the Economy"

(6) with a paradox:

Our scientists and engineers could make a kitchen table fly — if we gave them enough time and money. That's America's competence. Toss a social problem at us, and we fumble almost every time.

— Ira Mothner, "Cities"

(7) with unusual details presented in an unusual frame or style:

FADE IN . . . lone stranger . . . mean, ugly, handsome-ugly lonely stranger . . . skyline . . . mean, ugly, handsome-ugly lonely skyline . . . out of shadows comes a man . . . pow, bam, sock . . . four-letter words . . . smash to the groin . . . pow, bam, sock . . . lone stranger pulls a gun . . . pow . . . man bites the asphalt . . . bam, sock . . . lone stranger walks on . . . mean, ugly, handsome-ugly lonely lone stranger . . . out of shadows comes a girl, beautiful-anonymous, big-bosomed boy-body, all hair and mouth, no forehead, no hips . . . pow, bam, sock . . . five-letter words . . . smooch to the groin . . . pow, bam, sock . . . pop-art penthouse . . . bare shoulders, bare thighs, bare everything . . . FADE OUT.

> — Judith Crist, "Movies: Where Anything Goes"

(8) with narrative exposition that puts the audience into context:

An elderly school bus, painted like a fluorescent Easter egg in orange, chartreuse, cerise, white, green, blue, and, yes, black, was parked outside the solitary mountain cabin, which made it an easy guess that Ken Kesey, the novelist turned psychedelic Hotspur, was inside. So, of course, was Neal Cassady, the Tristram Shandy of the Beat Generation, prototype hero of Jack Kerouac's *On the Road,* who had sworn off allegiance to Kerouac when the beat scene became menopausal and signed up as the driver of Kesey's fun and games bus, which is rumored to run on LSD. Except for these notorious luminaries, the Summit Meeting of the leaders of the new hippie subculture, convened in the lowlands of California's High Sierras during an early spring weekend last month, seemed a little like an Appalachian Mafia gathering without Joe Bananas.

> — Warren Hinckle, "A Social History of the Hippies"

(9) with a metaphorical or an ironical statement:

The war of the generations has been going on a long time, and it is unlikely that anything really new can be contributed to it. But I should like to say a word on behalf of the elderly, remembering, of course, that whatever I say is suspect as reactionary, fuddy-duddy or dead.

> — Spencer Brown, "The Younger Generation"

(10) with a dramatic statement:

It is clear that America as it now exists must be destroyed. There is no other way. It is impossible to live within this country and not become a thief or a murderer. Young blacks and young whites are beginning to say NO to thievery and murder. Black Power confronts White Power openly, and as the SNCC poet Worth Long cried: "We have found you out, false-faced America. We have found you out!"

> — Julius Lester, "Look Out, Whitey! Black Power's
> Gon Get Your Mama"

These illustrations by no means exhaust the possible techniques for capturing the interest of your audience, but they should give you some ideas to experiment with in your own writing. If you give enough thought to the nature of your subject matter, it should give you a hint as to how to appeal to the audience. Warren Hinckle's essay on the writers in the "hippie" movement begins with the technique of narration because his interest is in bringing alive with details a historical development. Julius Lester's essay concerns an emotional topic — the social relationships between the races — and it begins with a dramatic statement that threatens the security of any American who reads it. He has our attention. We're listening carefully to a statement on a subject many Americans prefer to avoid.

In addition to the appeal to the interest of the audience, the introduction should demonstrate the significance of the subject matter to the audience. Spencer Brown demonstrates the significance of his material by suggesting the generation "gap" is a "war" that must be understood not only in terms of the young but also from the perspective of the elderly. Whatever the subject matter, you must relate it to your audience; they must become active participants in the process. Judith Crist achieves this goal, among others, in her opener. We have said that the techniques of stream-of-consciousness and seemingly random associations are not usually ones you will need to use. But here, Crist, by giving us a compact narrative sequence of images and directions, comes close to suggesting that what she renders has become a universal occurrence in our films and so is of grave significance. The sequence has overtones of a dream or nightmare, moreover, and these overtones are in keeping with the overall ethical stance of Crist's essay. But be careful if you try this technique; done poorly, it can be trite and boring.

Another feature associated with the introduction is a clear thesis statement, which will usually indicate the shape or process of argument at the same time it indicates the thesis itself. A student writing about Dee Brown's *Bury My Heart At Wounded Knee,* the chapter on "The Battle at Little Big Horn," adopted this as a thesis: "Dee Brown's essay tells how American Indians have been ill-treated by the United States government, the U.S. Army, and the American public." Not only does this sentence express a proposition; it also suggests an order in which the material can be treated. In the completed essay there were paragraphs on each of the three items listed: government, army, and public. As theses often do, this clear thesis statement in the student's paper came at the end of the introductory material and offered a strong transition from the introduction to the body of the essay. Another example of a clearly defined proposition is the last sentence of Aubrey Singer's introductory paragraph.

All in all there are three important features of introductory paragraphs. If you neglect just one of these — capturing audience interest, demonstrating significance, presenting a clear thesis statement — your introduction will not be as effective as it might be.

EXERCISES

Write an introductory paragraph directed toward a specific audience that introduces each of the following propositions and uses a different method of audience appeal (straightforward statement, anecdote, play on words, and so on) for each.

1. Teachers should be willing to extend help outside the classroom.
2. Education should take place outside as well as in the classroom.
3. There are advantages for a student who lives at home (or in a dormitory) during his or her first year of college.
4. College should be primarily an intellectual experience.
5. College athletics perform an important role in the campus environment.

Obviously, you may have to alter the proposition to fit the particular method of audience appeal. Your intent should be to practice using different kinds of essay openings in order to gain more flexibility as a writer.

CONCLUDING PARAGRAPHS

Like the introductory paragraph, the concluding paragraph has a special rhetorical and structural function. There are times when the last thing you say to your audience may be as important as, or more important than, the first few words. In that case, try to make the final paragraph a restatement of the major points you have given in the body of the essay. You may also alter an essay's tone at the end in order to appeal to the audience in a specific way. Effective conclusions often reverse the tone of an opening. If you begin blandly, factually, unemotionally, but you want to move your audience to some action, then you may want to raise the emotional level at the end — arouse anger, desire, hostility, sorrow, conscience, whatever suits your purpose. On the other hand, if you have begun with an impassioned appeal to your audience, it is often helpful to return to it in conclusion — thus giving your essay a harmonious, circular integrity. The following introduction by Spencer Brown begins with a metaphor or war, and he repeats it in his conclusion; this technique has the effect of "closure," of rounding off a subject.

> We cannot win, and society can only lose, if we alternate old-fashioned repression with the new-fashioned appeasement. There are probably just as many wicked young people as wicked old people, and just as many virtuous people in both camps. Our young people have a right to look to us for balance, common sense and a sense of humor. With these unspectacular but indispensable qualities we can call off the war and proceed with the job of education.
>
> — Spencer Brown, "The Younger Generation"

By shifting from the metaphor of *war* to one of *job* — the last sentence — Brown subtly changes his tone and shows that there is a more humane and constructive way for the two generations to see each other.

It is important to consider your audience and to select and arrange your material carefully in order to make the most appropriate effect. In the speech we looked at in the previous chapter, Kennedy's visionary appeal to the role of art in a democratic culture is appropriate because it suggests that poetry is available to all of us. It leaves the audience exalted, makes them feel they have capabilities they have never tapped. Kennedy's vision offers a humane ideal, and that seems more appropriate than the old standard appeals to class, race, national origin, or material self-interest. You may also end your essay effectively with a quotation, anecdote, speculative question, or descriptive passage. The following illustrations of techniques for conclusions are taken from essays from which you have already seen the introductions. You may conclude:

(1) with a humorous twist or play on familiar words or rhythms:

> The danger in the hippie movement is more than overcrowded streets and possible hunger riots this summer. If more and more youngsters begin to share the hippie political posture of unrelenting quietism, the future of activist, serious politics is bound to be affected. The hippies have shown that it can be pleasant to drop out of the arduous task of attempting to steer a difficult unrewarding society. But when that is done, you leave the driving to the Hell's Angels.
>
> — Warren Hinckle, "A Social History of the Hippies"

(2) with repetition for rhetorical effect:

> It won't get done tomorrow. But we *can* change our cities, we *can* change the quality of life in the ghettos, we *can* change the slums. We *can* make cities that will be the pride of this rural-loving nation.

> — Ira Mothner, "Cities"

(3) with a relevant, appropriate, striking, ironic, or other quotation:

> It is beyond argument that the generation attuned to rock, pot and sex will drastically change the world it grew up in. The question is: How and to what purpose? Columbia sociologist Amitai Etzioni applauds the idealism of the young but argues that "they need more time and energy for reflection" as well as more opportunities for authentic service. Ultimately, the greater danger of the counterculture is its self-proclaimed flight from reason, its exaltation of self over society, its Dionysian anarchism. Historian Roszak points out that the rock revolutionaries bear a certain resemblance to the early Christians, who, in a religious cause, rejected the glory that was Greece and the grandeur of Rome. Ultimately, they brought down a decaying pagan empire and built another in its place. But the Second Comings of history carry with them no guarantees of success, and a revolution based on unreason may just as easily bring a New Barbarism rather than the New Jerusalem. As Yeats so pointedly asked:

> And what rough beast, its hour come round at last,
> Slouches toward Bethlehem to be born?

> — *Time* Essay, "The Message of History's Biggest Happening"

Compare the introductory passages with these conclusions. Notice the consistency of tone and historical approach, for example, in both the introduction and conclusion in the *Time* essay. But notice, too, that Hinckle moves from the immediacy of narrative description to a metaphor linking Kesey's bus to the Greyhound, whose driver has been replaced by a Hell's Angel. It's a topical allusion ("Leave the driving to us") that suggests the danger Hinckle sees in a movement usually thought to be quite benign. These two examples suggest that you must adjust your material to fit *your* purposes.

One last point. The transitional signal that you are concluding should be considered in light of your audience. Some audiences like the obvious, so you might simply say by way of introducing the concluding paragraph, "In conclusion." Usually, the shorter the essay the less need there is for such devices, but at the end of a long essay (as at the end of a long speech or sermon) your audience may find great relief in those two words.

EXERCISES

Analyze the following student introductory and concluding paragraphs for their strengths and weaknesses.

Introductory Paragraph

Culture, according to Lionel Trilling, is a prison. Perhaps "prison" is too strong a term, but we all realize that our actions, beliefs, and attitudes are often conditioned and hence limited to a large extent by the culture in which we live. There is a way, however, to lessen the impact of cultural control on us and that is to understand exactly what culture is. Culture, by definition, is the way of life of a people, a sum of their learned behavior patterns, attitudes, and material things. A way to understand culture is to approach it through its building blocks; that is, through the pieces and parts that it constitutes such as rituals, norms, values, and mores.

Concluding Paragraph

These four building blocks by no means exhaust the wall of culture. Such pieces as inhibition, behavior, conformity, peer, myth, and ethic contribute to the totality of our responses in any culture. However, our understanding of ritual, norms, values, and mores does give us some insights into how culture works and how it conditions our behavior. By understanding these characteristics we have at least a "key" in our hand to unlock the cultural prison if we so desire. The knowledge of culture like all knowledge ultimately frees us.

MIDDLES: PATTERNS FOR DEVELOPMENT

The body or the middle part of your essay normally is formed by a sequence of paragraphs designed to achieve your purpose, which ordinarily will be either to explain (the rhetorical term for which is *exposition*) or to convince (*argumentation*). These paragraphs are organized around a limited number of major ideas and presented in some unified conceptual framework usually announced or hinted at in the introductory sentence(s) or paragraph(s). If you are writing a short, five-paragraph essay on the career of a ballplayer, for example, you probably will find that three paragraphs will form a middle, the body of the essay, and that these can be focused *chronologically* if your intent is to show the development of his talent, from high school glory through minor-league struggles on to major-league triumph, each stage in the chronological sequence being narrowed down to one climactic game: pitching a no-hitter in the state championship finals, being bombed out in his minor-league debut, and finally winning the last game of a world series. You could shift the focus of your paragraphs, however, and emphasize instead the roles of three people who had important influences on him: a parent, a teacher or coach, a wise friend of the family. With this focus, your structural principle may be chronological, but it will be involved too with the concept of *significance*. This way you may more effectively present your essay's thesis by showing that it was not a coach (paragraph one), not the father (paragraph two), but the ballplayer's mother (paragraph three) who had the most important impact on the subsequent career.

Structure, in middles as in the whole essay, is thus conceptual. It is not a matter of physical arrangement of paragraphs on pages, in various shapes or configurations, but is a matter of ideas, concepts, or principles that allow — indeed, force — a reader's mind to focus on the pattern of your thinking, expressed most succinctly in your thesis. When you successfully have provided such a structure, a reader of your essay will read it feeling that each paragraph is anticipated in, grows out of, or is otherwise connected to the preceding one. In addition, when the sequence is ended, your reader will feel the essay is coming to a concluding paragraph or statement. In your essays, then, middles are always taking your reader somewhere: they are the steps that get the reader from the introduction to the conclusion and make the whole jaunt worth his or her time.

Our point here should be fairly obvious: all discourse — not just poetry — gains its coherence because it mirrors what Kenneth Burke calls "patterns of experience." If it does not mirror these patterns, it is incoherent or, at the very least, unsatisfying, in just the same sense that we feel an unresolved chord is unsatisfying. Seemingly, this argument is unassailable, even on biological grounds. The human mechanism is so organized that it can perceive the world only in certain ways; most obviously all perception has a spatial and temporal orientation. But we can borrow terms from the arts to describe other *forms* of experience: climax, resolution, counterpoint, modulation, tension, and so on. Now this inquiry would be futile if it were impossible to find some finite number of patterns in discourse; that is, an infinite series of discrete items always implies precisely lack of meaningful pattern.

— W. Ross Winterowd, *Rhetoric: A Synthesis* (1968)

Much thought will have gone into your essay by the time you are able to state your thesis and formulate the pattern upon which it will be constructed. But at this point in the writing process you are still concerned more with large units than with small ones: several paragraphs, not just one, many potential sentences, not the one actual sentence you must eventually write, add to, and then add to again and again before your essay is concluded. You must get to this next stage sooner or later, however, so you will have to decide *how* each paragraph itself will be developed after your pattern or organization has told you *what* should be in it. Decisions at this stage will usually be made on the spot, as you begin to formulate — in your mind or on paper — actual sentences. These decisions will be made on the basis of your experience in communication, for that experience will prompt you to ask and answer certain questions, which in turn will lead you to employ specific techniques of development.

Do your thesis and purpose require you to use words your reader is not likely to understand? If so, you need to define terms. Do thesis and purpose force you to deal in abstractions? You can decide to help your reader by giving examples and illustrations. Would it be helpful to show the reader a comparison or a contrast in order to develop an idea, a theme, an argument? Is a situation you are explaining so complex that you need to reduce it to simpler terms? Perhaps then an analogy will help. Or perhaps the best way to get at a conclusion is to present the data first. Then you may want to take your reader through an inductive

The relationship between writer, subject, and audience, which serves as the basis for our choice of form, is relative; it consists of three independent variables, and a change in any one of them may result in a change of form. A basic distinction between exposition and argument is that in argument the audience is not expected to accept at face value what the writer has to propose. There may be several reasons for their scepticism: the audience may not accept him as an authority (they may not know him, for example, or they may be fellow-experts); or his proposition may not be immediately acceptable, as when alternative propositions have already been advanced; or his proposition may seem contrary to common sense, accepted knowledge, or common practice. Then his job is to argue his proposition as convincingly and persuasively as possible.

— N. Friedman and C. A. McLaughlin, *Logic, Rhetoric, and Style* (1963)

61

sequence that will move from a possible thesis to a conclusion, as a scientist begins with a hypothesis and works from details to a thesis.

From your accumulated experience you *know* these patterns of problem and solution, but you probably are not always conscious that you know them. They are part of our cultural heritage, not precisely aspects of language itself but formal elements of our inherited rhetorical systems. As formal elements, each technique has its own set of mechanisms that alerts readers to it and allows them to realize when it has fulfilled its capabilities. And, as formal elements, each pattern can often be used to shape and develop all three levels of essay structure: the sentence, the paragraph, and the whole essay.

DEFINITION

One of the initial responsibilities the writer has to consider is whether there are any words that might need to be explained and defined for the audience. Depending on the purpose of the writer and the material itself, the process of *definition* can be achieved in a single sentence, a full paragraph, or even an entire essay. In essence, definition is a method for seeking an answer to the question, What is it? The word itself derives from the Latin *de* and *finire* meaning "to set a limit"; thus, when we set out to define a word or an idea we attempt to establish boundaries for it; these boundaries relate in some way to the common usage of the term or to the reality it represents. That is why we have just defined the word *definition* and why you will need frequently to define words for your readers. If your reader can't say, "I speak your language," then you must say, "I'll teach my language to you."

How can we go about achieving understanding through definition? There are a number of ways, of course, but three basic techniques are important: the use of the synonym, of logical definitions, and of extended definitions. The first, most obvious, and commonest method of defining is by synonym; this method generally means an appeal to the dictionary. Thus, an unfamiliar word like *exegesis* might be explained by the better-known and better-understood *interpretation*. Definition by synonym may have the virtue of ready availability; but it may also have certain marked disadvantages. For one thing, no two words are ever precisely synonymous, as anyone who arbitrarily uses a thesaurus, without recourse also to a dictionary, will know. For another, the simplest dictionary or equivalency definition may set up boundaries — but they are the boundaries of conventional usage that are notoriously shifting and unstable. For example, a word like *world* can be confusing in certain contexts, for synonyms include *universe, cosmos, kingdom,* and the like. To the astronomer, these words have very precise meanings, and they do not include the meaning involved in the title of the popular daytime soap opera, *As the World Turns.* Synonyms can be of considerable help in clarifying meaning, but one must be wary of relying upon them exclusively.

To extend the dictionary definition, you might use an example (*exemplification* is in itself a pattern of development, so be aware of the ways patterns can combine). We may not know the strictly literary meaning of the term *novel,* but if we are told that *Moll Flanders, The Scarlet Letter, The Portrait of a Lady,* and *Fear of Flying* are novels, we may gain some rudimentary understanding of the term: we may have read one of these, but if not, we may turn to the examples themselves to test abstraction against concrete reading experience. For definition by example to be effective, you must consider your audience. Will they know the examples and understand the characteristic features of them? To assure your success you may need to give several examples, ones that range across the limits of the term as well as the experiences of the audience. You do not know *Moll Flanders,* perhaps, but you do know *Fear of Flying, The Scarlet Letter* but not *The Portrait of a Lady*: that is okay. You can begin to understand the term from what you know of what we give you.

We know that the dictionary is concerned with the origin of words, their historical progress, and their present conventional usage. Despite the examples it can give, the dictionary cannot easily go beyond the word to consider many special relationships between the word and the thing it

---

Until we examine the way language works, we usually assume that words have definite, permanent meanings. We feel that, as long as our grammar and punctuation are adequate, what we are trying to say should be obvious to all people of good will. However, when dealing with issues of some consequence, we soon learn that different people use the same words in widely different ways. . . . Once a writer realizes that such differences exist, he will feel obligated to make clear what his *own* vantage point is, what ideas and aspiration *he* reads into a term. The first step is to become aware of the types of words that are most likely to need such narrowing down; that is, words in need of definition.

— Hans P. Guth, *A Short New Rhetoric* (1964)

defines. Thus, let's suppose our purpose, occasion, and thesis require more than the dictionary and a few examples can provide. Suppose we need to define words and ideas that include difficult concepts as part of their essential meaning. What then can we do?

A more intensive means of explaining words is through logical definition. In this pattern (which is the same process as the general pattern of *classification* and *division*), the term to be defined is placed in a class or category, usually called the *genus*, based on likenesses or commonality of traits. Next, the special characteristics of the term are enumerated and specified for the purpose of distinguishing it from other members of the same class (*differentia*). The novel, for instance, belongs to the class *narrative*, differentiated from biography by being *fiction*, from metrical fictional narrative (*The Iliad, Evangeline*) by being in *prose*, and from prose fictional narrative romance by being about a real world essentially contemporaneous with its authorship. Carried out this far, the definition may begin to eliminate some of the examples a broader definition would permit: *The Scarlet Letter,* for instance, would drop out because of the last differentia. Let's take another example. In *The Making of a Counter Culture*, Theodore Roszak defines two distinct cultures: the existing culture, which he calls the "technocracy," and an emerging "counter culture." Here are his definitions of the two terms using the logical method:

Technocracy: "By the technocracy, I mean that social form in which an industrial society reaches the peak of its organizational integration."

Genus: "Social form"

Differentia: "an industrial society reaches the peak. . ."

Counter Culture: "A culture so radically disaffiliated from the mainstream assumptions of our society that it scarcely looks to many as a culture at all, but takes on the alarming appearance of a barbaric intrusion."

Genus: "A culture"

Differentia: "disaffiliated from the mainstream . . ."

The process of finding a class, establishing boundaries around the word being defined, and separating it from all other members of that class is particularly important when we want our audience to understand a concept in a special way. In his *Rhetoric,* Aristotle wanted to be certain that his audience understood the range and significance of his concept of rhetoric: "The art of discovering all the possible means of persuasion on any subject whatsoever." The *genus* in which he puts rhetoric is *art;* he then separates rhetoric as a specific *art* from all other forms of art by establishing a boundary: rhetoric is the art that discovers all the possible means of persuasion on any subject whatsoever. Other arts do other things: rhetoric specifically discovers means of persuasion, but it *includes* the other arts. Frequently, the differentia become a series of details or illustrations, perhaps carried to several levels, that help to clarify the genus or class of the term being defined. William G. Carleton in his essay "The Passing of Bughouse Square," after putting "bughouse" in its class, goes on to distinguish it from all others in its class by using a series of details and illustrations:

> Now, what is a bughouse square? A bughouse square is [class follows] a public street-intersection or mall or park in a large city where [primary differentia follow] gregarious, imaginative, exhibitionistic, and auto-compulsive "ism" peddlers, agitators, soapboxes, folk evangelists, teachers, showmen, faddists, cultists, cranks, crackpots, dreamers and self-proclaimed messiahs congregate [secondary differentia follow] to impress one another and to display their wares.

What are the faults the careful writer should learn to avoid and the reader to distinguish in methods of definition? A common flaw is the *circular definition;* that is one in which the term being defined or some form of it appears in the definition itself. To define *democracy* as "that sort of state in which all people are treated democratically" is useless and frustrating. Another sort of error is that occasioned by *overrestriction* in definition. Overrestriction occurs when the definition given for a term is too narrow to encompass all you intend the term to denote in your essay. Though not to the scholarly specialist in prose fiction, our last definition of *novel* is too restrictive for the general reader, because there would be little reason to exclude *The Scarlet Letter.* Or, if you are writing an essay on different types of education, to define *student* as "someone who gains his education at an accredited school" is only partly believable, for it rules out other important possibilities for the word. What of the many persons who attend unaccredited institutions? What of the self-educated? What of those educated by their experiences — students of life? Your definition is satisfactory as far as it takes us, but obviously that is not far enough. *Overinclusion* is the opposite of overrestriction. In errors of this kind the definition given is too sweeping, including possibilities not denoted by the word to be defined. If we define a *student* as "an individual associated with the field of learning" we are, once again, accurate to a degree. If we are deciding on GI benefits for the Veterans' Administration, however, our definition is faulty because it includes too many people not denoted by the word *student,* such as teachers and school administrators, as well as authors, editors, book publishers, and others "associated" with fields of learning.

EXERCISES

1. Consider whether the following are satisfactory definitions. Underline the *genus* and circle the *differentia.*
   a. Democracy is a form of government that is controlled by the people.
   b. Courage is the quality of being courageous.
   c. Inflation is an economic condition in which the increase of money and credit relative to available commodities results in a continuous increase in prices.
   d. Baseball is a game played by nine people.
   e. A rock opera is a musical composition that tells a story.

2. Select five of the terms below and write a logical definition for each. Underline the *genus* and circle the *differentia.*

rhetoric	parapsychology	poetry
psychology	clairvoyance	drama
social science	telepathy	symbol
science	psychokinesis	rite of passage
humanities	precognition	allegory

There is a process of definition that can often eliminate some of the inherent ambiguities and uncertainties found in nominal dictionary definitions and logical definitions. You can develop the *extended definition* by using the nominal and logical methods in conjunction with other rhetorical methods. By extending the definition of a word, you can create a pattern of development for paragraphs and even whole essays. You will turn to the extended definition when you wish to explore completely a term being defined, often in order to introduce a new meaning, or to alter the audience's whole attitude toward a term. R. D. Laing, in *The Politics of Experience,* wanted to change the public attitude toward schizophrenia, so he went to the dictionary for an etymology: the

> Lexicographers, or nominal definers, try to find many or all the contexts for a word before setting out to define it. The contexts they find dictate the definitions they compose — for a meaning can exist only in relation to other meanings. Similarly, real definers must sift their experience to think of all the contexts in which they have observed the thing which interests them — for a thing can exist only in relation to other things. Since nobody's contexts, and nobody's equipment for distinguishing them, are the same as yours, the truth is forever just on the verge of being stated.
>
> — Leo Rockas, *Modes of Rhetoric* (1964)

word is derived from a combination of words (*schizo* + *phrenos*) that originally meant *cleave, split, broken* and *mind, soul, heart.* Laing suggests that we ought to see schizophrenia not as madness or insanity but as a form of a *broken heart.* Seen this way, the word cannot have only the adverse connotations usually associated with the phenomenon of "split personality" or dissociation from reality.

BUILDING PARAGRAPHS USING DEFINITION

Just as the essay is controlled by a *thesis statement,* the paragraph is controlled by a *topic sentence.* This sentence usually comes early in the paragraph and establishes the content and often the structure as well. If the function of the paragraph is to define a term and extend the definition (this situation often occurs in essay exams), then the first sentence can be used as the logical definition in addition to acting as the topic sentence. The following paragraph written by a student is an example of this method used to define the term *ethnocentrism* (the major structural concepts are noted in the margin):

¹Ethnocentrism is [genus follows] the doctrine that [differentia follows] one's own culture is inherently superior to others. ²In other words, ethnocentrism is the measuring and judging of the ways of thinking and acting of others in terms of our own standards and norms. ³For example, when most of us in our culture think of the Eskimo custom of putting their very old people out to die,

Topic Sentence

Restatement

Example

our values would lead us to believe that the Eskimo is uncivilized. [4]But when we make a value judgment such as this, we have not taken into account the Eskimos' attitudes toward the community and the individual. [5]Their culture feels that the existence of the community is more important than the survival of the individual. [6]Therefore, when an individual becomes a burden to the group, the Eskimo community feels it has no other choice but to let that person die. [7]We are guilty of *ethnocentrism* when we judge them solely by our standards rather than taking into account the Eskimos' standards and judging them on that basis.

Conclusion

After establishing the definition-topic in the first sentence, the writer obviously thought the material to be sufficiently complex to put it "In other words." He then extends the definition by an example (sentences 3 through 6). The seventh sentence acts as a kind of summary-conclusion. One of the reasons the idea is so easy to follow is that the sentences are connected by marked transitions — "In other words," "For example," "But," and "Therefore" — that contribute to a coherent flow of language and idea. This kind of developmental pattern — topic-restatement-example-summary — used to build paragraphs is probably the most common when using definition.

A more complicated illustration of an extended definition using an example is the following paragraph from "Letter from a Birmingham Jail" by Martin Luther King, Jr.:

[1]How does one determine whether a law is just or unjust? [2]A just law is a manmade code that squares with the moral law of God. [3]An unjust law is a code that is out of harmony with the moral law. [4]To put it in the terms of St. Thomas Aquinas: An unjust law is a human law that is not rooted in eternal law and natural law. [5]Any law that uplifts human personality is just. [6]Any law that degrades human personality is unjust. [7]All segregation statutes are unjust because segregation distorts the soul and damages the personality. [8]It gives the segregator a false sense of superiority and the segregated a false sense of inferiority. [9]Segregation, to use the terminology of the Jewish philosopher Martin Buber, substitutes an "I-it" relationship for an "I-thou" relationship and ends up relegating persons to the status of things. [10]Hence, segregation is not only politically, economically, and sociologically unsound, it is morally wrong and sinful. [11]Paul Tillich has said that sin is separation. [12]Is not segregation an existential expression of

man's tragic separation, his awful estrangement, his terrible sinfulness? [13]Thus it is that I can urge men to obey the 1954 decision of the Supreme Court, for it is morally right: and I can urge them to disobey segregation ordinances, for they are morally wrong.

The *topic sentence* is expressed through a question in the first sentence; the definition of the term *unjust* is established in sentences 2 through 6 (sentence 4 is a restatement using the words of St. Thomas Acquinas). Beginning with sentence 6, Dr. King builds his paragraph using the example of segregation as an "unjust law." The last sentence (13) acts as a concluding statement. Although the subject matter is considerably more complex, this paragraph is built essentially the same way as the previous one — topic sentence-definition-restatement-example-conclusion. Obviously, all paragraphs that are developed extending a definition are not built using an example. As you become more aware of other developmental devices in the succeeding sections (especially, analysis, comparison and contrast, and cause and effect), you should be able to use them to extend your definition.

BUILDING ESSAYS USING DEFINITION

The process of definition by example can be used not only to develop a paragraph but also to develop an essay. If our object were to define *myth*, for example, we could establish a brief definition in the introduction: call it "A narrative in which the individual's central dream-like concerns are united with society, time, and the universe." This definition could then be expanded, first, by illustrations drawn from a variety of narrative works, such as *Ulysses, Paradise Lost,* and Ingmar Bergman's film *The Seventh Seal,* as well as *Moby Dick, American Grafitti,* and *Jaws.* Second, once you have introduced your material to your audience, established your intent, and nominally defined your term, then you can build a whole essay on explanations of the series of illustrations, each of which might explain further a separate aspect of the idea or concept being defined.

Another example of extending a definition to build an essay is demonstrated in the following essay about *rites of passage* written by a student. In the essay, the student defines *rites of passage* in the introductory material and then extends the definition by drawing upon examples from her readings. The important structural concepts are outlined in the margin.

Rites of Passage

Anthropologists have found that in all cultures both past and present certain changes in individuals are marked by rituals. These rituals known as *rites of passage* are important ways of externally relating to our particular society as well as signalling internal changes. By definition, a *rite of passage* is a ceremony that marks a change in an individual's life. It is like a bridge; once you have crossed the bridge you cannot go back. These ceremonies or bridges can be either formal external rituals, such as a wedding, or informal psychological experience, such as an awareness of independence or responsibility. To better understand the different kinds of rites of passage, examples from Margaret Mead's *Coming of Age in Samoa* and Nathaniel Hawthorne's "My Kinsman, Major Molineux" will be helpful.

In Samoa, according to Margaret Mead, rites of passage take place through external changes associated with role. From the time a child is born until after puberty, there is no ceremonial importance. At the age of six or seven years, a child must perform the job of baby tending. In addition, she develops a number of simple techniques consisting of weaving square balls from palm leaves, making pinwheels and breaking open coconuts, cleaning the house and bringing water from the sea. As soon as the girls are strong enough to carry heavy loads, they learn to weave fish baskets and to gather and arrange the bundles of fagots used in torchlight fishing. In the house she learns to weave the venetian blinds and the more difficult floor mats that are made from palm leaves. At the age of seven, the little girls are just beginning to be ashamed in the presence of older men.

These are some of the stages the girls go through until the age of fifteen or sixteen when they change their social role and attain a rite of passage. At this point they are placed into adult groupings, and are invested with definite obligations and privileges in the community. For exam-

Audience appeal step

Demonstration of significance

Definition of term

Thesis statement and structural intent

Topic sentence

Developed by a series of details and examples ordered on a chronological sequence of experiences that happen to the girls in Samoa

ple, some girls are placed as village servants or called village princesses. Their obligations are to wait upon strangers, spread their beds, make their Kava, dance when they wish and rise from their sleep to serve either the visitors or their own chief. In this capacity, the girls are obliged to serve the social needs of the women as well as the men. It is obvious from their duties that the rites of passage of the girls at about the age of fifteen bring about a dramatic change in their status and role, a change that is essentially external and social.

Series of examples

Conclusion

If the rite of passage is external and unique to the Samoan girls, then the rite of passage that Robin goes through in "My Kinsman, Major Molineux" is internal and universal. The story by Nathaniel Hawthorne is a clear illustration of a young man's passage from innocence to an awareness of adult responsibility. This initiation into the adult world takes place in a single day and each character plays a symbolic role in this transition. Robin begins his rite of passage when he leaves his sheltered home in the country and crosses the mythical river to arrive in a complex city world. His initial encounter with the old man and the innkeeper makes Robin's outlook on life look foolish. Though somewhat disillusioned he chooses to ignore these experiences because of his innocence. His naiveness is presented through the conversation with the woman in red. She claims to be the Major's innkeeper but in reality she is a prostitute; however, Robin eventually realizes this and resists the temptation. Later, on three different occasions, Robin is threatened by the presence of a man whose features—the protruding bumps on his forehead and two-toned complexion of fiery red and black—resemble that of the devil and probably symbolize the evil we are all capable of. While waiting for the procession, Robin keeps the company of a kind old man who serves as the guide he has longed for. Through the old man, the most important aspect of Robin's initiation into manhood is formulated. After confronting his

Transitional sentence

Topic sentence

Series of details and examples based on chronological order

tarred and feathered kinsman and laughing hysteri-
cally, he comes to an understanding of self and
others. This understanding is his realization of the
nature of revolution, change, human nature, and
his responsibilities as an adult. He is quite capable **Conclusion**
without his uncle and his passage from depen-
dence to independence is complete.

    The above examples show the variety of rites
of passage that individuals go through. For the **Summary sentences**
Samoan girls the passage is from tending children
to fulfilling a community responsibility. For Robin
the passage is a personal and psychological ceremony from youth to adulthood, from innocence to
awareness. All of us go through a series of rites of **Personal appeal and**
passage that mark our development both socially **return to audience**
(confirmation, bar mitzvah, graduation, marriage, **appeal step**
divorce, etc.) and individually (first "joint," first
sexual experience, first experience with the unknown, etc.). These passages essentially represent
who and *what* we are.

    We must make it clear at this point that essays can be and usually are
extended using a variety of developmental principles. The more sophisticated our understanding of structure and developmental principles
becomes, the more sophisticated we will be in our use of them. An
example of a more complex approach to extending a definition is Laurence Sears's essay, "Liberals and Conservatives." His introduction establishes his intention to use a process of definition:

> It is one of the significant facts of our time that there is a growing concern
> with the meaning of political conservatism, and is a dissatisfaction with the
> way that the term is popularly used. To a large degree both "liberal" and
> "conservative" are today little more than honorific terms used to give a
> comfortable glow of satisfaction, or else epithets designed to destroy the
> influence of those with whom we disagree. But even though the concepts
> are blurred, nonetheless one assumption is held in common, that *either* one
> *or* the other is the true belief, and that, although we may tolerate the
> opposite and mistaken view, *we* hold the truth and must be ready to do
> battle for it. It is the right versus the wrong. But there is another position
> which holds: (1) that it is one of the urgent tasks of our time to get these
> terms sharply defined; and (2) that when we do so, we will find that each

position holds both a profound and partial truth. That view needs reexamination today.

In this paragraph of introduction, Sears arouses audience interest by demonstrating the significance of his subject and producing a purpose and a thesis; he then goes on to build the body of his essay around an extended definition of *conservative,* using in the process the rhetorical methods of *example* (historical) and *comparison and contrast* (conservative versus the liberal position).

Bear in mind that definition can also be used in poetry as well as prose. Indeed, a poem often tries to do what a good extended definition does, which is to bring out the emotional nuances of a word. Sometimes the poet simply sets about to explain or explore a term in the context of a particular feeling and event. For instance, Gerard Manley Hopkins in his poem "Spring" defines his subject in the first stanza with a series of images and illustrations as they evoke the natural world; in the second stanza he extends the definition by contrasting these images to the present condition of man.

Spring

Nothing is so beautiful as spring —
   When weeds, in wheels, shoot long and lovely and lush;
   Thrush's eggs look like little low heavens, and though
Through the echoing timber does so rinse and wring
The ear, it strikes like lightnings to hear him sing;
   The glassy peartree leaves and blooms, they brush
   The descending blue; that blue is all in a rush
With richness; the racing lambs too have fair their fling.

What is all this juice and all this joy?
   A strain of the earth's sweet being in the beginning
In Eden garden. — Have, get, before it cloy,
Before it cloud, Christ, lord, and sour with sinning,
   Innocent mind and Mayday in girl and boy,
Most, O maid's child, thy choice and worthy the winning.

— Gerard Manley Hopkins

Definition is a useful rhetorical method partly because it combines so readily with other methods: we see Sears define *conservative,* for example, through the method of *comparison and contrast*; much of Dr. King's definition was presented through the analytic method of classification and division. The discussions that follow deal with other developmental patterns you may use as further methods to extend definitions.

EXERCISES

1. Select key terms from your other courses and define them in paragraph form, extending the definition with a series of illustrations. Begin each of the paragraphs with the definition. Use the paragraph on *ethnocentrism* as a model (page 67).

2. Write an essay defining the term *rites of passage*. Introduce your subject by appealing to your audience, giving some background information about the concept, defining the term logically ("A ritual marking an important change in an individual's life"), and establishing a thesis that suggests the intent. Follow this introductory material with a series of paragraphs that extends the term through illustration. In other words, extend the definition by explaining how certain characters in particular literary works went through a rite of passage *or* select an event-experience from your own life that could be considered as "marking an important change"—perhaps going to college or your first journey away from home. Do not forget to write a conclusion, and place an appropriate title on the essay. The essay on page 70 can be used as a guide.

EXAMPLE AND ILLUSTRATION

Unlike the pattern of definition, which can be a structural end in itself, the pattern of *example and illustration* contributes a part to a larger structural whole. It is simply a building block for constructing sentences and paragraphs. Your goal in using example or illustration is to clarify abstract material by making it more concrete. The more concrete the material you present, the more effective your writing is likely to be. In the development of a sentence or a paragraph, example and illustration usually follow a proposition: a thesis or a topic clause or a sentence like the logical definition of "ethnocentrism" (cited in the previous exercises). Essentially, the pattern is *tell and show*: the idea precedes the thing. The following paragraph from Margaret Mead's *Culture and Commitment* illustrates the development of a topic sentence through example:

Within two decades, 1940–1960, events occurred that have irrevocably altered man's relationships to other men and to the natural world. The invention of the computer, the successful splitting of the atom and the invention of fission and fusion bombs, the discovery of the biochemistry of the living cell, the exploration of the planet's surface, the extreme acceleration of population growth and the recognition of the certainty of catastrophe if it continues, the breakdown of the organization of cities, the destruction of the natural environment, the linking up of all parts of the world by means of jet flights and television, the preparations for the building of satellites and the first steps into space, the newly realized possibilities of unlimited energy and synthetic raw materials and, in the more advanced countries, the transformation of man's age-old problems of production into problems of distribution and consumption—all these have brought about a drastic, irreversible division between the generations.

This paragraph is comprised of only two sentences: the thesis (#1) and (#2) the inventory of the events and the changed relationships that result. Combining example with cause and effect helps Margaret Mead argue effectively her proposition that events between 1940 and 1960 "have irrevocably altered man's relationships to other men and to the natural world." Her method of heaping up examples (though we might disagree with the appropriateness of some) generates remarkable force in the paragraph.

The following paragraph by Carl Jung, from *Man and His Symbols,* is also built on the principle of example, but it is a bit more complex than the preceding one:

There are many reasons why we forget things that we have noticed or experienced; and there are just as many ways in which they may be recalled to mind. An interesting example is that of cryptomnesia, or "concealed recollection." An author may be writing steadily to a preconceived plan, working out an argument or developing the line of a story, when he suddenly runs off at a tangent. Perhaps a fresh idea has occurred to him, or a different image, or a whole new subplot. If you ask him what prompted the digression, he will not be able to tell you. He may not even have noticed the change, though he has now produced material that is entirely fresh and apparently unknown to him before. Yet it can sometimes be shown convincingly that what he has written bears a striking similarity to the work of another author—a work that he believes he has never seen.

Jung establishes the paragraph thesis or topic sentence in his first sentence, then he develops that thesis with the example of the phenomenon known as "cryptomnesia." As we have suggested, a writer may find it necessary to give examples to clarify a difficult or unfamiliar term. Jung's example is really a little story, a narrative illustration of a process that can occur in memory when *both* recollection and forgetting are functioning. As each succeeding sentence explains the cryptomnesia, Jung's paragraph becomes vividly concrete. As Jung has done, you can often extend a paragraph to considerable length using this method, though you will want to continue with the example only as long as necessary to achieve clarity.

Development using the pattern of example and illustration does not always have to follow the sequence of topic sentence then illustration/ example. The pattern may prevail in a series of paragraphs, the method becoming a kind of Chinese box, examples within examples within examples. In other words, a paragraph developed by example may also be part of a sequence of paragraphs that offers illustrations of a thesis stated in an earlier part of the essay. This kind of paragraph is exemplified in Alvin Toffler's *Future Shock*:

> In *War With the Newts,* Karel Capet's marvelous but little-known novel, man brings about the destruction of civilization through his attempt to domesticate a variety of salamander. Today, among other things, man is learning to exploit animals and fish in ways that would have made Capet smile wryly. Trained pigeons are used to identify and eliminate defective pills from drug factory assembly lines. In the Ukraine, Soviet scientists employ a particular species of fish to clear the algae off the filters in pumping stations. Dolphins have been trained to carry tools to "aquanauts" submerged off the coast of California, and to ward off sharks who approach the work zone. Others have been trained to ram submerged mines, thereby detonating them and committing suicide on man's behalf — a use that provoked a slight furor over interspecies ethics.

The topic sentence of this paragraph is the second one, but the paragraph's purpose comes from an assertion made in a previous paragraph concerning man's domination of nature. Consequently, the development of this paragraph by a series of examples of man's uses of nature is offered as further proof of his original proposition. Toffler's paragraph also shows that the arrangement of examples in a paragraph is often important. Toffler's examples move from man's less obviously destructive treatment of other species (the pigeons and fish) to the more destructive (the "suicide"/murder of the dolphins). This rhetorical order obviously has an emotional effect, and Toffler uses it to evoke in readers feelings of concern or guilt for man's misdeeds. The paragraph quoted from Margaret Mead is basically arranged chronologically; that order — rather than one based on ethical values — is more in keeping with her historical survey of the events of 1940–1960. It is important to remember that, while the process of example and illustration is simple to use, it is also an effective means of making your material concrete for your audience. Whenever your material seems to be climbing the ladder of abstraction, it is always a good idea to yank it down with the concrete weight of an example or illustration, or at least give it a load of meaning to carry up with it.

You must be able to use all patterns of development in conjunction with one another, for in even a single sentence you may need to go from definition to example, to cause and effect to analogy. In your use of example/illustration you may find it necessary to include sentences and paragraphs that themselves include several other patterns of development. Nowhere is this more likely to be true than when you use a special type of example or illustration found in the use of testimony or an appeal to authority. Frequently, in the development of a paragraph you will turn to the testimony of another person to help prove your thesis or proposition. You may have many reasons for doing so. Perhaps your self-interest makes your own testimony suspect; the objective testimony of another may settle that problem. Perhaps you simply have no direct experience of the subject; a statement by someone else who has had the experience can resolve that problem. Perhaps the issue itself is one that has generated conflicting interpretations; turning to authorities who speak for your thesis can help (though, in fairness, you ought to acknowledge the other side's authorities also). In a way, your use of exemplary or illustrative testimony is like that of an attorney in court who may need eyewitnesses, character witnesses, expert authorities (in medicine or ballistics, for instance), and the like. Like the lawyer, you must create a framework of statement or argumentation in order for your reader (as a kind of jury) to reach the hoped-for conclusions. Illustrative testimony may be rather simple and short, a statement that puts briefly the essential position for which you are arguing, or it may be a lengthy commentary, one that represents your more complete argument. An example of the former, a statement that encapsulates the essential position of the argument, can be seen in Dr. Ann Faraday's *Dream Power:*

> The layman probably has little idea of the intense mental activity that goes
> on continuously in the waking mind. Research on the psychology of

perception has shown that even an apparently simple observation has already been thoroughly processed in terms of our past experience and present preoccupations *before we even become aware of it.* The poet William Blake was speaking the simple truth when he wrote, "The fool sees not the same tree as the wise man sees." My perception of a tree depends upon all the hundreds of experiences I have had with trees in the past — the tree in the back garden of my childhood home, the tree in the woods under which a small boy kissed me, the tree out of which I fell and broke my arm, and so on. My perception also depends on my present mood and feelings: when I am in love, a tree which I normally regard with indifference becomes suffused with light and life. Of course, our varying perceptions of the same object have enough in common to enable us to communicate our thoughts about it, but they differ in detail according to our individual experiences.

The paragraph is built primarily of the topic sentence and the examples from personal experiences of the author. The quotation from Blake captures succinctly Dr. Faraday's main idea and, at the same time, provides the sort of validation only a poet renowned for his mystic experiences can offer. Though this quotation is embedded in the middle of her paragraph, Dr. Faraday might have begun the paragraph or ended with it. You are not compelled to use such quotations in one location or another.

A fuller, more complete use by Dr. Faraday of testimony as illustration occurs in the following paragraph:

Cars, trains, and airplanes as instruments of power can represent the energy of the impulses, particularly the sexual impulses. A passage from Desmond Morris's book *The Human Zoo* illustrates this point nicely: ". . . sport cars . . . have always radiated bold, aggressive masculinity and have been considerably aided in this by their phallic qualities. Like a baboon's penis, they stick out in front, they are long, smooth and shiny, they thrust forward with great vigour and they are frequently bright red in color. A man sitting in his open sports car is like a piece of highly stylized phallic sculpture. His body has disappeared and all that can be seen are a tiny head and hands surmounting a long, glistening penis. . . . Even ordinary motor cars have their phallic qualities, and this may explain to some extent why male drivers become so aggressive and so eager to overtake one another, despite considerable risks and despite the fact that they all meet up again at the next set of traffic lights, or at best, only cut a few seconds off their journey."

In this instance Dr. Faraday not only uses Morris as an authority to back up her position concerning the interpretation of dream images; she also permits the vivid imagery of his statement to *develop* her own argument. Implicit in her choice of Desmond Morris is his presumed authority on the subject of man and his symbols. But many readers would not accept Morris as such an authority, for to them he is merely a popularizer of ideas buried in relatively inaccessible scholarly journals. Your testimony must be carefully selected on the basis of actual authority and the kind of appeal it will have to your audience. Popular readers of Dr. Faraday's book would be more amenable to Morris' testimony than specialists in psychology, biology, or zoology, even though the specialists themselves might agree wholeheartedly with the propositions Faraday presents and Morris supports.

An extended use of testimony and authority in combination with other methods is the research essay. Sometimes you will approach a particular subject by collecting testimony from "authorities" either through personal contact (field work) or research in the library. Your essay is then developed from the arrangement of the testimonial data collected in your research. For example, if you were to identify or explain some cultural change—say the role of women in our culture from 1950 to 1970—you would probably go to the library and do some research on women and their roles in the 50s and 60s. Using the examples, illustrations, and ideas collected from your library research, you might then interview various women—younger ones who represent the contemporary generation and older ones who have experienced both the earlier period and the contemporary. The conclusions drawn from your data might lead you to use one of several other structural patterns. The ideas and experiences of the sources-authorities from the 1950s might be compared and contrasted to those of the 1970s. Or you might decide, instead, to analyze the categories of change: appearance, manners, language, career. Or you might prefer to define *women* for the 50s and 70s.

However you use your examples of testimony and authority, you should recognize that they are an *extension* of your own personal re-sources. Authorities are good only so long as they are reliable, to you and your audience. They must remain only *examples* and *illustrations* that support your own theses or propositions. They offer bridges to data, wisdom, opinion beyond your own range of personal experience, but you do yourself no good in your writing when dubious sources invite suspicion and distrust.

ANALYSIS: CLASSIFICATION AND DIVISION

The developmental process of definition is designed to establish the limits of a word or idea; within these limits we tend to comprehend meaning in its broad outlines before we understand its parts. There is a reversal of this method in the process of understanding and communicating that involves reducing a subject, group, or object to its constituent parts or locating its appropriate categories or divisions. The method of *classification and division* is based on the idea that, by understanding the characteristic parts of something, we can understand its totality. In *Motivation and Personality,* for example, Abraham Maslow explains the basic needs of a human being by identifying eight categories: physiological needs, and the needs for safety, love, self-esteem, information, self-actualization, understanding, and beauty. Another example of identifying constituent elements occurs when we analyze the language of film by dividing the medium of the shot into image, movement, time, space, color, and sound. There is little doubt that in our everyday lives we informally use this analytical process. Each time we budget our paycheck, plan a work-study schedule, or explain the functions of a piece of machinery, we are engaged in some form of classification or division or categorization.

Analysis depends on the structure of the object, event, or idea analyzed and the purposes prompting the analysis. Different interests and purposes, according to Brooks and Warren (*Modern Rhetoric,* 1958), can dictate different analyses of the same item. The botanist might regard an apple as a botanical structure and therefore identify its parts as stem, skin, flesh, seeds, and so forth; but a chemist might regard it as a chemical structure and reduce it to certain elemental formulas, or a painter might regard it as an aesthetic structure composed of shape, texture, and color. Each person might perform the reductive analysis in terms of a particular interest, but the purpose prompting the analysis would determine the kind of structure identified. The kind of structure would in turn determine the constituent parts of the structure.

In more formal writing such as a composition or essay exam, analysis by classification and division can be used as the basis for extending a definition, developing a paragraph, or structuring an entire essay. When used to extend a definition, such analysis usually constitutes the body of the essay. After you have defined a word or concept in your introductory material, you would then extend its meaning by identifying its relevant parts and developing each in a separate paragraph or some parts in several paragraphs. The pattern holding the essay together, giving it its coherence, would be analysis, though your purpose is to define a particular term. The following student essay is an example of the interaction of various developmental patterns. The overall intent of the essay is to define the term *culture*. The term is extended through the body of the essay by breaking culture down (analysis) into three aspects or "tools" (goals, values, and rituals) that govern the overall arrangement of the paragraphs; the body consists of three paragraphs, each concerned with one of the "tools." In addition, the paragraphs themselves are generally constructed on the principle of comparison and contrast that is used to compare the two cultures in the film *Walkabout,* which provides the basis for another developmental pattern—example and illustration (the basic structure concepts are identified in the margin).

The Tools of Culture

"Culture is an instrument wielded by professors to manufacture professors, who when their turn comes will manufacture professors." This quote by Simone Weil metaphorically states that people of a culture manufacture and shape people into a specific cultural mold. The cultural shaping process is so complete that we often find it difficult to read the codes of other cultures. To understand any culture it is useful to examine it comparatively with others from a peripheral view. The term *culture,* by definition, is the way of life of a people, a sum of their learned behavior patterns, attitudes, and material values. Perhaps cultures differ because of the many different tools which are used to define each individual culture. A few of these tools used for defining cultures are goals, values, and rituals. A good source for understanding how these "tools" operate to define a culture is the film *Walkabout,* because it offers a comparative view of two distinct cultures.

One of the most important tools that defines a culture is its goals, or its objectives. The apparent goals of the white culture as generally revealed in *Walkabout* are wealth, success, and education. Almost every individual, we can assume, feels that striving towards these goals will eventually lead to prominence and acceptance in the white society. On the other hand, the goals of the Aborigine are

Audience appeal steps

Demonstration of significance

Definition of term

Thesis statement and structural intent

Topic sentence

Contrast

to become self-sufficient and live in complete harmony with nature. The reasons for these extreme differences in goals are that the white culture is technologically advanced, which leads to large societies and higher education. The Aborigine lives in a culture which is not concerned with technology, and is basically concerned with his survival.

A second and equally relevant tool for defining a culture is its values or morals. The values of the white culture are obviously far more materialistic than those of the Aborigine. In *Walkabout,* the white culture is generally surrounded by confining walls and tall concrete buildings. They reside in close quarters, cook with mass produced man-made stoves, and swim in pools of chlorinated water. The Aborigine is far more integrated with nature. He kills his own food and cooks it over his own fire, kindled by the rubbing together of two sticks. The Aborigine lives with nature; he cleans his body by swimming in fresh pools and he sleeps on the earth under the open sky. The Aborigine would never kill an animal for pleasure or sport as the white man does. This point was raised in the film dramatically when the Aborigine was hunting for food and sees white men shooting down animals randomly for sport, not for survival. Although the family of the Aborigine is not included in the film, I would surmise that he lives with all his relatives in an extended family situation and that these people are his primary group. In the white culture, as we know, there has developed the nuclear family (mother, father, children) whose other relatives do not play a very important role in shaping the values of an individual as they do in an extended family.

A third tool used in the definition of a culture is ritual, or "rites of passage." Rituals play an extremely important part in the life of a people such as the Aborigine. During the film, *Walkabout,* the Aborigine is going through a very significant ritual, his rite of passage into manhood, where he

Topic sentence

Concrete details

Contrast

Example

Topic sentence

must survive on his own in the desert for a spec-
ified period of time. Another ritual performed was   **Examples**
the mating ritual to the white girl. A culture, such
as the Aborigine, usually experiences many rituals
such as the coming of age, courting, birth, death,
and even rites for seasons. Although the white   **Contrast**
culture does not have explicit rituals such as these,
there are still marriage rituals, baptizing, funerals,
Bar Mitzvahs, etc. The rituals of the white culture
would appear to be far more unstructured than
those of the Aborigine, which partially explains
the white girl's utter confusion toward the mating
ritual the Aborigine performs.

    All three of these cultural tools — goals, values,
rituals — help define a culture that is passed down   **Summary**
from generation to generation. Cultures differ be-
cause of the varying emphasis and influence of
each of the cultural tools. There are several more   **Return to audience**
tools in the cultural tool box that are often used to   **appeal step**
define culture; some of these are ideals, mores,
norms, etc. The key to understanding all cultures
is to study the different influences each of the
cultural tools exercises on personality and development.

BUILDING PARAGRAPHS USING ANALYSIS

The analytical method can also be used as a structural pattern to
build a paragraph. In this form, the *topic sentence* usually acts as the basis
for the division or classification of the subject matter to be discussed.
The following paragraph (written by a student as part of a final-exam
question) establishes the division of the subject (an effective writer) in
the topic sentence and is built through a discussion of each division (the
structural concepts are outlined in the margin).

    Every writer to be effective must achieve three   **Topic**
basic things — an understanding of human na-   **sentence**
ture, an attitude toward the subject matter (tone),
and a relationship with the audience (voice). Of   **First**
the three responsibilities, the understanding of   **division**
human nature is the most complex and difficult to

achieve. Nevertheless, it usually becomes clear through experience and hard philosophical inquiry and is eventually labeled the writer's *vision*. J. D. Salinger's vision (*The Catcher in the Rye*), for example, concludes that man is essentially good and society is corrupt. On the other hand, William Golding's vision (*Lord of the Flies*) concludes that society is necessarily good while man is innately evil. In addition to "vision" a writer must take an attitude toward his subject matter — stylistically, considered *tone*. This tone can be serious, half serious, detached, light, suspenseful, playful, ironical, or satirical. And, finally, the writer must take an attitude toward his audience — stylistically, called *voice* — that is in harmony with his attitude toward the subject matter. If you engage in a dialog about some scientific principle with an audience that expects you to use a calm "voice" of reason, then the tone you take toward the subject matter should be serious. When the three responsibilities are fulfilled by the writer and are working effectively then the chances are the communication process will be successful.

Example

Contrast

Second division

Third division

Conclusion

Although we may not necessarily agree with the content of the paragraph, the presentation structurally is clear and effective. One reason that the idea flows as coherently as it does is the use of structural transitions that mark the divisions ("Of the three," "In addition to," "And, finally").

Another example of analysis as the basis for building a paragraph occurs in Robert Hunter's *The Storming of the Mind:*

The three stages of the holistic consciousness which has been developing in the postwar period may broadly be categorized as being cultural, political, and environmental. At each stage, the assault widens. Its sphere of action expands. Initially, expressed through the Beat Generation, it found itself in an attack upon the values, mores, concepts, and attitudes of the dominant culture. At the second stage, nothing has changed — the assault is against the same cultural bastions, but the new consciousness has begun to move on other fronts: the conflict spills over into the political arena. Now, as the third stage begins to congeal, we see that the conflict has expanded again. While it has shed nothing — it is still both cultural and political — it has achieved a far greater definition. Not only has the new consciousness at this stage transcended the cultural limitations of its incubator, not only has it outgrown the old political categories, but now, having passed through the "outer walls" of one-dimensional society, it finds itself at the innermost gate, confronted with the real beast astride the throne of the technological order: pure operationalism itself.

The paragraph develops by dividing "holistic consciousness" into three distinct areas, with each area designated as a "stage." These stages are identified by what is included in the thought process involved; discussed in serial or chronological order, they become a set of building blocks for the paragraph. Transitions signal the stages of the process at work ("Initially," "At the second stage," "Now, as the third stage begins"). You should have little trouble following Hunter's explanation of a development that in itself is rather complex, even if you don't have the slightest idea what "holistic consciousness" actually is (an illustration like this suggests how important terms can be, for a definition, of course, looms in its background).

BUILDING ESSAYS USING ANALYSIS

Development by classification and division, like most methods, may be part of a larger structure, or it may be a dominating structure in itself. The following essay written by a student uses the divisions of human needs established by Abraham Maslow (page 80) as the basis for the structure. Selecting just two of the *needs* — physiological and love — the student shows in two different sources how the mother's inability to provide these needs has a damaging effect on the child (the structural concepts are outlined in the margin).

The Mother and Human Needs

Every human requires certain basic needs to become a socially adjusted adult. These needs, according to Abraham Maslow, are ranged in eight categories — physiological, safety, love, esteem, self-actualization, knowledge, information, and beauty. As a primary agent of socialization, the mother plays an important role in fulfilling these needs. Therefore, the perfect mother would totally satisfy all of these needs for a stable develop-

(margin notes) **Audience appeal step**

Demonstration of significance

ment of her child's personality. Yet, not all mothers implement these essentials. The result may be a child's physical or emotional derangement. The readings, "Final Note on Extreme Isolation" and *A Taste of Honey*, have been consulted to gain a better understanding of the effect of the mother's behavior toward fulfilling the basic needs of physiology and love as they relate to the formation of the child's personality.

Thesis statement and structural intent

The physiological needs of food, water, sex, sleep, and shelter, according to Maslow, are "the most crucial for survival"; "if these needs go unsatisfied, they can dominate the psychological life of the individual." In the study, "Final Note on Extreme Isolation," Kingsley Davis analyzes what happens to a child, Anna, who does not receive these needs from her mother. Anna, being born an illegitimate child, received a minimal amount of physical attention. Her mother was a farm girl who was not at all interested in the welfare of the child. By the age of eight weeks Anna had been moved three times to three different homes and had contacted impetigo, vaginitis, umbilical hernia, and a skin rash. After being placed in a foster home until her mother could no longer pay the bill, Anna was brought to her grandfather's house where she was shut up in an attic. She received only enough care to keep her alive. She appeared to have been seldomly moved from one position to another, her clothing and bedding were filthy, and she had no instruction or friendly attention. Her mother would sometimes go out at night leaving her totally unattended. Because of these actions, she at the age of six could not walk, talk, or do anything that showed any significant intelligence. In addition, she was in an extremely emaciated, undernourished condition, with skeleton-like legs and a bloated abdomen. She was fed on virtually nothing but cow's milk while under her mother's care. Eventually, after six years of this kind of existence, Anna was "rescued" and placed under a doctor's

Definition of need

Topic sentence

Chronological ordering of details

Cause and effect

care. Even though she did progress to the intellec-
-tual level of eighteen months in the next four
years, the damage had been done. She died when
she was ten. It is clear that the mother's failure to **Conclusion**
provide Anna with the necessary physiological
needs led to her early death.

Another important basic need is love which **Definition**
Maslow defines as that state of "being deeply un- **of need**
derstood and deeply accepted." A good example **Topic**
of a mother's failure to fulfill this need is seen in **sentence**
S. Dalaney's *A Taste of Honey*. Jo, the daughter, is
portrayed as a girl who can fend for herself, but at
the same time needs someone to care for her and
love her. The mother, Helen, is a lower-class
whore, who has a "money" head. Their relation- **Details**
ship is destructive with a continuous flow of un- **and**
kind words between them. Jo has some artistic **examples**
talent but is not given any encouragement and so
she turns to other outlets to fulfill herself. Jo needs
a "taste" of love, which her mother refuses to provide and so she reaches out to Jimmy (a sailor) for
it. During this time she is in bliss, even ignoring
her environment of filthy rooms, factories and
being poor. Later, after Jimmy ships out, she finds
a friend in Geof, a potential artist who, like Jo
(unmarried, pregnant, carrying a Black child), is
an outcast of society. Jo and Geof are able to live
together because they have something in common,
loneliness and "uniqueness." However, Jo's feelings of hate and insecurity undermine any happiness she might have. Because Helen never gave **Conclusion**
her the necessary love, Jo is doomed to repeat her
mother's mistakes, and to live a lonely and desperate life.

In conclusion, the absence of a maternal concern for the fulfillment of the basic human needs
has a great impact toward the development of the
child. In Anna's case, her mother deprived her of **Summary**
the fundamental physiological need; therefore,
her personality did not have a chance to develop.
In Jo's case, Helen's neglect in fulfilling the need

of love and belongingness resulted in her pessimis- **Return to**
tic attitude. It is obvious that without the fulfill- **audience**
ment of these needs, the child has great difficulty **appeal**
making the proper adjustments to his or her society.

The writer could have used all eight of the basic human needs if time
and space had allowed. Each need could have been represented in a
paragraph that could have been developed using an example from
various literary sources. The important point to note is that each paragraph would reflect a particular division.

Another example of analysis to build an essay occurs in Charles
Reich's *The Greening of America*. Here he builds an essay showing how
skiing can be turned into an activity that would make it part of a "real"
culture. Following an introductory paragraph, Reich isolates five aspects
of the activity of skiing; he then makes each element the focus of one of
the five paragraphs that constitute the middle of the essay. An outline of
the essay's development, including introductory sentences for each paragraph and elements italicized, goes like this:

Paragraph 1: "Perhaps he might become interested in the *history* of
skiing. . . ."

Paragraph 2: "The skier is to some extent dependent upon *weather*,
and he might develop his knowledge of, and consciousness of, weather."

Paragraph 3: "Then there is the study of *nature* in winter. . . ."

Paragraph 4: "*Geography and travel* are another aspect of skiing."

Paragraph 5: "We have said all this without even mentioning other
people and their role in skiing."

This visual scheme shows how each of the paragraphs contributes to the
analytical process. Reich then completes the process with a summary
paragraph, beginning: "These are some of the ways in which an activity
now an example of false culture and the consumer ethic might become
an activity of genuine use." Here he ties the subject of skiing back to his
initial concern with "genuine" activities in a "real" culture. The five
aspects (history, weather, nature, geography, and people) suggest how
skiing (an *activity*) can become not just a *pastime* but a genuine element in
our *culture*.

One of the strengths of analysis by classification and division lies in
the emphasis it can bring when categories and purposes work together.
Classification and division may give you sequences that need only be

enumerated, but others may allow you to use a chronological order that permits a semblance of narrative (or "story"), and yet others may allow you to use a principle of climax, as you shift from least to most important. Transitions that signal this analytical process ("the first stage," "the second stage," etc.: "A further characteristic," "Another part," "In addition to," "Along with," "A more important aspect," etc.) are easily followed and manipulated. Nevertheless, there are certain pitfalls you should avoid and certain guidelines you should follow. Your analysis should be logically sound: You must employ only one principle for each classification or division, and classes or parts must be mutually exclusive. Do not start writing about the chemical elements of the apple and include shape or weight or color as classifying aspects. Further, depending on the extent of information your purposes require, such analysis should be complete. Completeness in this method of development is generally a matter of degree, and inevitably becomes a matter of judgment.

Virtually any subject can be carried through a number of stages or levels if the analyst is ingenious enough. But it is your responsibility as a writer to determine the number of levels appropriate to your audience and purpose. In a general explanation of the committee structure of the United States Senate, you might find sufficient a simple classification of those committees and their predominant functions. But if the writer is politically sophisticated and is writing for an audience that is not, he or she might wish to continue the analysis through subcommittees, individual efforts, delegated responsibilities, and on to an insider's view of political decisions made in backrooms, on jetplanes, or on spacious golf courses. Again, the lengths one goes to finally depend on purpose and audience.

EXERCISES

1. Write a paragraph using analysis by classification and division by extending each of the following topic sentences:

   a. A football team usually consists of three squads of players: the offense, defense, and a specialty unit. (If you prefer, use any other "team" or performance that can be broken down into its unit parts.)

   b. Success in college is predicated on your ability to study, take exams, and write effective papers. (Break down the concept of "success," as you understand it, into its constituent parts.)

2. Using Maslow's list of human needs as a guideline (page 80), list five of his or five of your own that you think are necessary for your physical and/or psychological happiness. Select three of these needs and write an essay explaining how they have or have not been fulfilled in your life. Reminders:

   a. Be sure to write an introduction in which you have an audience appeal step, a demonstration of significance, a listing of your basic needs, and a thesis and structural intent that states explicitly which ones you are going to discuss.

   b. Be sure each paragraph has a topic sentence and is developed using concrete details and examples.

   c. Write a conclusion that summarizes your material and returns to the audience appeal step.

3. Write an essay arguing for or against or explaining one of the propositions derived from the following quote:

> Mysticism, supernaturalism, occultism, are flourishing today because many people are disillusioned by the deterioration of our moral standards, the social and economic inequities, the excessive permissiveness and punishments, the hypocrisy and the corruption of people in high places. This makes people feel disoriented, powerless, and tempts them to regress into mysticism, to gain a sense of belonging and of bliss. We see it in the emotionally sick, the dropouts, the disenfranchised, and the hard-drug users, among others.
>
> — Dr. R. R. Greenson, "A Psychoanalyst's Indictment of 'The Exorcist'"

Propositions (these are just guidelines; create your own if you wish):

   a. The belief in the supernatural is the result of a general disenchantment with the social, economic, and political structures.

   b. People are turning to more exotic forms of spiritualism because orthodox religion is inadequate.

   c. Supernaturalism is a popular topic in films, television, and other media.

Procedure:

   a. Develop your essay using the process of analysis; that is, the *body* of your essay should reflect how the content can be broken down to better understand it.

   b. Use transitions that signal the pattern of the analytic thought process; in other words, begin your paragraphs with something like, "One reason there is a belief in supernaturalism . . ."; "Another reason . . ."; "A further reason . . . ," etc.

    c. Write an introduction that has an audience appeal step, background material (if necessary), a thesis statement, and an indication of a structural plan or method.

    d. Write a conclusion and give a title to the essay.

4. Write an essay in which you argue for the meaning of the following poem by using the process of analysis. Your responsibility is to identify units that help you to understand the poem; for instance, obvious divisions are the poem's four stanzas, each of which can be discussed in a paragraph in your essay; another classification, a bit more complicated, could be based on the elements of structure, style, and theme. Be sure your essay has an introduction, conclusion, and title. Also quote specific lines, phrases, and words that will help present your argument as concretely as possible.

Dover Beach

The sea is calm tonight.
The tide is full, the moon lies fair
Upon the straits; — on the French coast the light
Gleams and is gone; the cliffs of England stand,
Glimmering and vast, out in the tranquil bay.
Come to the window, sweet is the night-air!
Only, from the long line of spray
Where the sea meets the moon-blanch'd land,
Listen! you hear the grating roar
Of pebbles which the waves draw back, and fling,
At their return, up the high strand,
Begin, and cease, and then again begin,
With tremulous cadence slow, and bring
the eternal note of sadness in.

Sophocles long ago
Heard it on the Aegean, and it brought
Into his mind the turbid ebb and flow
Of human misery; we
Find also in the sound a thought,
Hearing it by this distant northern sea.

The Sea of Faith
Was once, too, at the full, and round earth's shore

Lay like the folds of a bright girdle furl'd.
But now I only hear
Its melancholy, long, withdrawing roar,
Retreating, to the breath
Of the night-wind, down the vast edges drear
And naked shingles of the world.

Ah, love, let us be true
To one another! for the world, which seems
To lie before us like a land of dreams,
So various, so beautiful, so new,
Hath really neither joy, nor love, nor light,
Nor certitude, nor peace, nor help for pain;
And we are here as on a darkling plain
Swept with confused alarms of struggle and flight,
Where ignorant armies clash by night.

— Matthew Arnold

COMPARISON AND CONTRAST

Another fundamental pattern of development is *comparison and contrast*. This device seems inherent in the nature of thought and language, which rely heavily on systems of opposition and apposition. One sure way for trying to understand something is to compare and contrast it with a similar thing. This process is essentially what is known in grammar as *apposition*, the placing next to a word another word or words that mean(s) the same thing, done usually because we feel our audience does not know the word: Dom DiMaggio, younger brother of Yankee baseball great Joe DiMaggio, . . . ; Carl Jung, a colleague of Sigmund Freud and leading theorist of archetypal theory in psychology, . . . (etc.). *Apposition* itself, however, can also refer to what we think of as *opposition*, for it also means to set something against something else — to establish an association of *dis*similarity as well as identity. *Comparison and contrast*, then, really are only two different faces of the same coin. Knowledge and understanding build on the known and the understood, learning itself being a search for appositional connections. When we see a thing we do not know, we try to connect it, put it into apposition, to something we do. In language, at the level of style, the process of comparison begins with simile and metaphor (see our discussion of the pattern of analogy later in this chapter); the process of contrast begins with the grammatical form known as antithesis. But for our purposes, comparison and contrast is a method of *structure*. We will analyze it as a way to develop paragraphs and as a pattern with which to develop a whole essay.

As a rhetorical technique, comparison and contrast implies the treatment of one subject through reference to one or more subjects; thus, X may be juxtaposed with Y to establish likenesses and differences between the two. Comparison usually is thought to deal with the former (the likenesses) and contrast with the latter (the differences), but both words actually mean "to set side by side," since apposition and opposition also have similar meanings. Like the principle of analysis (classification and division) discussed in the preceding section, the principle of comparison and contrast seems to be built into our thinking processes; we use it regularly to make judgments on a multitude of subjects. Is the National Baseball League superior to the American League? Is French wine better than American wine? Is Richard Brautigan better than Kurt Vonnegut, Jr. as a writer? Our responses (which will not necessarily be final answers) to questions of this sort must inevitably grow out of our judgments of likenesses and differences, comparisons and contrasts.

The structure of comparison and contrast has at least two fundamental uses in the rhetorical process: to clarify a hazy or obscure subject through reference to a more familiar one and to examine two subjects by setting them side by side and pointing out similarities and differences. In the first use, our supposition is that the unfamiliar can often be explained in light of the familiar. Thus, one might explain the sport of soccer by comparing and contrasting it with football. Both are team sports played on an outdoor field, both employ a ball, and both involve body contact. But the lengths of the fields differ, the numbers of men per team differ, and equipment, shapes of the balls, types of body contact, and scoring systems all differ. The audience's knowledge of American football is presumed and is used as a base for the explanation of soccer. (One wit has said, "In soccer you kick anything that moves. If it doesn't move, you kick it until it does.") The second role of comparison and contrast is useful for the appraisal of two subjects presumed to be equally well known to, and understood by, the audience. Two writers could be compared and contrasted for their styles and social views, presuming the audience's familiarity with both authors.

You must take care with the organizational patterns of comparison and contrast on two different levels. First, you should see that each subject of the comparison and contrast is a member of the same class; only then can comparison and contrast be developed along clearly defined lines. A random listing of the characteristics of the subjects is by itself not enough. Second, you should select a set of traits pertinent to both and that you can expand according to a pattern discernible to your audience. Suppose you are trying to decide which of two schools you wish to attend after high school graduation. You have ruled out two-year colleges, so there is no chance you will relate schools which do not belong to the same class, called *university*. In comparing and contrasting two universities, you might establish four criteria or traits to serve as the basis for your decision: (1) admission requirements, (2) tuition costs, (3) library holdings, and (4) sports facilities. The four criteria then provide you with the unifying set of principles around which you can proceed with comparison and contrast. Following this process through may allow you to decide where to go; following it certainly will give you a coherent structure for your essay.

Once you have done these two things, a third step appears: You should give careful consideration to the manner of developing the essay *after* your principles of relation have been established. Two means — the *continuous* and the *discontinuous* — are available for broad structural patterns. Your choice here — as with most writing decisions — depends upon the complexity of the subject matter, your purpose, and the audience. In the *continuous*, the comparison and contrast takes place continuously in the same paragraph (a-b, a-b, a-b pattern), and in the *discontinuous* it takes place in separate paragraphs (a-a-a, b-b-b pattern). The essay concerning which of the two universities to attend could be organized by comparison and contrast in the following ways:

(1) Continuous (a-b, a-b, a-b, a-b)

Paragraph 1: Compare the two universities for admission requirements.

Paragraph 2: Compare the two universities for tuition costs.

Paragraph 3: Compare and contrast the two universities for library holdings.

Paragraph 4: Compare and contrast the two universities for success of athletic teams.

(2) Discontinuous (a-a-a-a, b-b-b-b)

Paragraph 1: Establish the characteristics of one of the universities in the areas of admissions, tuition, library holdings, and success of athletic teams.

Paragraph 2: Compare and contrast the second university for the characteristics of admissions, tuition, library holdings, and success of athletic teams.

Everything the Power of the World does is done in a circle. The sky is round, and I have heard that the earth is round like a ball, and so are all the stars. The wind, in its greatest power, whirls. Birds make their nests in circles, for theirs is the same religion as ours. The sun comes forth and goes down again in a circle. The moon does the same, and both are round. Even the seasons form a great circle in their changing, and always come back again to where they were. The life of a man is a circle from childhood to childhood, and so it is in everything where power moves. Our tepees were round like the nests of birds, and these were always set in a circle, the nation's hoop, a nest of many nests, where the Great Spirit meant for us to hatch our children.

— Black Elk, *Black Elk Speaks* by John Neihardt (1961)

While neither of the two patterns is inherently superior, the *discontinuous* method is likely to be more effective when the subject matter is simple, for the obvious reason the audience will be able to recall the pertinent facts on one school while reading about the other. The *continuous* pattern usually works best on subjects of greater complexity that are treated in more detail. If all you want to include about admission is the particular standard tests required, you might as well put this information in with that from other categories in a *discontinuous* form. But if the level of your approach requires the names of the tests (ACT, College Board), the minimal scores, class rank, financial needs or abilities, geographic restrictions, and the like, you probably should organize your details in a *continuous* pattern.

BUILDING PARAGRAPHS USING COMPARISON AND CONTRAST

When using comparison and contrast to build a paragraph, it is important to identify the points (usually two) to be compared in the *topic sentence*. Then, develop the paragraph by establishing one side of the comparison fully before going on to the other side. The following paragraph demonstrates the comparison and contrast structural principle.

A responsibility we have as writers today is to understand the workings of the mind. Recent findings have clearly shown that the brain is di-

Topic sentence
Basis for the comparison

95

vided into two hemispheres. Further, it has been demonstrated that each hemisphere has its own communication system. The left hemisphere (if you are right-handed) is the control center for the kinds of communication we associate with logic. It understands and interprets experience in the linear, highly formalized, methods of deductive, inductive, and analytical discourse. Obviously, "left" thinking is the most basic and influential of Western culture. In contrast, the right hemisphere of the brain (if you are right handed) is the garden where the nonlogical forms of communication grow. Such forms as metaphor, rhythm, symbol, clairvoyance, ESP, dreams, telepathy, and hallucinations are characteristic of the "right" side. As a culture, we have not done much to integrate the nonlogical forms with the logical forms in our everyday activities. As writers, however, it is our "duty" to understand the two sources of communication and to bring them into a balance in our lives.

One side of the comparison

Transition and other side of comparison and contrast

Conclusion

The key to controlling the comparison and contrast process in the paragraph is the structural transition ("In contrast"), which clearly signals that the other side of the subject is to be explored.

BUILDING ESSAYS USING COMPARISON AND CONTRAST

As we said earlier, one consideration in using the comparison and contrast method is the decision whether to use a *continuous* or a *discontinuous* approach. This decision can be made only after examining the material you plan to use and the audience to whom it is directed. Following is a short essay* demonstrating the *discontinuous* method:

There is a widely held belief that language is the cohesive that holds societies together. When

Audience appeal

* The material, from an earlier chapter, represents an example of how a relatively small building block in a larger context (in this instance, a chapter) can function as a complete essay.

man assembled his language, he built his cities and civilizations. How and why man first used language is a matter of conjecture. However, there are two contrasting theories as to how we as children acquire and first learn to use language.

Thesis statement

On the one hand, one group of philosophers — those called empiricists and, more recently, behavioralists such as B. F. Skinner — says that a child learns language as a habit: words are repeated by the parents, and repeated again, and eventually the child begins to imitate them. As a matter of fact, Claude Lévi-Strauss, an anthropologist, has conjectured that the environment is so influential in the shaping of language that there is even a relationship between food and resources and linguistic forms. He has found that certain primitive cultures with meager food resources have very complex grammars, as if the complexity of the linguistic form makes up for the absence of resources. Other, resource-rich cultures use words sparingly; they rely on understatement and grammatical simplicity. Americans, for example, like to think of themselves as a laconic, tight-lipped nation of Gary Cooper-Clint Eastwood types. Indeed, at one time in our history foreign travelers to this country *have* been struck by our silences as much as by our speeches.

Topic sentence

On the other hand, there is the position of the influential MIT linguist Noam Chomsky. Chomsky argues that the principles of language are present in the mind at birth, and that the four to five thousand known languages all rest on the same principles. Thus, determined by our chromosomes at birth, these principles he identifies as "linguistic universals," "biological properties of the human mind." Chomsky believes a child "knows" — not consciously, of course, but instinctually — the principles of language before he says his first word, largely because the categories of perception become grammatical categories as well. The interplay of these preexisting, embedded structures

Transition

Topic sentence

97

with his environment ultimately allows the child to acquire knowledge of a specific language.

Regardless of how we learn it — by imitation **Summary** or by filling in imprinted channels there in the human brain cortex from the beginning — language gives us a reciprocal relationship with our environment. It is our way to understand and order the world around us, but it also *shapes* our way of looking at the world. As our language al- **Conclusion** ters, our perception of the world alters and our selves, our identities, alter, as well.

The following student essay is an example of how the *continuous* comparison and contrast pattern can be effectively used. Included is the introductory paragraph and an outline of the body:

Folk and Urban Society

In most Western societies there are essentially two distinct life styles that people tend to choose. They are known as "folk" and "urban" societies and each has its own particular advantages and disadvantages. The folk society, on the one hand, is limited in geographical area, isolated in its relationships with other societies, and is static in its attitude toward change. On the other hand, the urban society is essentially the antithesis of the folk as it is generally larger, is heterogeneous in that many different kinds of people inhabit the area, and allows for diversity among its inhabitants. These are the essential differences between the two societies and from these differences the advantages and disadvantages of each arise.

Outline of Body

Paragraph 1: A comparison and contrast of the two cultures for advantages and disadvantages of geographical size.

Paragraph 2: A comparison and contrast of the two cultures for advantages and disadvantages in relation to other societies.

Paragraph 3: A comparison and contrast of the two cultures for advantages and disadvantages in attitude toward change.

The subject matter was sufficiently complex that the student chose to use the continuous structure. The advantage of his choice is that it does not overload the reader with too much different material at one time. This student kept in mind, moreover, the use of structural signals, such as "On the other hand," as transitions. Like other patterns of development, the pattern of comparison and contrast has its own set of sign posts, and this student used them to help guide the reader through the essay. Such transitional words* include for comparison, *similarly, parallel to, analogous to, compared to, corresponding to, allied to, associated with, coupled with, much the same as, approximately like,* and, for contrast, *unlike, antithetical to, in contrast to, diametrically opposed, inversely, contrary to, in opposition to, counter to,* and *conversely.*

Comparison and contrast can be an energetic rhetorical device when tone comes into play over the rigors of logic or system. For example, in Dorothy Lee's *Freedom and Culture*, a Wintu (California) Indian opposes the attitudes toward the environment of her culture with those of the white man:

> The white people never cared for land or deer or bear. When we Indians kill meat, we eat it all up. When we dig roots, we make little holes. . . . We shake down acorns and pinenuts. We don't chop down the trees. We only use dead wood. But the white people plow up the ground, pull up the trees, kill everything. The tree says, "Don't. I am sore. Don't hurt me." But they chop it down and cut it up. The spirit of the land hates them. The Indians never hurt anything, but the white people destroy all. They blast rocks and scatter them on the ground. The rock says, "Don't! You are hurting me." But the white people pay no attention. When the Indians use rocks, they take little round ones for their cooking. . . . How can the spirit of the earth like the white man? Everywhere the white man has touched it, it is sore.

The paragraph dramatically establishes a contrast, with one side of the relation largely implied in the first, or topic, sentence. A clear order emerges, but it seems far less important than tone, connotation, imagery. The method here — *we* versus *they* — is both ancient and effective, for it grows out of that fearful primary dichotomy of self versus other.

In *The Greening of America*, Charles Reich also uses informal comparison and contrast to develop an idea:

> There is a crucial parallel between the contemporary condemnation of the average man and the prejudices that once were held against the "nigger." The black was once blamed for having all sorts of supposed deficiencies of

---

* Most of the terms in this list reflect the kinds of transitions that are often associated with the spoken word. As beginning writers, we must become sensitive to using transitions associated with speech before we can use the more literary ones naturally.

> Normal babies are born turned on. Most adults are CLOSED OFF:
> Alive in every sense. In a caught intentions
> state of undifferentiated being: *bound being*, inhibition
> OPEN . . . egoless, timeless, the ego. Chronic excessive
> wordless, process muscular tension . . .
> of direct experience. unreleased. Caught
> Naked, uninhibited; in words, indirect experience,
> without distinction between self conditioned, automatic
> and the world: paradise. behavior concept dominated,
> Unself consciousness expanding. defensive
> Biological self-regulation: a sense of separation,
> balance-tension-satisfaction- goal oriented, accomplishment
> balance: total involvement: oriented. Depression,
> flow. the burden of time.
>
> — Bernard Gunther, *How the West Is One* (1972)

character and intellect. But in the case of black people, the existence of centuries of deprivation and discrimination has gradually come to be seen in relation to these judgments, and with that insight has come a new recognition, by blacks and whites alike, of the black man's worth. But when we talk about the worker, we entirely fail to relate his present "nature" to the deprivation that he has undergone. We do not relate his "character" to the fact that he has been subjected to the enslavement of personality. Why have we refused to acknowledge that the white man has been systematically niggerized, that what we see as his shortcomings are the inevitable products of a systematic process of destruction?

Reich compares the white worker's condition to that of the black in order to reveal how the worker, too, has been a victim. One principle of comparison and contrast is that it ought to relate interesting, often emotionally tinged items. The comparisons by the Wintu Indian and Charles Reich generate a strong response because the structure of comparison and contrast can bear the tone it demands for handling their content and purpose.

Two principles should be observed in the use of comparison and contrast. First, be certain that your subjects have enough in common to make comparison and contrast reasonable. Political systems are better and more easily compared with other political systems, and ideologies with ideologies. Second, remember that effective comparison and contrast acknowledges *both* similarity and difference; if you are not aware of both, your reader may discover that your whole thesis is undercut by, say, differences that are sharper than the similarities upon which you focus. Be sure *your* purpose is not sabotaged by ignoring one or the other. To describe baseball and cricket as similar because they are team sports played on an outdoor field with a bat and ball would be to ignore several crucial differences between them. But if your purpose is to distinguish between games like baseball and cricket and games like football and soccer, then you may want to go no further than this.

Any choice you make concerning structure should be made after an examination of your subject matter, your purpose, and your audience. Frequently, in essay exams and assigned composition topics, one structural pattern or another will be inherent in the question or topic itself. The student essay discussed earlier was the result of an essay question that read: "Discuss the advantages and disadvantages of the 'folk' and 'urban' societies." The structural pattern of comparison and contrast is built into the question. But had the question been, "What are some of the features of 'folk' and 'urban' societies?", classification and division would offer an overall structure, and the use of examples and definitions would probably fill out specific paragraphs within the whole. If the question had been, "What are 'folk' and 'urban' societies?", *definition* would offer an inclusive structure, with example, classification and division, and comparison and contrast secondary structural choices or options for paragraphs within it.

EXERCISES

1. Using the content of the following excerpt from Philip Slater's *The Pursuit of Loneliness* as a departure point, write an essay comparing and contrasting (use *continuous* or *discontinuous* form) selected features of the "old" and "new" cultures. Be sure to use appropriate transitions to signal the comparison and contrast process.

    There are an almost infinite number of polarities by means of which one can differentiate between the old and the new cultures. The old culture, when forced to choose, tends to give preference to property rights over personal rights, technological requirements over human needs, competition over cooperation, violence over sexuality, concentration over distribution, the producer over the consumer, means over ends, secrecy over openness, social forms over personal expression, striving over gratification, Oedipal love over communal love, and so on. The new counterculture tends to reverse all of these priorities.

Procedure:
a. Select one or more differences between the cultures cited above. Be as concrete as possible by using examples, illustrations, and details. Perhaps a few personal experiences could be added.
b. Write an introduction and a conclusion.
c. Use a title.

2. *Interdisciplinary topics.* Using the structural principle of comparison and contrast, write an essay arguing for or against one of the following propositions or topics. Be sure to include a title, introduction, and conclusion, and use as many specific examples as you can to develop your thesis.
a. "Man is a complex organism, responding in predictable ways to his environment — freedom of choice, dignity, and humanism are absurd and empty concepts." Compare two different psychological positions such as those of Freud and B. F. Skinner as they would relate to the above proposition.
b. What we call American culture is in reality only a series of subcultures.
c. Each human being is essentially a product of environment (culture) rather than heredity (biology).
d. Compare and contrast the advantages and disadvantages of individuals who live in either a rural or urban society.
e. Disobedience, the rarest and most courageous of the virtues, is seldom distinguished from neglect, the laziest and commonest of the vices.
f. Compare and contrast two poems, stories, or films for their meanings and/or character.
g. The modern theory of combustion is somewhat superior to the phlogiston theory.

METAPHOR AND ANALOGY

As a means of rhetorical development, the analogy has a close affinity to comparison and contrast and simile and metaphor. Though not limited to one function, analogy, like comparison, is a structural device for larger verbal units, and simile and metaphor are primarily

> The basic distinction between grammar and rhetoric might be compared with the game of football. The "grammar" of the game would be the rules and conventions that determine the conduct of the game, including the system of scoring. The "rhetoric" of the game would be the knowledge of strategy and maneuver that leads to effective play and a winning game. To play the game correctly would not *necessarily* be to play it effectively, though effective play would certainly have to conform to the rules of the game.
>
> — C. Brooks and R. P. Warren, *Modern Rhetoric* (1958)

stylistic devices used in smaller verbal units. The simile is an explicit comparison of two unlike things employing either of the words *like* or *as*. The metaphor is an implicit comparison of basically unlike things; neither "like" nor "as" is used to draw attention to the comparison. The sentence, "The sun arched like a golden ball through the sky," is a simile. By slightly altering the same sentence to, "The golden ball arched through the sky," we change the simile into a metaphor; and though the objects of the comparison (sun, ball) remain the same, in the first instance comparison is explicit, in the second implicit. Of these two terms, *metaphor* is the more inclusive, for it is often used generically to refer to all figurative language. A *simile* may thus be called a *metaphor*, but we do not normally refer any more to *metaphor* as *simile*. In a general way, both simile and metaphor are analogies, and all three involve comparisons. All are structural devices, and one or the other may serve well throughout a sentence, several sentences, a paragraph, or a whole essay.

Linguists agree that all language is basically metaphorical or figurative, for it is built up from comparisons of one thing to other things. Much of our commonplace language is fundamentally metaphorical: chairs have *legs*, decisions *hinge* on, movies have *stars*, time *flies*, traffic *roars* (you can probably *drum up* even more examples for yourself). Slang, jargon, and colloquial language are replete with metaphor, for the most part used unconsciously. Louis Untermeyer suggests the importance of the role of metaphor in our everyday lives:

Even while he scorns poetry, the ordinary man helps himself to its properties and symbols; his daily life is unthinkable without metaphor. Having "slept like a log," he gets up in the morning "fresh as a daisy" or "fit as a fiddle"; he "wolfs down" breakfast, "hungry as a bear," with his wife, who has a "tongue like vinegar," but a "heart of gold." He gets into his car, which "eats up the miles," "steps on the gas," and, as it "purrs" along through the "hum" of traffic, he reaches his office where he is "as busy as a one-armed paper hanger with the hives." Life, for the average man, is not "a bed of roses," his competitor is "sly as a fox" and his own clerks are "slow as molasses in January." But "the day's grind" is finally done and, though it is "raining cats and dogs," he arrives home "happy as a lark."

When we observe that someone "wolfs down" breakfast or has "a heart of gold" we are, perhaps, being rather trite, but we are, consciously or not, depending on metaphor to help express our meaning.

A skillful writer employs metaphor and analogy to achieve clarity or to touch one's emotions. In expository and some persuasive writing, the primary purpose of these types of figurative language is to achieve clarity rather than to appeal to emotions: we all thus use *analogy*. The purpose of analogy is largely structural rather than emotive: it is used to make clear to the audience one idea or object by close comparison to another. The workings of the human heart may be explained to a lay audience by likening the heart to a pump. The functions of a pump are similar enough to the action of the heart to make such an analogy useful and to clarify some of the mysteries of the latter. Similarly, in order to explain the complex workings of language, Ludwig Wittgenstein uses an analogy of game:

> Doesn't the analogy between language and games throw light here? We can easily imagine people amusing themselves in a field by playing with a ball so as to start various existing games, but playing many without finishing them and in between throwing the ball aimlessly into the air, chasing one another with the ball and bombarding one another for a joke and so on. And now someone says: The whole time they are playing a ball-game and following definite rules at every throw.
>
> And is there not also the case where we play and make up the rules as we go along? And there is even one where we alter them as we go along.

Wittgenstein's analogy suggests many features about one activity (language) that we normally associate only with another (game). It helps us because we may understand games better than we understand language. Like games, language operates normally through rules, or conventions of syntax, meaning, number, function, and the like; but we can be (as we usually are) unconscious of the rules, rules can be suspended for any reason at any time, and we can change the rules: give the batter four strikes, let *ain't* be a formal verb. Language, Wittgenstein says, permits an element of play. Metaphor, as a "play on words," often begins in verbal play.

BUILDING PARAGRAPHS USING ANALOGY

The development of a paragraph using the process of analogy depends on the availability of relevant points of comparison and how far you want to extend them. You must choose items for your analogies that have a sufficient number of comparative features, and you must consider the points of similarity only as far as needed to clarify your argument. The following paragraph, by Susanne K. Langer from *Philosophy in a New Key*, explains the workings of the human mind through an analogy to a "grammar-bound island":

> At best, human thought is but a tiny, grammar-bound island, in the midst of a sea of feeling expressed by "Oh'oh" and sheer babble. The island has a periphery, perhaps, of mud — factual and hypothetical concepts broken down by the motional tides into the "material modex," a mixture of meaning and nonsense. Most of us live the better part of our lives on this mud-flat; but in artistic moods we take to the deep, where we flounder about with symptomatic cries that sound like propositions about life and death, good and evil, substance, beauty, and other nonexistent topics.

Langer's explanation gains concreteness and clarity through her analogy. The extension of the points of similarity from the island to the mud-flats to the "deep" helps us understand the mysterious qualities of the human thought process, but Langer's purpose permits her to drop the analogy after a brief space. Robert Hunter, in *The Storming of the Mind*, pursues a different analogy, but on a similar subject, much farther:

> . . . We have been moving even deeper into the largely uncharted seas of the psyche. We find ourselves being pulled, in our search for the new world of consciousness, ever closer to the line etched in our minds by Western thought beyond which the universe is assumed to end, the line separating the cognitive world from the intuitive — a line not unlike the one appearing on ancient sea charts, indicating nothing about the regions beyond except that "Here be monsters." This is the one region never deeply penetrated or mapped by white adventurers and certainly never — until recently — "colonized." Here is a whole uncivilized continent, a primitive world. And advancing, tapping a whole new complex of resources, coming into contact with ancient wisdoms, and finally, setting up colonies of their own. Like their white ancestors, they are for the most part fleeing from tyranny and oppression — in this case the tyranny of a mode of consciousness. They come riding new currents of rhythm, many borne

by very "high" winds indeed, propelled by LSD, pot, hashish, peyote, mescaline, others guided by astrological charts or the *I Ching* — if they make use of ancient maps it is only because the West has failed to provide them with new ones.

Hunter establishes a clear line of development through his analogy. Perhaps above all Hunter makes us *see* and commands our interest as he explains the search for the inner world, for a new consciousness, where the landscape is just as dramatic and fraught with just as many dangers as the search for geographical worlds.

BUILDING ESSAYS USING ANALOGY

An analogy may be usefully employed for the development of a single paragraph or a series of paragraphs. How much space you devote to it depends on your rhetorical purposes and needs. Consider the effectiveness of the following argument for the reduction of armaments by the United States on the hope that the Soviet Union would do likewise. This example is quite complex, for the two paragraphs stretch a simple metaphor into an extended analogy that ends by sounding like a parable:

Imagine two husky men standing facing each other near the middle, but on opposite sides, of a long and rigid seesaw balanced over an abyss. As either man takes a step outward, the other must compensate with a nearly equal step outward on his side or the balance will be destroyed. The farther out they move, the greater the unbalancing effect of each step, and the more agile and quick to react both men must become in order to maintain the precarious equilibrium. To make the situation even worse, both of these husky men realize that this teetering board has some limit to its tensile strength — at some point it is certain to crack, dropping them both to destruction. So both men are frightened, but neither is willing to admit it for fear the other might take advantage of him.

How are these two men to escape from this dangerous situation, a situation in which the fate of each is bound up with that of the other? One reasonable solution immediately presents itself: let them agree to walk slowly and carefully toward the center of the teetering board in unison. To do this they must trust each other. But these men do not trust each other, and each imagines the other to be irrational enough to destroy them both unless he (Ego) preserves the balance. But now let us suppose that it occurs to one of these men that perhaps the other is just as frightened as he is and would also welcome some way of escaping from this intolerable situation. So this man decides to gamble on his new insight and calls out loudly, "I am taking a small step *toward* you!" The other man, rather than have the precarious balance upset, also takes a tentative step forward, whereupon the first takes another, larger step. Thus they work their ways back to safety by a series of unilateral, yet reciprocal steps — very much as they originally moved out against each other.

Metaphor, analogy, and parable all have roots in words that mean *to compare*. Since one side of the comparison here is left unstated (the countries that are *like* these two men), this analogy seems an extended metaphor (also called, in poetry, a *conceit*); since it is also a didactic *story*, the two paragraphs become a parable as well. Nowhere is the relation between the U.S. and the U.S.S.R. mentioned, but once these nations are plugged into the roles of the two balancing men the clarity and force of the analogy illuminates the argument for disarmament. In Chapter 13 of Matthew in *The New Testament*, Christ employs several parables (built on a base of metaphor/analogy) to explain difficult concepts; these parables are analogies developed through a narrative (chronological) sequence. Two short ones are these:

> The Kingdom of heaven is like a grain of mustard seed, which a man took, and sowed in his field: which indeed is the least of all seeds: but when it is grown, it is the greatest among herbs, and becometh a tree, so that the birds of the air come and lodge in the branches thereof.

> The Kingdom of heaven is like unto leaven, which a woman took, and hid in three measures of meal, till the whole was leavened.

In the following essay from *Walden* Henry David Thoreau observes a battle between two ant armies and sees this war analogous to human wars. As you read, underline the words and phrases that directly compare the ants to humans (for example, the classical reference to "the legions of these Myrmidons," and "the red republican" and "the black imperialists"). Also, be sure to underline those words that are commonly used to describe human war scenes ("the ground was already strewn with the dead and dying," "engaged in deadly combat," and so forth).

The Battle of the Ants

One day when I went out to my wood-pile, or rather my pile of stumps, I observed two large ants, the one red, the other much larger, nearly half an inch long, and black, fiercely contending with one another.

Having once got hold they never let go, but struggled and wrestled and rolled on the chips incessantly. Looking farther, I was surprised to find that the chips were covered with such combatants, that it was not a *duellum*, but a *bellum*, a war between the two races of ants, the red always pitted against the black, and frequently two red ones to one black. The legions of these Myrmidons covered all the hills and vales in my wood-yard, and the ground was already strewn with the dead and dying, both red and black. It was the only battle which I have ever witnessed, the only battle-field I ever trod while the battle was raging; internecine war; the red republicans on the one hand, and the black imperialists on the other. On every side they were engaged in deadly combat, yet without any noise that I could hear, and human soldiers never fought so resolutely. I watched a couple that were fast locked in each other's embraces, in a little sunny valley amid the chips, now at noonday prepared to fight till the sun went down, or life went out. The smaller red champion had fastened himself like a vice to his adversary's front, and through all the tumblings on that field never for an instant ceased to gnaw at one of his feelers near the root, having already caused the other to go by the board; while the stronger black one dashed him from side to side, and, as I saw on looking nearer, had already divested him of several of his members. They fought with more pertinacity than bulldogs. Neither manifested the least disposition to retreat. It was evident that their battle-cry was "Conquer or die." In the meanwhile there came along a single red ant on the hillside of this valley, evidently full of excitement, who either had despatched his foe, or had not yet taken part in the battle; probably the latter, for he had lost none of his limbs; whose mother had charged him to return with his shield or upon it. Or perchance he was some Achilles, who had nourished his wrath apart, and had now come to avenge or rescue his Patroclus. He saw this unequal combat from afar — for the blacks were nearly twice the size of the red — he drew near with rapid pace till he stood on his guard within half an inch of the combatants; then, watching his opportunity, he sprang upon the black warrior, and commenced his operations near the root of his right fore leg, leaving the foe to select among his own members; and so there were three united for life, as if a new kind of attraction had been invented which put all other locks and cements to shame. I should not have wondered by this time to find that they had their respective musical bands stationed on some eminent chip, and playing their national airs the while, to excite the slow and cheer the dying combatants. I was myself excited somewhat even as if they had been men. The more you think of it, the less the difference. And certainly there is not the fight recorded in Concord history, at least, if in the history of America, that will bear a moment's comparison with this, whether for the numbers engaged in it, or for the patriotism and heroism displayed. For numbers and for carnage it was an Austerlitz or Dresden. Concord Fight! Two killed on the patriots' side, and Luther Blanchard wounded! Why here every ant was a Buttrick — "Fire! for God's sake fire!" — and thousands shared the fate of Davis and Hosmer. There was not one hireling there. I have no doubt that it was a principle they fought for, as much as our ancestors, and not to avoid a three-penny tax on their tea; and the results of this battle will be as important and memorable to those whom it concerns as those of the battle of Bunker Hill, at least.

I took up the chip on which the three I have particularly described were struggling, carried into my house, and placed it under a tumbler on my window-sill, in order to see the issue. Holding a microscope to the first-mentioned red ant, I saw that, though he was assiduously gnawing at the near fore leg of his enemy, having severed his remaining feeler, his own breast was all torn away, exposing what vitals he had there to the jaws of the black warrior, whose breastplate was apparently too thick for him to pierce; and the dark carbuncles of the sufferer's eyes shone with ferocity such as war only could excite. They struggled half an hour longer under the tumbler, and when I looked again the black soldier had severed the heads of his foes from their bodies, and the still living heads were hanging on either side of him like ghastly trophies of his saddle-bow, still apparently as firmly fastened as ever, and he was endeavoring with feeble struggles, being without feelers, and with only the remnant of a leg, and I know not how many other wounds, to divest himself of them; which at length, after half an hour more, he accomplished. I raised the glass, and he went off over the window-sill in that crippled state. Whether he finally survived that combat, and spent the remainder of his days in some Hôtel des Invalides, I do not know; but I thought that his industry would not be worth much thereafter. I never learned which party was victorious, nor the cause of the war, but I felt for the rest of that day as if I had my feelings excited and harrowed by witnessing the struggle, the ferocity and carnage, of a human battle before my door.

— Henry David Thoreau

Analogy, metaphor, simile, and parable can appeal both to a reader's feelings and to his reason at the same time. Consider the effect you would achieve by describing a building as a "grey smudge on the horizon." Clearly, such an image will evoke a particular — and usually negative — response in the mind of your audience; you can reverse that effect by picturing the same building as "a bright tower on the horizon." Both uses of metaphorical language evoke emotions — one of rejection, the other of approval. Both appeals working together achieve your persuasive and descriptive purposes more effectively than either alone.

> Don Juan stated that in order to arrive at "seeing" one first had to "stop the world." "Stopping the world" was indeed an appropriate rendition of certain states of awareness in which the reality of everyday life is altered because the flow of interpretation, which ordinarily runs uninterruptedly, has been stopped by a set of circumstances alien to that flow. In my case the set of circumstances alien to my normal flow of interpretations was the sorcery description of the world. Don Juan's precondition for "stopping the world" was that one had to be convinced; in other words, one had to learn the new description in a total sense, for the purpose of pitting it against the old one, and in that way break the dogmatic certainty, which we all share, that the validity of our perceptions, or our reality of the world, is not to be questioned.
>
> — Carlos Castaneda, *Journey to Ixtlan* (1972)

Metaphor and analogy are possibly the most effective rhetorical devices in our language. They seem integral to thought itself. Both have inherent within them the idea of tying together two seemingly unrelated objects or concepts. In the hands of the skillful writer, metaphors become the major device by which to show the links between individual experience and nature and the universe at large. A metaphor often is at the very center of our thinking about a subject, and writers frequently call attention to their central metaphors, as, for example, in chapter or book titles. The titles of many books we have referred to — including *The Greening of America*, *Where the Wasteland Ends*, *The Storming of the Mind*, and *To A Dancing God* — represent effective metaphors at work.

It is often difficult to separate objective and subjective uses of language. Not even the analogies of Susanne Langer or Robert Hunter are without emotional impact, though the main purposes of their analogies remain clarifying ones. In poetry and imaginative prose, on the other hand, figurative language may have its sole purpose in the emotional response it can arouse. In the following poem by an unknown early English poet, the essential metaphor is developed primarily for the emotional context surrounding an idea:

> O Western wind, when wilt thou blow,
>   That the small rain down can rain?
> Christ, that my love were in my arms,
>   And I in my bed again!

The poem seems to be the plea of a speaker (perhaps a soldier) to return home to his love. The emotional force of the poem is carried by the implicit comparison between the man's plight and the plight of a barren winter landscape. In his juxtaposition (a Latin word combining *juxta* [near] and *position*) of nature and self, the speaker equates the coming of the western wind and "the small rain" it brings with a return to his love. Not only do the wind and rain signal the coming of spring, the rebirth of life in nature, but they also suggest his longing and physical desire ("And I in my bed again!"). Nature, the earth, and waiting for rain, all connect the renewal of life with the renewal of love for which the speaker hopes. Does this seem a lot of meaning for four short lines to carry? It is. But of course that's why we use figurative language, for it offers "pictures" worth many, many words, and it depicts feelings that can be represented in no other way while expressing an abstract idea. Regardless of how metaphor and analogy are employed, whether for achieving clarity only or for emotional appeal as well, they serve rhetorically important functions.

EXERCISES

1. Analyze the effectiveness of the following analogies in terms of their logical (objective) and emotional (subjective) qualities:

   a. Nothing in progression (i.e., nothing changing, growing) can rest on its original plan. We may as well think of rocking a grown man in the cradle of an infant.

   — Edmund Burke

   b. The process of communication, like a great river, is continually shaping and changing our lives. Like a river, the process of communication can be dammed only momentarily. Television is the most powerful medium of mass communication man has ever toyed with. In its brief years, we have only begun to explore its vast social force. In denying people access to this medium, just as in damming a river, these forces can spill over and inundate a society. We see these forces today on our campuses, and have seen them in our ghettos.

   — Tommy Smothers

   c. Cape Cod is the bared and bended arm of Massachusetts; the shoulder is at Buzzard's Bay; the elbow, or crazy-bone, at Cape Mallebarre; the wrist at Truro; and the sandy fist at Provincetown, — behind which the

111

State stands on her guard, with her back to the Green Mountains, and her feet planted on the floor of the ocean, like an athlete protecting her Bay, — boxing with northeast storms, and, ever and anon, heaving up her Atlantic adversary from the lap of the earth, — ready to thrust forward her other fist, which keeps guard the while upon her breast at Cape Ann.

— Henry David Thoreau

d. In the field of world policy I would dedicate this Nation to the policy of good neighbor — the neighbor who resolutely respects himself and because he does so, respects the rights of others — the neighbor who respects his obligations and respects the sanctity of his agreements in and with a world of neighbors.

— Franklin D. Roosevelt

e. She regarded him with her kindly glances, which made something glow and expand within his chest. It was a delicious feeling, even though it did cut one's breath short now and then. Ecstatically he drank in the sound of her tranquil, seductive talk full of innocent gaiety and of spiritual quietude. His passion appeared to him to flame up and envelop her in blue fiery tongues from head to foot and over her head, while her soul appeared in the center like a big white rose. . . .

— Joseph Conrad

f. For a strange thing has happened — while all the other arts were born naked, this the movies, the youngest, has been born fully-clothed. It can say everything before it has anything to say. It is as if the savage tribe, instead of finding two bars of iron to play with, had found scattering the seashore, fiddles, flutes, saxophones, trumpets, grand pianos by Erard and Bedhstein, and had begun with incredible energy, but without knowing a note of music, to hammer and thump upon them all at the same time.

— Virginia Woolf

g. Western Europe is a patient in an iron lung. American economic and military aid provide it with oxygen, but it cannot live and breathe by itself. The sickness which paralyses it is not of an economic nature. Nor is it social strife; nor the Communist phantom creed. These are symptoms of the disease, but not its cause. The cause is both deeper and simpler: Europe has lost faith in itself.

— Arthur Koestler

2. Write a short essay analyzing the connection between metaphor and meaning in the following poem:

The Tyger

Tyger! Tyger! burning bright
In the forests of the night,
What immortal hand or eye
Could frame thy fearful symmetry?

In what distant deeps or skies
Burnt the fire of thine eyes?
On what wings dare he aspire?
What the hand dare seize the fire?

And what shoulder, & what art,
Could twist the sinews of thy heart?
And when thy heart began to beat,
What dread hand? & what dread feet?

What the hammer? what the chain?
In what furnace was thy brain?
What the anvil? what dread grasp
Dare its deadly terrors clasp?

When the stars threw down their spears,
And water'd heaven with their tears,
Did he smile his work to see?
Did he who made the Lamb make thee?

Tyger! Tyger! burning bright
In the forests of the night,
What immortal hand or eye
Dare frame thy fearful symmetry?

— William Blake

3. Write a paragraph or an essay in which you explain a concept from one of your other courses using an analogy to help clarify it. For example, you could use the idea that society is like a living organism and then go on to explain that relationship.

4. Analyze the following speech for its pattern of analogy through which Ulysses gives reasons to the Greek army for their failure to capture Troy. When you read through the poem the first time, mark words you do not understand and then look them up in your dictionary: when you do not find the exact words, look at words in the dictionary close to their roots and be aware of meanings in the contexts of the whole:

113

from **Troilus and Cressida**

The specialty of rule hath been neglected.
And, look, how many Grecian tents do stand
Hollow upon this plain, so many hollow factions.
When that the general is not like the hive
To whom the foragers shall all repair,
What honey is expected? Degree being vizarded,
The unworthiest shows as fairly in the mask.
The heavens themselves, the planets and this centre,
Observe degree, priority and place,
Insisture, course, proportion, season, form,
Office, and custom, in all line of order:
And therefore is the glorious planet Sol
In noble eminence enthroned and sphered
Amidst the other; whose medicinable eye
Corrects the ill aspects of planets evil,
And posts like the commandment of a king,
Sans check to good and bad: but when the planets
In evil mixture to disorder wander,
What plagues and what portents, what mutiny,
What raging of the sea, shaking of earth,
Commotion in the winds, frights, changes, horrors,
Divert and crack, rend and deracinate
The unity and married calm of states
Quite from their fixture! O, when degree is shaked,
Which is the ladder to all high designs,
The enterprise is sick! How could communities,
Degrees in schools and brotherhoods in cities,
Peaceful commerce from dividable shores,
The primogenitive and due of birth,
Prerogative of age, crowns, sceptres, laurels,
But by degree, stand in authentic place?
Take but degree away, untune that string,
And, hark, what discord follows! each thing meets
In mere oppugnancy: the bounded waters
Should lift their bosoms higher than the shores,
And make a sop of all this solid globe:
Strength should be lord of imbecility,
And the rude son should strike his father dead:
Force should be right; or rather, right and wrong,
Between whose endless jar justice resides,

Should lose their names, and so should justice too.
Then every thing includes itself in power,
Power into will, will into appetite;
And appetite, an universal wolf,
So doubly seconded with will and power,
Must make perforce an universal prey,
And last eat up himself. Great Agamemnon,
This chaos, when degree is suffocate,
Follows the choking.
And this neglection of degree it is
That by a pace goes backward, with a purpose
It hath to climb. The general's disdain'd
By him one step below; he by the next;
That next by him beneath: so every step,
Exampled by the first pace that is sick
Of his superior, grows to an envious fever
Of pale and bloodless emulation:
And 'tis this fever that keeps Troy on foot,
Not her own sinews.

— William Shakespeare

CAUSE AND EFFECT

Observers suggest that a characteristic of contemporary culture is a widespread rebellion against logic as the dominating mode for organizing one's life. Some say the rebellion is justifiable, that we have for too long given too high a priority to the processes of logic. According to S. Giedion (*Sign, Image, Symbol*), the reaction against logic occurred because modern man has realized it is limited to only a portion of our total human experience:

As we become aware of the multilayered fabric of the soul, we try to ascertain not only the limits within which logical argument operates as a reliable tool, but also the areas in which that tool cannot be used, areas of different psychic dimensions. The laws of logic have colored philosophic thought ever since the Renaissance, especially since the seventeenth century. This influence is closely paralleled in the optical sphere by the influence of perspective on our view of the world. It is just these narrow criteria of logical cause and effect and of optical perspective that the present period resents and rebels against.

> Rhetoric, dealing as it does with persuasion, is involved with human relations: man persuading man to act, to think, to agree, to enjoy. The rhetorician must establish a contact, therefore, and must do this in an effective way, a way in which his purpose is likely to be achieved. The most basic contact is on the level of reason. In all our actions — at least in our important and deliberate actions — we act according to reason. Or, to put it another way, we don't consciously act in an unreasonable way. Our actions may at times appear unreasonable to others, but they at least *seem* reasonable to us.
>
> — E. V. Stackpoole and W. Ross Winterowd, *The Relevance of Rhetoric* (1966)

This rebellion, taken to its extreme, would lead to complete dependence upon another mode of ordering experience, one that glorifies the emotional, intuitive, and mystical. Aspects of experience such as feelings, hunches, are important parapsychological phenomena, but they comprise just one dimension of our capabilities. Like logic, they, too, represent only a *mode*, one way of doing or being. Men and women are capable of a great range of experiences, so, for the total being, the extreme of one is as bad as the extreme of the other. It is the balance of the two — the logical and the nonlogical — that creates the sense of wholeness of the individual. Our dreams are sometimes just as capable of instructing us as our logic; our logical capabilities frequently are all we have with which to cope with some experiences. If we are able to handle the paralogical tools of analogy and figurative language in our lives and our writing, we must at the same time be able to handle the tools of logic, of reason.

The system of logic in Western culture consists of two kinds: deductive and inductive. Robert M. Pirsig, in his novel *Zen and the Art of Motorcycle Maintenance,* uses the motorcycle as an example of the two kinds of reasoning:

Two kinds of logic are used, inductive and deductive. Inductive inferences start with observations of the machine and arrive at general conclusions. For example, if the cycle goes over a bump and the engine misfires, and then goes over a long smooth stretch of road and there is no misfiring, and then goes over a fourth bump and the engine misfires again, one can logically conclude that the misfiring is caused by the bumps. That is induction: reasoning from particular experiences to general truths. Deductive inferences do the reverse. They start with general knowledge and predict a specific observation. For example, if, from reading the hierarchy of facts about the machine, the mechanic knows the horn of the cycle is powered exclusively by electricity from the battery, then he can logically infer that if the battery is dead the horn will not work. That is deduction.

Of the two kinds of reasoning, *induction* has dominated the other from the seventeenth century on. Its rise to authority closely parallels the rise of science, and the inductive method has been identified with the "scientific method" itself despite the fact that both deduction and induction are combined in it. The method of inductive reasoning does offer a powerful mode for organizing and analyzing much of our experience and the objective data of the world, so it is important that we understand and use it whenever our material, purpose, and audience require it. As Pirsig indicates, *induction* proceeds from the particular to the general, from the part to the whole. Using this process, you collect facts, figures, observations, all kinds of particulars about a subject, then you make an inductive "leap": you formulate a generalization from the material collected.

Our uses of inductive reasoning are often not infallible. We commit errors of all sorts, yet we must rely on induction in our lives, otherwise all our experience becomes useless. Who would drive down a road at night and go speeding over the top of a hill if he couldn't infer from the data of his experience that the road would continue on the other side? The Roadrunner's battles with the Coyote, in the cartoons, joke with our attitudes toward roads, hills, perspectives, inferences, and most of us laugh when the bird goes speeding off down a road that is merely sketched in on a backdrop made by *the properly incredulous Coyote*. Induction is simply a way of arriving at probabilities; there are few certainties in our lives so, like it or not, we must lead our lives along lines of probabilities. In those cartoons, we *are* the Coyote, but we *pull* for the Roadrunner because we too would like to be less bounded by those drawn lines of logic and perspective.

The most common form of induction that we can use for developing a particular paragraph and a whole essay is *cause and effect*. The reasoning of *why* things happen — as well as questions about the *relationship* between things — constitutes the cause-and-effect process. By observing effects we can often arrive at the cause, or by observing a series of causes we can project or infer — make an inductive "leap" to — a conclusion about the effects. This process, reasoning from cause to effect or effect to cause, is accepted and applied by all of us — unconsciously and often erroneously — every day of our lives. Why (cause) did the Yankees fail to

An error causing grief in our time is the idea that culture and civilization are recent acquisitions, and that all previous cultures were but crude gestures laying the groundwork for our own enlightened emergence into truth. Erickson denies that primitive societies are "infantile stages of mankind," or arrested deviations from the "proud progressive norms which we represent." They are, he states, a "complete form of mature human living." Levy-Bruhl spoke of prehistoric man not as a *protoscientist* who arrived at false conclusions, but another type of man entirely, whose mental life differed from ours in kind. I would qualify this by observing that primitive man is not so much a different type as of a different esthetic bent. Lévi-Strauss finds archaic cultures a unified, coherent, intellectual scheme, based on different logical premises from our own. Jensen deplores the theory that early man arrived at totally erroneous conclusions regarding cause and effect.

— Joseph Chilton Pearce, *The Crack in the Cosmic Egg* (1971)

win the divisional title this year (effect)? Most assuredly, we argue, because of a change in their coaching staff. Clearly, the Republican party (cause) was responsible for the Depression (effect) of the thirties; they were in office, weren't they? Surely we must all starve (effect) in the near future; the world is becoming grossly overpopulated (cause). These questions and answers suggest the most likely faults that may occur in inductive reasoning: (1) ignoring the possibility of multiple causes for a single effect; (2) fastening on an inadequate cause or causes; (3) accepting improbable causes from among the ones possible; (4) invoking the *post hoc ergo propter hoc* ("after this, therefore because of this") fallacy that assigns an effect to a cause merely on the basis of the latter's preceding the former.

BUILDING PARAGRAPHS USING CAUSE AND EFFECT

When you use cause and effect to develop an essay or paragraph, you must think carefully if you are going to avoid the simple-minded faults of our common speech. You may analyze either from cause(s) to effect(s) or from effect(s) to cause(s), but you must make clear which set you are using; your transitional or keying words can identify for your audience your particular method. The following paragraph, written by a student, offers a clear example of how cause and effect can be employed to build a paragraph:

> [1]One troublesome problem facing educators today is the significant drop in SAT (Scholastic Aptitude Test) scores over the past ten years. [2]The actual decline from 1963 to 1975 in the verbal part of the test is from a 479 average to a 434 average while the decline in the mathematical part is from a 502 average to a 472 average. [3]The reasons for this decline can probably be attributed to the following causes: (1) a lack of discipline in the classroom, (2) increased parental permissiveness, (3) decline in reading and writing abilities, (4) limitations imposed on teaching professions, and (5) reduction of money spent on education. [4]In addition to these causes there is another that might be the most significant of them all — the phenomenal viewing of television over the past decade. [5]Because of this, some people are persuaded that students are more tuned into the oral-aural approach than they are to the printed word; hence, the test because of its form fails to measure the "real" ability of the student. [6]Whatever the cause or causes it is obvious that a rigid reexamination of our educational system is in order.

Topic sentence

Effects

Causes

Conclusion

After establishing the topic in the first sentence, the writer presents the *effects* in terms of the comparative SAT scores in sentence 2. Beginning with the third sentence, the pattern of development shifts to classifying the *causes* and continues through sentences 4 and 5. The paragraph ends with a call for action.

Another illustration of the cause-and-effect developmental pattern is the following paragraph from *My Several Worlds* written by Pearl Buck:

And speaking of cruelty, this is perhaps the place to mention the cruelty to animals which shocks so many foreigners when they visit China. There is indeed a vast difference between the way in which animals are treated in China and the way in which they are treated in the West. Animals are not petted and fondled and made much of by the Chinese. On the contrary, Chinese visitors in the United States are usually shocked and disgusted by the affection with which animals are treated, an emotion which the

Chinese feel should be reserved for human beings. I believe in kindness toward animals and human beings and I used to wonder why my Chinese friends, whom I knew to be merciful and considerate toward people, could be quite indifferent to suffering animals. The cause, I discovered as I grew older, lay in the permeating of Chinese thought by Buddhist theory. Though most Chinese were not religious and therefore not Buddhist, the doctrine of the reincarnation of the human soul influenced their thinking, and the essence of that theory is that an evil human being after death becomes an animal in his next incarnation. Therefore every animal was once a wicked human being. While the average Chinese might deny direct belief in this theory, the pervading belief led him to feel contempt for animals.

The paragraph is nicely balanced. By comparison with Westerners, it establishes that the Chinese have a different attitude toward animals (effect). In sentence five, Pearl Buck begins to explain that Chinese cruelty toward animals comes from vestiges of Buddhist beliefs in reincarnation. Hence, the first four sentences explain the effect, the last four sentences explain the cause, and we are signaled of the shift by the transition (the pivotal phrase is "The cause") from one part to the other. Is Pearl Buck's reasoning flawless? No. But it seems adequate, it acknowledges the complexity of causes and effects, it seems probable enough as we judge it from our own knowledge and experience, and it is not a feeble *post hoc* argument. Her conclusions can be disputed, of course, but most of us, for the time being, will accept them.

BUILDING ESSAYS USING CAUSE AND EFFECT

The structural principle of *cause and effect* can also be used to develop an essay. The following student essay is built on this pattern.

A Look in the Mirror

The study of psychology represents an attempt to understand, predict, and control behavior. Psychology, as a science, seeks to establish general principles relating to human behavior, and this effort must be directed toward broad areas in as much as there is a great deal of variance in behavior. Additionally, no two individuals are entirely alike, so psychologists, while relying to a great extent on established theories of behavior, must be constantly receptive to the particular traits characteristic of any one person.

How, then, do we come to be so unique and to possess an individual identity as opposed to shallow, unemotional, and unimaginative nonentities? From the moment of birth (indeed, some say from conception) we are constantly receiving stimulus from our environment and others. From a steady interaction, we develop ideas and the capacity for response and initiative. We progress through successive stages of development, from ability to distinguish between ourselves and the outside world, to our ability to respond and act in our environment, to our capability for social interaction. Psychology has been able to identify and define specific forms of development, critical areas of psychological growth. To better understand a few of these concepts, I will identify some of the factors involved in *my* psychological development and demonstrate their significance as they relate to the formation of an "individual" person. To this end, I will describe my present attitude [effect] toward my status as a student. Later, I will show how certain influences in my personal development [causes] have generally formed and shaped these current ideas.

To begin, a great many of the attitudes I've formed to date are brought into play with my perceptions and feelings as a student. Of primary importance is a strong desire for new and rewarding stimulus. The acquisition of new knowledge takes a central role in most of my activities. As each bit of information is received, it serves to strengthen and enhance what has been learned in the past. The assimilation of new concepts becomes a means of providing direction and substance for past abstractions. I find the general atmosphere that is encountered in a learning environment to be personally rewarding in that it provides an outlet for intellectual activity that might otherwise have to be reduced to a subordinate level. A constant subliminal state of awareness is a prospect which I find abhorrent. Thus, my position as student not only provides a fair amount of the stimulation which I deem to be crucial to living in the present, but it presents an opportunity to gain the tools that will be necessary in future endeavors along the same lines. In addition, the present environment gives rise to opportunities for competition not only with others, but with prescribed standards of achievement. This need for some basis of comparison, a relative indication of personal merit, is only of secondary importance but is somewhat rewarding nevertheless.

From where do these assumptions take root? An individual does not randomly decide at some predetermined stage to adopt a particular doctrine of behavior. They are the sum of what we learn in the process of our physical, cognitive, and social development. A partial explanation of what psychology has learned about these processes may be demonstrated by forming a *probable* model of what direction my early years took and relating this to the present perceptions as described. Since it is likely that most of my perceptions were derived from factors common to each of them, I have chosen not to make concrete and absolute distinctions be-

121

tween effect to a particular cause. I presume that one cause may have many effects and that these occur simultaneously. Therefore, to list the causes in each separate case would, I feel, be redundant.

I can remember practically nothing of my life up to the age of five. Psychology has determined that these forgotten years probably formed the singularly most critical period of my life. In these years parents must maintain a fine balance of interaction with their child. At first, they serve as caretakers by maintaining absolute control of the child's environment. They must provide the child with a sense of security and, at the same time, provide enough stimulation so that the child does not become lethargic. They must inhibit certain behavior such as destructive or dangerous activities without being overly repressive or protective. In this manner the child develops a sense of self-confidence and a degree of independence. The parents must make certain social demands on the child, such as toilet training, without being overly strict and instilling too great a sense of shame or guilt or implying inferiority. These years set the pattern for such concepts as conscience, personal identity, and motivation. I can assume that my parents were able to fulfill these responsibilities quite well, because I entered the first grade in school very eager to learn, with a high degree of motivation.

With my first year in school, my parents were intent upon setting a pattern that would guide me in later years. I entered school fully aware that I was expected to put forth my best effort. My parents chose a parochial school, not primarily because of the religious nature, but because they felt the first year to be most important, and they were convinced that this particular school would teach discipline and responsibility. Also, they considered the staff to be especially dedicated and qualified. My parents spent a great deal of time with me explaining the importance of education, the necessity for always trying my best, and pointing out that while achievement and reward in the form of good grades were important, of *most* importance was the effort extended and the ability to assume responsibility. They taught me that by working hard I could learn a great deal that would always benefit me, and gave me a belief that a person could advance as far as he wanted, the limits of achievement being determined by the individual himself. I was constantly supplied with new stimulus, new ideas, and new opportunities. In order to maintain all this I was rewarded with such things as recognition and feelings of personal esteem. I wanted to please everyone, and the result was an overwhelmingly successful year in which I was recognized by relatives, friends, and the school, all of whom encouraged me even further. Obviously, my first year played an instrumental part in my later development. I was able to develop decidedly positive attitudes in regard to school. After all, school was fun, "good" people received praise, and authorities were there to *help*. These ideas persisted in later years.

Still another important factor in my development related to my environment. Our family moved so often that by the age of sixteen I had seen all but three states and had visited several foreign countries. Since we always lived near government bases, the other children were always from a wide variety of backgrounds. Additionally, there was a necessity for the ability to adapt to constantly changing environments. This was not overly difficult since most of the other children were in the same position. The unity among these kids was phenomenal, and most of our time was spent exchanging information on different cultures, people, and interests. It is a popular misconception that military and government dependents are constantly suffering from a state of "culture shock," are generally shiftless, restless, and lack a sense of security and direction. I found exactly the opposite to be true. The input of new stimuli was always at a tremendous level, and this certainly bears direct relevance to my present desires for the same quantity and quality of new stimulus. As to the popular contention regarding a lack of security and direction, the prevailing atmosphere was always one of belonging to a large "family," and most of the "parents" of this family were inspirational in their dedication to high ideals of public service and responsibility. (Also in direct contrast to popular theory.) Perhaps all this accounts for my attitude of trying to retain an "open" mind and a dedication to *principles* rather than to particular *institutions*. Institutions may be adapted to contemporary modes, while basic principles will generally remain unchanged. A parallel situation exists in regard to my future aspirations, which brings us to the final purpose of this essay.

Psychology proposes that we are all in some manner directed by developmental forces over which we have little control. The preceding account of my own circumstance tends to support this. If this is indeed true, then I am thankful for the foresight and efforts of those who have guided me thus far. I only hope that I can use what they have taught me to achieve in my own life what they have instilled as a model for behavior and direction. This can be done, I believe, by remaining receptive to changing circumstance and, more importantly, by retaining and adhering to the underlying principles in the face of it. I believe that we have a responsibility to live up to our fullest potential, not merely for our own benefit, but so that others may benefit as well. Perhaps this is too ambitious but, as it was told to me years ago, our limits are, for the most part, self-imposed.

The essay is structurally effective because it clearly defines the transition (the paragraph that begins, "From where do these assumptions take root?) between the *effect* (the discussion of the present in terms of being a student) and the *causes* (the past experiences). In using the cause-and-effect principle, you must clearly establish the cause(s) or effect(s) in a paragraph or series of paragraphs and then, through an effective transition, move on to discuss the effect(s) or cause(s).

A more complex example of the inductive process is Arthur Schlesinger, Jr.'s essay, "The Crisis of American Masculinity." He first identifies through examples the various aspects of the masculine crisis and then makes an inductive "leap" to the cause of the crisis. Here is Schlesinger's introductory paragraph on the nature of the problem (the effect):

> What has happened to the American Male? For a long time, he seemed utterly confident in his manhood, sure of his masculine role in society, easy and definite in his sense of sexual identity. The frontiersmen of James Fenimore Cooper, for example, never had any concern about masculinity; they were men, and it did not occur to them to think twice about it. Even well into the twentieth century, the heroes of Dreiser, of Fitzgerald, of Hemingway remain men. But one begins to detect a new theme emerging in some of these authors, especially in Hemingway: the theme of the male hero increasingly preoccupied with proving his virility to himself. And by mid-century, the male role had plainly lost its rugged clarity of outline. Today men are more and more conscious of maleness not as fact but as a problem. The ways by which American men affirm their masculinity are uncertain and obscure. There are multiplying signs, indeed, that something has gone badly wrong with the American male's conception of himself.

Schlesinger then develops his essay in ways we can outline as follows:

Part I. Schlesinger enumerates *effects* of the masculine crisis (we include in our outline the topics of each paragraph):

    Paragraph 1: "On the most superficial level, the roles of male and female are increasingly merged in the American household."

    Paragraph 2: "Consider the theatre, that faithful mirror of a society's preoccupations."

    Paragraph 3: "Or consider the movies."

    Paragraph 4: "Psychoanalysis backs up the theatre and the movies in emphasizing the obsession of the American male with his manhood."

Part II. Schlesinger considers possible *causes* of the masculine crisis:

Paragraph 5: "Male anxiety, many observers have declared, is simply the result of female aggression. . . ."

Paragraph 6: "Why is the American man so unsure today about his masculine identity?"

Part III. Schlesinger suggests some *remedies* for the crisis:

Paragraph 7: "For men to become men again, in short, their task is to recover a sense of individual spontaneity."

Paragraph 8: "I should like to mention three such techniques: satire, art, and politics."

By establishing the effects, the observed experiences around him, the author is able to suggest a conclusion about the essential causes for the condition of the American male. Cause and effect as a form of inductive reasoning moves from an observed set of causes or effects to some conclusion about the effect or cause. But as the outline of Schlesinger's essay may suggest, it is difficult and sometimes impossible to examine every particular cause or effect. Therefore, at some point in our reasoning we must "leap" from the effects, across the gap in our information, to a conclusion about causes. The more effects and causes located before you leap, the shorter the gap and the more accurate your reasoning is likely to be. To protect the validity of your generalizations, where there are gaps in data, you must usually qualify your generalizations with words such as *often, sometimes, frequently, many times, perhaps,* and the like. Remember, too, the potential fallacies and hazards inherent in analysis by cause and effect. What follows amounts to a set of strictures intended as guidelines for you when you employ cause-and-effect reasoning as the basis for your essays.

The seventeenth-century English philosopher John Locke defined *cause* as "that which makes any other thing . . . begin to be." But Locke was fully aware that when we claim or imply that something makes something else "begin to be" we inevitably simplify a complex relationship; that is, we point to only one of a series of factors which often work in conjunction to create the effect. It would release us from a considerable burden of reason and proof if causes and effects occurred in isolation, but this is seldom the case. More often than not, surrounding conditions and circumstances influence the relationship. If a match were struck in a vacuum, it would not ignite, because one contributing factor (or cause) for fire is oxygen. Even the most predictable relationships are not always as obvious as they seem, and the astute writer will take care to discuss as many of those contributing factors and conditions as are necessary to establish firmly his principle of cause and effect. As we are writing this, two major league baseball managers have just been fired by club owners. Both are to some extent the victims of faulty cause-and-effect reasoning of this sort. They are made the guilty causes of the teams' failure to ascend to first place in their division, but any reasonably intelligent baseball fan could point out that other causes coexist in each situation: inferior players in key positions, failures of players to reach the performance levels of previous years, injuries to regulars, and so on.

Another problem arises when we understand that *point of view* can frequently influence our identification of a cause. Let us consider again our earlier example of the Republican Party and the Depression. A Democrat might very well be tempted to lay the blame for those difficult times squarely in the lap of the Republican administration. An economist might ignore the political issues and attribute cause to rampant speculation on the stock market, which led to the crash of 1929. An ecologist might say that, though the stock market fell, it would have recovered quickly were it not for the dust bowls caused by the droughts in the Midwest during the 30s. A temperance man might suggest the Depression was not economic so much as moral, that it grew out of the moral bankruptcy of Prohibition and the gangsterism of the 30s. With an "effect" as widespread as the Depression, possible points of view, then, are endless, and the examples suggest that the causes of an effect can easily be defined in a number of ways, though some ways must remain more probable and adequate than others. For a *full* discussion of the Depression, you would need to consider virtually all of these. The writer must take into account the points of view that serve his or her purposes, but the writer must also be constantly aware of how a particular *stance* influences the view of a cause postulated for a given effect.

Another common fallacy, referred to earlier in this section, is the assumption that a sequence of events in time implies a necessary causal relationship. It must be remembered that cause-and-effect reasoning is dependent on a linear concept of time. Effects cannot precede cause(s); cause(s) must precede effects. An easy illustration of the *post hoc* fallacy can be taken from superstition: We walk under a ladder today and a misfortune befalls us tomorrow. But did that which came *before* cause that which came *after*? Only the most credulous, we say, would fix the blame on our walking under the ladder, but in the next breath we argue that inflation is patently the fault of the administration in office because it came after their election. Or, says a friend in reference to the firing of one those baseball managers: "The real reason Billy Martin got the axe

> Perhaps when we ceased to measure time by the sun and the seasons, it was wisdom that suffered, the sense of the organic rhythm of birth, maturation, and death which governs all life. There is an ancient tradition which defines wisdom as the sense of timeliness and appropriateness. Ecclesiastes states the point well: "For everything there is a season, and a time for every matter under heaven": the wise man knows what time it is in his own life and in the life of the community. . . . Education, which aims at wholeness, must teach a man to tell time.
>
> — Sam Keen, *To A Dancing God* (1970)

from the Texas Rangers was that he appeared on the cover of *Sports Illustrated*. Happens every time."

Hasty generalization in causal analysis may lead us to overlook all the potential contributing factors. If, on a given day, thirty dorm students come down with symptoms of ptomaine poisoning, it might give us pause before taking our dinner at the dorm's cafeteria. Yet the question may not concern the cafeteria at all, but only what foods can be safely eaten there: hot meals, leftovers, cold cuts, sandwiches? What about the water system? We must not neglect noting that ninety other students left the cafeteria in good health, that students often snack elsewhere, and that *hysterical* symptoms can readily occur in large numbers of people confined together. This latter was actually the case one summer in a program of intensive teaching. Students were kept closely confined and rigorously monitored in the program, and when one student developed symptoms, many others in the group soon developed similar "symptoms" — no doubt from assuming it was the food — and a hysterical epidemic, brief but powerful, resulted. So be wary of premature "leaps" to the most obvious conclusion, regardless of your subjects.

Finally, once the writer has skirted these several dangers in inductive reasoning, he or she must offer the audience one thing more: evidence for the contention that a stated cause produces a stated effect. It is not enough merely to claim that a poet's tangled love life affected his work. Surely we can be expected to offer some proof for that claim. We might make connections between the poet's biography and certain elements of his poetry, locate letters and notes that suggest such a relationship, and offer close analysis of relevant lines in his poems.

Most of our lives are spent acting and reacting inductively. We see all about us effects, ranging from the mundane to the cosmic, for which we try to locate causes: Why the successes of some friends, the failures of others, our own successes and failures; why the efficiency of some machines, teams, procedures, or techniques, the inefficiency of others? Inductive reasoning will give us only so many and often only partial answers to all our "whys." But just because Carlos Casteneda (from one perspective) and Thomas S. Kuhn (from another) teach us to be skeptical of logic is no reason to abandon it altogether. The mystic way is only another mode for us to try to answer our basic questions in a universe that does not provide ultimate answers. Ours, for better or worse, is the situation that Frost, in another poem, calls "The Trial by Existence."

EXERCISES

1. The structural basis of the following sermon by John Donne is a cause-to-effect pattern. Explain how each of the paragraphs contributes to that pattern. Then decide whether the logic Donne uses is adequate for your view of the issues at stake.

Meditation

Nunc lento sonitu dicunt, Morieris.

*Now, this bell tolling softly for another says
to me, Thou must die.*

Perchance he for whom this bell tolls may be so ill, as that he knows not it tolls for him. And perchance I may think myself so much better than I am, as that they who are about me and see my state may have caused it to toll for me, and I know not that. The church is catholic, universal; so are all her actions. All that she does belongs to all. When she baptizes a child, that action concerns me. For that child is thereby connected to that head which is my head too and engraffed into that body whereof I am a member. And when she buries a man, that action concerns me. All mankind is of one author and is one volume. When one man dies, one chapter is not torn out of the book, but translated into a better language. And every chapter must be so translated. God employs several translators; some pieces are translated by age, some by sickness, some by war, some by justice. But God's hand is in every translation, and his hand shall bind up all our scattered leaves again for that library where every book shall lie open to one another.

As, therefore, the bell that rings to a sermon calls not upon the preacher only, but upon the congregation to come, so this bell calls us all. But how much more me, who am brought so near the door by this sickness. There was a contention as far as a suit (in which both piety and dignity, religion, and estimation were mingled) which of the religious orders should ring to prayers first in the morning, and it was determined that they should ring first that rose earliest. If we understand aright the dignity of this bell that tolls for our evening prayer, we would be glad to make it ours by rising early in that application, that it might be ours, as well as his whose indeed it is. The bell doth toll for him that thinks it doth. And though it intermit again, yet from that minute that that occasion wrought upon him, he is united to God.

Who casts not up his eye to the sun when it rises? But who takes off his eye from a comet when that breaks out? Who bends not his ear to any bell, which upon any occasion rings? But who can remove it from that bell which is passing a piece of himself out of this world? No man is an island, entire of itself. Every man is a piece of the continent, a part of the main. If a clod be washed away by the sea, Europe is the less, as well as if a promontory were, as well as if a manor of thy friend's or of thine own were. Any man's death diminishes me, because I am involved in mankind. And therefore never send to know for whom the bell tolls: it tolls for thee.

Neither can we call this a begging of misery or a borrowing of misery, as though we were not miserable enough of ourselves but must fetch in more from the next house in taking upon us the misery of our neighbors. Truly, it were an excusable covetousness if we did. For affliction is a treasure, and scarce any man hath enough of it. No man hath affliction enough that is not matured and ripened by it, and made fit for God by that affliction. If a man carry treasure in bullion or in a wedge of gold and have none coined into current moneys, his treasure will not defray him as he travels. Tribulation is treasure in the nature of it, but it is not current money in the use of it, except we get nearer and nearer our home, heaven, by it. Another man may be sick too, and sick to death, and this affliction may lie in his bowels as gold in a mine and be of no use to him. But this bell that tells me of his affliction, digs out and applies that gold to me, if by this consideration of another's danger, I take mine own into contemplation and so secure myself by making my recourse to my God, who is our only security.

— John Donne

2. Write an essay establishing the causes (the reasons why) for the following series of "effects" as seen by Bob Greene in his essay, "The National Binge." Perhaps a particular point of view, such as that of a psychologist, sociologist, theologian, or philosopher, would be helpful in your exploration of cause.

It is . . . an amphetamine age, an era of giddy excess, when we have all become so dulled to the concept of the quiet and the normal that there is nothing left to do but demand more, wait for the next, greater excitement — and don't look back. We are in the middle of a giant drunk, a monumental, dizzying speed trip, and nowhere is there the recognition that it cannot go on indefinitely. Nowhere is there the thought that like all manic binges, this one will end, and that when it does there will most certainly be a price to be paid, a psychic hangover to remind us of exactly what we have all been through.

3. Frequently the writer of fiction indirectly uses the concept of cause and effect in his work. That is, a writer will create a series of "effects" or "causes" that make up the basis of the narrative action, and we as readers often have to infer the cause(s) or effect(s) of a particular character's actions. A clear example is James Joyce's short story, "Counterparts." The story presents a series of events that constitute the protagonist's activities for a day. The events (causes) — his boss scolds him; he is put down in an arm wrestling contest; a girl shuns him, etc. — begin to defeat the character. When he gets home, he beats one of his children, permitting Joyce to suggest that a chain of causes leads to a specific effect (the beating of the child). Write an essay tracing the chain of cause to effect or effect to cause in a story or play of your choice. *Or* write an essay tracing the cause(s) for your favorite team's success or failure last season.

4. Analyze the basis for the argument in the following poem by Andrew Marvell, which is based on a *hypothetical* situation (indicated by the subjunctive construction with which the poem opens: "Had we" meaning "If we had . . ."), rather than actual ones such as we dealt with previously.

To His Coy Mistress

Had we but world enough, and time,
This coyness, lady, were no crime.
We would sit down, and think which way
To walk, and pass our long love's day.
Thou by the Indian Ganges' side
Should'st rubies find: I by the tide

Of Humber would complain. I would
Love you ten years before the Flood,
And you should, if you please, refuse
Till the conversion of the Jews.
My vegetable love should grow
Vaster than empires and more slow:

An hundred years should go to praise
Thine eyes, and on thy forehead gaze.
Two hundred to adore each breast:
But thirty thousand to the rest.
An age at least to every part,
And the last age should show your heart.
For, lady, you deserve this state,
Nor would I love at lower rate.

   But at my back I always hear
Time's winged chariot hurrying near:
And yonder all before us lie
Deserts of vast eternity.
Thy beauty shall no more be found,
Nor, in thy marble vault, shall sound
My echoing song: then worms shall try
That long-preserv'd virginity:
And your quaint honour turn to dust;
And into ashes all my lust.
The grave's a fine and private place,
But none I think do there embrace.

   Now, therefore, while the youthful hue
Sits on thy skin like morning dew,
And while thy willing soul transpires
At every pore with instant fires,
Now let us sport us while we may;
And now, like am'rous birds of prey,
Rather at once our time devour,
Than languish in his slow-chappt pow'r.
Let us roll all our strength, and all
Our sweetness, up into one ball:
And tear our pleasures with rough strife,
Through the iron gates of life:
Thus, though we cannot make our sun
Stand still, yet we will make him run.

— Andrew Marvell

5. Using the concept that "everyone is unique" and that your uniqueness is a consequence of your genetic endowment, environment, and
   cumulative experiences since birth, write an essay that describes your
   feelings about particular aspects of your present self (effects) and

then go into the past to examine why you feel the way you do (causes). In short, explore what you are like now and how you grew to be this way. Choose two or three from the following list of areas that you might discuss for developing the first part of the essay:

a. your perceptions and feelings about yourself as a student
b. your perceptions and feelings about your body
c. your relationships with authority figures (parents, teachers, employers)
d. your relationships with brothers and sisters
e. your relationships with friends of the same and opposite sex
f. your ethnic, religious, or racial identity
g. your moral values and standards
h. any other aspect of yourself that seems pertinent

For the second part of the essay (tracing the causes), think back over your developmental history — the events and factors in your physical, intellectual, and social development that seem related to your present view of yourself. What were your "labels" as you were growing up? How were you described by your parents, teachers, and friends? Discuss some critical incidents or turning points in your childhood and early adolescence that relate to where you are now on the points you selected to address in part one of the essay.

For your conclusion, discuss the direction in which you would like to develop further.

If you have trouble visualizing the structure and content, turn to the essay on page 120 for a model.

DESCRIPTION AND NARRATION

Description and narration, as methods for the essayist, move authors and readers toward those realms we think of as "creative," for they help one imaginatively experience concrete "worlds" such as we find in poetry, fiction, and drama. The principles for description and narration are essentially the same once we understand that their basic dimensions are space and time. Objects we describe exist in space; events we narrate exist in time; and we write of space *in* time, just as we measure time by marks in space. In our presentation of objects and events, the qualities we should strive for — *unity*, *coherence*, and *emphasis* — are the same for both description and narration.

The most practicable way to achieve unity, coherence, and emphasis in both description and narration is to control *point of view*, which involves attitudes and space/time dimensions. A description or a narrative may be either objective or subjective. If it is objective, the description or narrative is presented without the intervention of attitudes, feelings, or beliefs. In an objective description you can achieve unity, coherence, and emphasis by locating your point of view and building around a particular fixed place from which you may develop your description in an orderly way using such principles as left-to-right, near-to-far, up-and-down (which are, of course, reversible): whatever relations are necessary or appropriate for your composition. Since childhood, we have been trained to perceive — and thus to conceive — in pictorial ways, and writers are adept at putting places, things, and people into such a frame, into a "picture," as it were. In the following description of a place, from his story "Amy Foster," novelist Joseph Conrad establishes clearly a near-to-distant organizational pattern (note our italicized words).

> *Beyond the sea wall* there curves for miles in a vast and regular sweep the barren beach of shingle, with the village of Brenzett standing out darkly *across the water*, a spire in a clump of trees; and *still further out* the perpendicular column of a lighthouse, looking *in the distance* no bigger than a lead pencil, marks the *vanishing point* of the land.

The eye is directed from a series of immediate objective details, starting with the sea wall and continuously moving out over the beach to the village, its spire and trees, until it reaches the distant pencil of a lighthouse. When we see the picture unfold before us, we feel that a dominant impression (unity), a consistency of parts (coherence), and a progressive order (emphasis) have all been achieved. And the "picture" is *objective* for the simple reason that Conrad's feelings or those of his narrator have played no part in the presentation. It is not, but it could have been, a scientist's view of a place.

In the passage from James Joyce's *Dubliners* that follows, the figurative language suggests a *subjective* relation between the things described and the "presenter":

> A fat brown goose lay at one end of the table and at the other end, on a bed of creased paper strewn with sprigs of parsley, lay a great ham, stripped of its outer skin and peppered over with crust crumbs, a neat paper frill round its shin and beside this was a round of spiced beef. Between these *rival ends* ran parallel lines of side-dishes: two little minsters of jelly, red and yellow; a shallow dish full of blocks of blancmange and red jam, a

large green leaf-shaped dish with a stalk-shaped handle, on which lay bunches of purple raisins and peeled almonds, a companion dish on which lay a solid rectangle of Smyrna figs, a dish of custard topped with grated nutmeg, a small bowl full of chocolates and sweets wrapped in gold and silver papers and a glass vase in which stood some tall celery stalks. In the centre of the table there stood, *as sentries* to a fruit-stand which upheld a pyramid of oranges and American apples, two squat old-fashioned decanters of cut glass, one containing port and the other dark sherry. On the closed square piano a pudding in a huge yellow dish *lay in waiting* and behind it were *three squads* of bottles of stout and ale and minerals, drawn up according to the *colours of their uniforms*, the first two black, with brown and red labels, the third and *smallest squad* white, with transverse green sashes.

Starting at the ends of the table, Joyce moves toward the center and finally away from the table to the piano top nearby. In the context of the description, the use of metaphor drawn from the military (note our italics) helps Joyce's reader imagine the exact arrangement of the dishes. But to the extent the metaphor takes on symbolic meanings, suggesting that the regimentation of the table reflects a regimented life for the people attending the dinner party, the passage becomes more subjective than Conrad's passage, though one is no more unified, coherent, or climactic than the other.

As these brief passages suggest, point of view in descriptions need not be stationary; you can combine a sense of narrative motion with static descriptive completeness by following an observer in motion. This is a "cinematic" technique existing in fiction long before motion pictures were invented. Such an organizational pattern can be illustrated from Washington Irving's "The Legend of Sleepy Hollow," in which Ichabod Crane's view takes in the home of prosperous Balthus Van Tassel:

It was one of those spacious farmhouses, with high-ridged but lowly-sloping roofs, built in the style handed down from the first Dutch settlers; the low projecting eaves forming a piazza along the front, capable of being closed up in bad weather. Under this were hung flails, harness, various utensils of husbandry, and nets for fishing in the neighboring river. Benches were built along the sides for summer use; and a great spinning-wheel at one end and a churn at the other, showed the various uses to which this important porch might be devoted. From this piazza the wondering Ichabod entered the hall, the centre of the mansion and place of usual residence. Here rows of resplendent pewter, ranged on a long dresser, dazzled his eyes. In one corner stood a huge bag of wool ready to be spun; in another, a quantity of linsey-woolsey just from the loom; ears of Indian corn, and strings of dried apples and peaches, hung in gay festoons along the wall, mingled with the gaud of red peppers; and a door left ajar gave him a peek into the best parlor, where the claw-footed chairs and dark mahogany tables shone like mirrors; and irons, with their accompanying shovel and tongs, glistened from their covert of asparagus tops; mock oranges and conch-shells decorated the mantel-piece; strings of various colored birds' eggs were suspended above it; a great ostrich egg was hung from the centre of the room, and a corner cupboard, knowingly left open, displayed immense treasures of old silver and well-mended china.

As we follow the movement of Ichabod, the spatial point of view shifts from a distant view of the house to a closer look at the piazza and finally into the house itself to look at the parlor. But because we see through the eyes of Crane, the passage has unity and coherence as well as the climactic order given by the movement from outside to inside.

Whether you decide a description should be *objective* or *subjective* will depend upon your purposes. As a contribution to expository and argumentative forms of discourse, description should generally appear to be objective. The composition of details presenting an object should be as specific and empirically verifiable as possible. With that composition the tone of the description should also be objective, but we know that in human endeavors total objectivity is impossible. Journalists, patent attorneys, scientists, and many others need the ability to write clear, accurate, objective descriptions, but most of us prefer the human interest of attitudes, feelings, beliefs, values. The following paragraph about starfish in *Wonders of the Great Barrier Reef* by Theodore Roughley offers an interesting objectivity in scientific exposition that also permits a human engagement in a few value-oriented words such as *remarkable* and *remarkably*.

Looked at from above, starfish are seen to be covered with a hard, leathery integument, but if turned over they will be found to have a groove extending along the whole length of each arm and meeting at the centrally situated mouth. These grooves are bordered by a great number of small, muscular tubes that can be stretched out or withdrawn at will; they are known as tube-feet and by their means the starfish is able to crawl about, though always very sluggishly. The tube-feet are remarkable little structures, unique in the animal world on account of the fact that their activities are dependent on a supply of water for their expansion and contraction. When the animal requires them to expand it pumps them full of water which distends them greatly and when it is necessary to contract them the water is withdrawn. Each is provided with a sucker-like extremity and walking is accomplished by pushing a series in the direction it is desired to take, attaching them to the surface and then contracting them to draw the body forward. The suction of the tube-feet is remarkably strong and if a starfish is pulled from a rock many of the feet will probably be found to remain adherent to it.

The scientific writer may occasionally utilize subjective elements, but another writer may actively cultivate feelings and attitudes toward a subject he or she happens also to be describing. In this sort of description, there is no longer that sense of detachment from the persons, places, or things being described; instead, there is a sense of a particular mind seeing them through the writer's own unique framework of perceptions. Roughley's starfish exists for everyone in all places and times, but in the following description from *The Road to Wigan Pier* the homes of British miners exist the way they do only in George Orwell's evocation of them (italics added to show attitudes, values, subjective relations):

I found great variation in the houses I visited. Some were as *decent* as one could possibly expect in the circumstances, some were so *appalling* that I have no hope of describing them adequately. To begin with, the *smell*, the dominant and essential thing, is *indescribable*. But the *squalor* and *confusion*! A tub full of *filthy* water here, a basin full of unwashed crocks there, more crocks *piled* in any odd corner, torn newspaper *littered* everywhere, and in the middle always the same *dreadful* table covered with *sticky* oilcloth and crowded with cooking pots and irons and half-darned stockings and pieces of *stale* bread and bits of cheese wrapped round with *greasy* newspaper! And the congestion in a tiny room where getting from one side to the other is a complicated voyage between pieces of furniture, with a line of damp washing getting you in the face every time you move and the children *as thick underfoot as toadstools*!

All these descriptions — of place (by Conrad, Irving, Orwell), of things (by Joyce, Roughley) — depend on other senses besides the visual for their effectiveness. By and large, though, descriptions must make us *see*, and they do so by detailing objects in item-lists (as in Joyce, Irving), by mentioning colors (see Joyce especially), by suggesting patterns or configurations (disorderly ones in Orwell; orderly ones in Joyce and Roughley; profuse ones in Irving), by indicating textures and shapes: in other words, by appealing to varieties of visual order. By introducing sensory impressions beyond the visual and the tactile, a good description can increase its emotional and subjective power, though it correspondingly loses objectivity. The subjective response is Faulkner's interest in the following passage from *Sartoris*; he has no need for objectivity:

> It was high here, and the air moved with grave coolness. On either hand lay a valley filled with silver mist and with whippoorwills; beyond these valleys the silver earth rolled on into the sky. Across it, mournful and far, a dog howled. Bayard's head was as cool and clear as a clapperless bell. Within it that face emerged clearly at last: those two eyes round with grave astonishment, winged serenely by two dark wings of hair. It was that Benbow girl, he said to himself, and he sat for a while, gazing into the sky. The lights on the town clock were steadfast and yellow and unwinking in the dissolving distance, but in all other directions the world rolled away in slumbrous ridges, milkily opaline.

Descriptions rely on a writer's ability to put unknowns into familiar contexts or language. Because people are among those objects we know best, in describing a person it is practicable to begin with an outstanding trait and then to move on to more specific details. It may be useful to describe a person in a progressive sequence in order to give unity, coherence, and emphasis. Try to select the details or traits that give the character his or her individualization. William Golding, in *Lord of the Flies*, is able to distinguish Simon from all the other boys by a few carefully chosen details:

> He was a small, skinny boy, his chin pointed, and his eyes so bright they had deceived Ralph into thinking him delightfully gay and wicked. The coarse mop of black hair was long and swung down, almost concealing a low, broad forehead. He wore the remains of shorts and his feet were bare like Jack's. Always darkish in colour, Simon was burned by the sun to a deep tan that glistened with sweat.

In descriptions of people, objectivity and subjectivity in point of view identify the writer's attitude toward the person being described. Like descriptions of objects and places, character descriptions can assume the objective stance of the reporter, but the more usual position is one that goes ahead and admits a shaping view — a bias, if you will, for or against. It is difficult for humans to regard other humans objectively. In "Waxworks at the Abbey," Virginia Woolf's impressionistic description of Queen Elizabeth's regal dominance reveals ambiguous feelings, admiration as well as hostility:

The Queen dominates the room as she once dominated England. Leaning a little forward so that she seems to beckon you to come to her, she stands, holding her sceptre in one hand, her orb in the other. It is a drawn, anguished figure, with the pursed look of someone who goes in perpetual dread of poison or of trap; yet forever braces herself to meet the terror unflinchingly. Her eyes are wide and vigilant; her nose thin as the beak of a hawk; her lips shut tight; her eyebrows arched; only the jowl gives the fine drawn face its massiveness. The orb and the sceptre are held in the long thin hands of an artist, as if the fingers thrilled at the touch of them. She is immensely intellectual, suffering, and tyrannical. She will not allow one to look elsewhere.

The paragraph following is an example of a more objective point of view. But though it is made up of factual statements that give the character sketch a certain empirical, verifiable credibility, the description by John Steinbeck of Peter Randall in *The Long Valley* nevertheless reveals a strong sense of the respect the character inspires:

Peter Randall was one of the most highly respected farmers of Monterey County. Once, before he was to make a little speech at a Masonic convention, the brother who introduced him referred to him as an example for young Masons of California to emulate. He was nearing fifty; his manner was grave and restrained, and he wore a carefully tended beard. From every gathering he reaped the authority that belongs to the bearded man. Peter's eyes were grave, too; blue and grave almost to the point of sorrowfulness. People knew there was force in him, but force held caged. Sometimes, for no apparent reason, the eyes grew sullen and mean, like the eyes of a bad dog; but that look soon passed, and the restraint and probity came back into his face. He was tall and broad. He held his shoulders back as though they were braced, and he sucked in his stomach like a soldier. Inasmuch as farmers are usually slouchy men, Peter gained an added respect because of his posture.

The re-creation of experience in its full immediacy, detail, and texture is generated by Tom Wolfe in his introduction to *The Kandy-Kolored Tangerine Flake-Streamline Baby*, a collection of essays illustrating the "new journalism" that subordinates idea to descriptive detail and narrative texture. Wolfe tells us he had gone to a hot rod and custom car show in New York City and vaguely discerned that the show had a meaning outside the usual "system of ideas" within which he and other journalists had grown accustomed to working. It had something to do with art and artists, for, he says, at the show were all these people who had starved, suffered, and created works to them as expressive as those of any painter or sculptor. Talking to these "artists," men such as Dale Alexander, Wolfe began to see that a new American art form was emerging, and he wanted to write about it.

> So I went over to *Esquire* magazine after a while and talked to them about this phenomenon, and they sent me out to California to take a look at the custom car world. Dale Alexander was from Detroit or some place, but the real center of the thing was in California, around Los Angeles. I started talking to a lot of these people, like George Barris and Ed Roth, and seeing what they were doing, and — well, eventually it became the story from which the title of this book was taken, "The Kandy-Kolored Tangerine-Flake Streamline Baby." But at first I couldn't even write the story. I came back to New York and just sat around worrying over the thing. I had a lot of trouble analyzing exactly what I had on my hands. By this time *Esquire* practically had a gun at my head because they had a two-page-wide color picture for the story locked into the printing presses and no story. Finally, I told Byron Dobell, the managing editor at *Esquire*, that I couldn't pull the thing together. O.K., he tells me, just type out my notes and send them over and he will get somebody else to write it. So about 8 o'clock that night I started typing the notes out in the form of a memorandum that began, "Dear Byron." I started typing away, starting right with the first time I saw any custom cars in California. I was started recording it all, and inside of a couple of hours, typing along like a madman, I could tell that something was beginning to happen. By midnight this memorandum to Byron was twenty pages long and I was still typing like a maniac. About 2 A.M. or something like that I turned on WABC, a radio station that plays rock and roll music all night long, and got a little more manic. I wrapped up the memorandum about 6:15 A.M., and by this time it was 49 pages long. I took it over to *Esquire* as soon as they opened up, about 9:30 A.M. About 4 P.M. I got a call from Byron Dobell. He told me they were striking out the "Dear Byron" at the top of the memorandum and running the rest of it in the magazine. That was the story, "The Kandy-Kolored Tangerine-Flake Streamline Baby."

As Wolfe tells us, he simply started writing down everything, and "the details themselves, when I wrote them down, suddenly made me see what was happening." This is the truth about ourselves and our experience that fiction writers have been teaching for centuries. So when your own experiences become the focal point for your writing, open yourself to the details and let their meaning develop through the unified, coherent, and climactic patterns available to description and narration.

Descriptions in and of themselves tend to be inert, for they largely depend upon *to be* verb forms and upon adjectives that point to static conditions rather than dynamic situations. That is one reason, in passages such as those by Irving, Joyce, and Orwell, writers so frequently combine descriptions with the movement of an observer, for that movement introduces action, and our attention is always drawn more to action than to stasis. Description thus seldom appears in good writing except in conjunction with narration. Modern writers are especially inclined to give brief patches of description along with sequences of narrative, the way things look joined with the way things happen. A good example of the combination occurs in the opening of Robert M. Pirsig's *Zen and the Art of Motorcycle Maintenance*. An important theme of the book (which may be treated as a novel or as autobiography) is the necessity of achieving a harmonious balance between the dynamic and the static aspects of one's life, aspects Pirsig's narrator associates with romantic and classic life views. In the book's opening, the narrator — father of eleven-year-old Chris — calls attention to the landscape he and the boy are traveling through:

> In the wind are pungent odors from the marshes by the road. We are in an area of the Central Plains filled with thousands of duck hunting sloughs, heading northwest from Minneapolis toward the Dakotas. This highway is an old concrete two-laner that hasn't had much traffic since a four-laner went in parallel to it several years ago. When we pass a marsh the air suddenly becomes cooler. Then, when we are past, it suddenly warms up again.
>
> I'm happy to be riding back into this country. It is a kind of nowhere, famous for nothing at all and has an appeal because of just that. Tensions disappear along old roads like this. We bump along the beat-up concrete between the cattails and stretches of meadow and then more cattails and marsh grass. Here and there is a stretch of open water and if you look closely you can see wild ducks at the edge of the cattails. And turtles. . . . There's a red-winged blackbird.
>
> I whack Chris's knee and point to it.
>
> "What!" he hollers.
>
> "Blackbird!"
>
> He says something I don't hear. "What?" I holler back.
>
> He grabs the back of my helmet and hollers up, "I've seen *lots* of those, Dad!"
>
> "Oh!" I holler back. Then I nod. At age eleven you don't get very impressed with red-winged blackbirds.

At this stage in the Minnesota-to-the-Pacific odyssey of the father and son, when neither is fully aware of the needs of the other, Chris dismisses his father's interest in the red-winged blackbird, just as the father dismisses the boy's lack of interest as merely a lack of experience. As it turns out, however, each is "burdened" by the other, as the present (son) is always connected to the past (father). Once father and son recognize their reciprocal needs and identities, they become freer simply to be themselves. Pirsig thus suggests this theme in his combining of description and narration at the book's end:

> We sleep and when we wake up I feel very rested, more rested than for a long time. I take Chris's jacket and mine and tuck them under the elastic cables holding down the pack on the cycle.
>
> It's so hot I feel like leaving this helmet off. I remember that in this state they're not required. I fasten it around one of the cables.
>
> "Put mine there too," Chris says.
>
> "You need it for safety."
>
> "You're not wearing yours."
>
> "All right," I agree, and stow his too.
>
> The road continues to twist and wind through the trees. It upswings around hairpins and glides into new scenes one after another around and through brush and then out into open spaces where we can see canyons stretch away below.
>
> "Beautiful!" I holler to Chris.
>
> "You don't need to shout," he says.
>
> "Oh," I say, and laugh. When the helmets are off you can talk in a conversational voice. After all these days!
>
> "Well, it's beautiful, anyway," I say.
>
> More trees and shrubs and groves. It's getting warmer. Chris hangs onto my shoulders now and I turn a little and see that he stands up on the foot pegs.
>
> "That's a little dangerous," I say.
>
> "No, it isn't. I can tell."
>
> He probably can. "Be careful anyway," I say.
>
> After a while when we cut sharp into a hairpin under some overhanging trees he says, "Oh," and then later on, "Ah," and then, "Wow." Some of these branches over the road are hanging so low they're going to conk him on the head if he isn't careful.
>
> "What's the matter?" I ask.
>
> "It's so different."
>
> "What?"

"Everything. I never could see over your shoulders before."

The sunlight makes strange and beautiful designs through the tree branches on the road. It flits light and dark into my eyes. We swing into a curve and then up into the open sunlight.

Pirsig suggests that we all live from moment to moment on a narrative edge where events are happening immediately, but these always flow back into reservoirs for experience, caches of data from the past that can be drawn upon in order to help one cope with the present. This reservoir in each of us is memory, and in our culture it is history. Some of our best writers are preoccupied by the relationship between memory and history, and passages in their works well illustrate the combinations of description and narration.

Narration permits a writer to manipulate experience, sharing this feature with memory itself; both are bounded by the *pastness* of events, but both can also unfold those events that are confined to the past in layers, levels, stages. We can start with the very beginning of a sequence and carry it through to its conclusion. So long as it is a complete event and our selection of phases in it is orderly and the event itself has a climactic structure, our narrative will be unified, coherent, and progressive. But most events are not structured this way in themselves; thus, we must restructure them so that when they go into our utterances — spoken or written — they will have these features. Usually, this means that we have to do some reordering of an action, experience, or event to reveal its unity, coherence, and completeness. You do this whenever you transform one of your experiences into an anecdote to tell your friends, and writers do this when they transform their experiences into essays (and poems, plays, stories, novels, autobiographies).

Narrative structure is achieved by the working of one's memory backward over one's experience. Narratives can be rendered without the appearance of reflectiveness, of one's having given thought to pattern in order to show structure and significance. Hemingway, among modern writers, is especially adept not only at transforming seemingly random experiences into unified, coherent, climactic narratives, but also doing so without revealing just how much planning must have gone into the writing. This passage from the autobiographical *Green Hills of Africa* illustrates how a writer can make an event seem remarkably immediate:

When I saw I was clear I got on one knee, saw the bull through the aperture, marvelling at how big he looked and then, remembering not to have it matter, that it was the same as any other shot, I saw the bead centered exactly where it should be just below the top of the shoulder and squeezed off. At the roar he jumped and was going into the brush, but I knew I had hit him. I shot at a show of gray between the trees as he went in and M'Cola was shouting, "Piga! Piga!" meaning, "He's hit! He's hit!" and the Roman was slapping me on the shoulder, then he had his toga up around his neck and was running naked, and the four of us were running now, full speed, like hounds, splashing across the stream, tearing up the bank, the Roman ahead, crashing naked through the brush, then stooping and holding up a leaf with bright blood, slamming me on the back, M'Cola saying, "Damu! Damu!" blood, blood, then the deep cut tracks off to the right, me reloading, we all trailing in a dead run, it almost dark in the timber, the Roman, confused a moment by the trail, making a cast off to the right, then picking up blood once more, then pulling me down again with a jerk on my arm and none of us breathing as we saw him standing in a clearing a hundred yards ahead, looking to me hard-hit and looking back, wide ears spread, big, gray, white-striped, his horns a marvel, as he looked straight toward us over his shoulder. I thought I must make absolutely sure this time, now, with the dark coming and I held my breath and shot him a touch behind the fore-shoulder. We heard the bullet smack and saw him buck heavily with the shot.

Enormous skill and craft go into the composition of a passage such as this, constructed by manipulating verb tenses to show the experience layered through time and by including description heavy with verbals (participles, especially) that show action: *shouting, slapping, running, splashing, tearing, crashing, stooping* and *holding, saying, reloading, trailing, picking, pulling* — all this primarily in one sentence beginning, "I shot," and ending, "as he looked straight toward us over his shoulder." This event is just one episode in a book-length narrative, but Hemingway makes it appear complete in itself (within just a few paragraphs) by suggesting how the shooting of the kudu consummates an initiating experience: Hemingway has been given lessons, he enacts them in the hunt, and he is recognized as a worthy by the men previously initiated (the two guides, M'Cola and "the Roman," a Wanderobo-Masai of massive dignity). To see this pattern at work, however, one should read all of Chapter 12 for the whole context.

Narrative writing can also be effective when it ranges more deliberately back and forth in time. William Styron, a writer interested in the relation between the personal past of memory and the cultural past of history, illustrates the multidimensional relations possible in narrative description. Explaining how he came to write the novel *The Confessions of Nat Turner* out of a fascination with the life of the black American rebel, Styron tells in "This Quiet Dust" of having recognized a long-abandoned home-site as perhaps the house of Turner's friends, the Whiteheads. Chauffered by the county sheriff, he had been searching the South-ampton region in Virginia for landmarks relating to the insurrection led by Nat Turner.

> I had been gazing out of the window, and now suddenly something caught my eye — something familiar, a brief flickering passage of a distant outline, a silhouette against the sun-splashed woods — and I asked the Sheriff to stop the car. He did, and as we backed up slowly through a cloud of dust, I recognized a house standing perhaps a quarter of a mile off the road, from this distance only a lopsided oblong sheltered by an enormous oak, but the whole tableau — the house and the glorious hovering tree and the stretch of woods beyond — so familiar to me that it might have been some home I passed every day. And of course now as recognition came flooding back, I knew whose house it was. For in *The Southampton Insurrection,* the indefatigable Drewry had included many photographs — amateurish, doubtless taken by himself, and suffering from the fuzzy offset reproduction of 1900. But they were clear enough to provide an unmistakable guide to the dwellings in question, and now as I again consulted the book I could see that this house — the monumental oak above it grown scant inches it seemed in sixty years — was the one referred to by Drewry as having belonged to Mrs. Catherine Whitehead.

Styron draws on his memory of pictures from the historical account of the insurrection by William S. Drewry, and shows how past and present can be folded one inside the other, an immediate event recalling one farther back in time and that one yet another even farther back. Poten-tially, this reach of memory and narrative is unlimited, but for structure to be comprehensible to us the reaching backwards must cease at some predetermined point, often then to be followed by a return to the threshold of the present on which the regression was begun. Styron continues:

> The approach to the house was by a rutted lane long ago abandoned and overgrown with lush weeds which made a soft, crushed, rasping sound as we rolled over them. Dogwood, white and pink, grew on either side of the lane, quite wild and wanton in lovely pastel splashes. Not far from the house a pole fence interrupted our way; the Sheriff stopped the car and we got out and stood there for a moment, looking at the place. It was quiet and still — so quiet that the sudden chant of a mockingbird in the woods was almost frightening — and we realized then that no one lived in the

house. Scoured by weather, paintless, worn down to the wintry gray of bone and with all the old mortar gone from between the timbers, it stood alone and desolate above its blasted, sagging front porch, the ancient door ajar like an open wound. Although never a manor house, it had once been a spacious and comfortable country home; now in near-ruin it sagged, finished, a shell, possessing only the most fragile profile of itself. As we drew closer still we could see that the entire house, from its upper story to the cellar, was filled with thousands of shucked ears of corn — feed for the malevolent-looking little razorback pigs which suddenly appeared in a tribe at the edge of the house, eying us, grunting. Mr. Seward sent them scampering with a shied stick and a farmer's sharp "Whoo!" I looked up at the house, trying to recollect its particular role in Nat's destiny, and then I remembered.

What Styron remembers, at a moment when an August day in 1831 "and this day seemed to meet and melt together, becoming almost one, and for a long moment indistinguishable," is associated with the most tragic aspect of our American past: slavery, with its "intermingled miseries, ambitions, frustrations, hopes, rages, and desires which caused this extraordinary black man to rise up out of those early mists of our history and strike down his oppressors with a fury of retribution unequaled before or since." Working out of the present back across the past, out of the immediate sensory details of his experience into the layered-over details of personal and cultural memories, Styron begins to show the uses and power of combined description and narration.

Regardless of whether you are presenting description or narration, you must remember that the principles of composition for handling time and space are interrelated. We experience the features of an object, place, or person during a sequence in time, so our descriptions are best laid out in unified, coherent, progressive presentations. We experience events in time, too, but against a background of spaces, so our narration of actions may often be presented most effectively in the context of places. To become more aware of ways in which you can accomplish better descriptive and narrative effects, pay close attention to media such as paintings, television and radio, and movies. Artists in each of these media are concerned to reveal the interrelationships of time and space and, especially, to overcome whatever limitations each medium might have. Writers, too, are faced with apparent limitations, for they have neither actual sound nor actual sights, neither words uttered in time nor pictures experienced, but in their medium — *language* — they can create virtual space and time.

EXERCISES

1. Describe in your own words a scene or scenes from a film you have watched.
2. Draw in words a portrait of a character you have met or read about.
3. Describe yourself as you think you really are, with all the insights that few people ever glimpse.
4. Describe a person you know revealing his or her inner qualities.
5. Describe an object first objectively and then subjectively.
6. Describe the same scene at two different times of day.
7. Narrate an episode about an experience you have had.
8. Read an article from a newspaper and recreate it in the form of a story.
9. Describe a scientific experiment you have performed.
10. Narrate the important events that took place on a specific day in your life. Try to give your material purpose and interest.
11. Write a description of one of your instructors (past or present). Concentrate on his or her appearance as it relates to the subject matter that he or she teaches (use the following student essay describing a rhetoric teacher as a model):

The Word and the Man

He entered the room. He didn't run. He didn't walk. With his usual gait, he floated across the room toward his chair. The effect was noticed on all the faces of the students as the facade of midmorning disinterest quickly changed to one of rekindled expectations. Around the corner, toward the blackboard, a quick adjustment of the chair to the front and center position, and he was down. As was customary, he set down a cup of yogurt and a spoon on the table in front of him. Facing the class, he conveyed the usual morning greetings and then proceeded to pry open the lid of the yogurt. After several sessions, such as the one above, one could unmistakably distinguish the fine line of character and image projected. The image of yogurt as conducive to good health only seemed to further complement his total appearance. It had, in fact, become his trademark.

The light, yet never flashy colors of his dress, the turtleneck shirt, the trim trousers, and tennis shoes, all outlining a slim build, reflected that image. A few grey hairs and a slightly receding hairline gave evidence to waning youth. But the perpetual light in his eyes and wide grin negated blatantly any lost youth and simply testified to a waxing level of vigor and activity reaching proportions previously unmatched.

Out of himself, he put forth all that his teachings stood for: the living embodiment of clarity, style, and organization. In organic form, by his very existence, he was a thesis statement for, in the most complimentary sense, his rhetorically succinct life.

12. Analyze the following passages for their descriptive and narrative effectiveness. Concentrate your analysis on point of view, appeal to the senses, metaphor (comparison), and subjective versus objective technique.

"Now, what I want is, Facts. Teach these boys and girls nothing but Facts. Facts alone are wanted in life. Plant nothing else, and root out everything else. You can only form the minds of reasoning animals upon Facts: nothing else will ever be of any service to them. This is the principle on which I bring up my own children. Stick to Facts, sir."

The scene was a plain, bare monotonous vault of a schoolroom, and the speaker's square forefinger emphasised his observations by underscoring every sentence with a line on the schoolmaster's sleeve. The emphasis was helped by the speaker's square wall of a forehead, which had his eyebrows for its base, while his eyes found commodious cellarage in two dark caves, overshadowed by the wall. The emphasis was helped by the speaker's mouth, which was wide, thin, and hard set. The emphasis was helped by the speaker's voice, which was inflexible, dry, and dictatorial. The emphasis was helped by the speaker's hair, which bristled on the skirts of his bald head, a plantation of firs to keep the wind from its shinning surface, all covered with knobs, like the crust of a plum pie, as if the head had scarcely warehouse-room for the hard facts stored inside. The speaker's obstinate carriage, square coat, square legs, square shoulders — yes, his very neckcloth, trained to take him by the throat with an unaccommodating grasp, like a stubborn fact, as it was — all helped with the emphasis.

"In this life, we want nothing but Facts, sir; nothing but Facts!"

The speaker, and the schoolmaster, and the third grown person present, all backed a little, and swept with their eyes the inclined plane of little vessels then and there arranged in order, ready to have imperial gallons of facts poured into them until they were full to the brim.

— Charles Dickens, *Hard Times*

The house of fiction has in short not one window, but a million — a number of possible windows not to be reckoned, rather; every one of which has been pierced, or is still pierceable, in its vast front, by the need of the individual vision and by the pressure of the individual will. These apertures, of dissimilar shape and size, hang so, all together over the human scene that we might have expected of them a greater sameness of report than we find. They are but windows at the best, mere holes in a dead wall, disconnected, perched aloft; they are not hinged doors opening straight upon life. But they have this mark of their own that at each of them stands a figure with a pair of eyes, or at least with a field-glass, which forms, again and again, for observation, a unique instrument, insuring to the person making use of it an impression distinct from every other. He and his neighbours are watching the same show, but one seeing more where the other sees less, one seeing black where the other sees white, one seeing big where the other sees small, one seeing coarse where the other sees fine. And so on, and so on; there is fortunately no saying on what, for the particular pair of eyes, the window may not open; "fortunately" by reason, precisely, of this incalculability of range. The spreading field, the human scene, is the "choice of subject"; the pierced aperture, either broad or balconied or slitlike and low-browed, is the "literary form"; but they are, singly or together, as nothing without the posted presence of the watcher — without, in other words, the consciousness of the artist. Tell me what the artist is, and I will tell you of what he has been conscious. Thereby I shall express to you at once his boundless freedom and his "moral" reference.

— Henry James, Preface to *The Portrait of the Lady*

This time the bear didn't strike him down. It caught the dog in both arms, almost loverlike, and they both went down. He was off the mule now. He drew back both hammers of the gun but he could see nothing but moiling spotted houndbodies until the bear surged up again. Boon was yelling something, he could not tell what; he could see Lion still clinging to the bear's throat and he saw the bear, half erect, strike one of the hounds with one paw and hurl it five or six feet and then, rising and rising as though it would never stop, stand erect again and begin to rake at Lion's belly with its forepaws. Then Boon was running. The boy saw the gleam of the blade in his hand and watched him leap among the hounds, hurdling them, kicking them aside as he ran, and fling himself astride the bear as he had hurled himself onto the mule, his legs locked around the bear's belly, his left arm under the bear's throat where Lion clung, and the glint of the knife as it rose and fell.

It fell just once. For an instant they almost resembled a piece of statuary: the clinging dog, the bear, the man astride its back, working and probing the buried blade. Then they went down, pulled over backward by Boon's weight, Boon underneath. It was the bear's back which reappeared first but at once Boon was astride it again. He had never released the knife and again the boy saw the almost infinitesimal movement of his arm and shoulder as he probed and sought; then the bear surged erect, raising with it the man and the dog too, and turned and still carrying the man and the dog it took two or three steps toward the woods on its hind feet as a man would have walked and crashed down. It didn't collapse, crumple. It fell all of apiece, as a tree falls, so that all three of them, man, dog and bear, seemed to bounce once.

— William Faulkner, "The Bear"

4

❧ STYLE ❧

The writer . . . needs to glance
in several directions as he writes.
He must keep an eye both on his audience
and on the nature of the occasion for his
writing. The tone of his voice must be tuned
to that audience and occasion.
But at the same time he must keep another eye
on that hard core of the self, the only source
of his distinction and identity, and attune his voice to its
deepest vibrations. And throughout the process he
must be alert to the runaway selves
that might move out and take over,
without so much as asking permission. He must
not dismiss these defiant selves
too quickly: they might reveal to him
much that he simply did not
— or refused to — know
before they appeared.

JAMES E. MILLER, JR.
Word, Self, Reality
(1972)

STYLE, RHYTHM, AND SELF

Style is that aspect of writing and speech which reflects our inner selves, our uniqueness, our distinctive voices. A personal style develops as both a resistance to and an acknowledgment of the pressure for uniformity and conformity every culture exerts upon its participants. Each epoch, each culture, group, and subgroup has a style. We may assimilate those styles, without caring to individualize them, or — more likely — without even being *aware* that we have absorbed them. But when this happens we have turned over our birthright to an institutional identity, for we do not have to let the forces of conformity crush our *personality*. We can employ only selected features of the verbal modes that surround us, that force themselves in upon our central selves, that — given the chance — will simply take over our core personality. Style resists this pressure, for each of us has or can have a unique style comprised of elements selected from the overall style(s) of our social contexts.

"Style is the man." "Style is choice." While we must understand that writing choices, like any choices we make, are surrounded by all sorts of uncontrolled and uncontrollable situations, we finally accept an *ethical* definition of style, a definition asserting that choices of style are choices of *character, personality, self-identity*. Style(s) should come from self-knowledge and ought to remain consistent with the knowledge we have of self. Style, as H. L. Mencken puts it, is as much an integral part of us as our skin is: though, unfortunately, sometimes "it hardens as the arteries harden," it "is always the outward and visible symbol of a man." Style, then, should reflect the development going on within each of us as we cope with those external pressures that would deny us individuality. Along with changes of age and circumstance, style has to accommodate the variety of open or mandated situations occurring each day of our lives. We do not speak or write the same way to our parents as we do to our roommate or our teachers, our friends or our sweetheart. Style has to adapt to meet the demands of different audiences and subjects, but it should do so without violating the central identity we value. Walker Gibson explains it in the following way:

Questions about style can most usefully be approached if we think of a style as the expression of a personality. I do not mean at all that our words necessarily reveal what we are "really like." I do mean that every writer and talker, more or less consciously, chooses a role which he thinks appropriate to express for a given time and situation. The personality I am expressing in this written sentence is not the same as the one I orally express to my three-year-old who at this moment is bent on climbing onto my typewriter. For each of these two situations, I choose a different "voice," a different mask, in order to accomplish what I want accomplished.

— Walker Gibson, *The Limits of Language*

No matter how many different "masks" we wear, there is a person, a "face," that ought to remain relatively visible, identifiable, and unchanged behind those masks. But this is a choice we make, for no law says we cannot dissemble, play false roles, don inauthentic masks. Nonetheless, in style "personality" is the consistent rhetorical stance, or attitude, that is directed toward all audiences, all subjects, toward people and language itself. At the point we begin to realize our personal style, says one writer,

. . . we are set on a tricky journey, a potholing discovery of our own personalities through our characteristic ways of using words. We are discovering our mind's favourite movements in approaching events, in making manageable shapes out of experience. These movements are likely to be expressed by the repeated use of the same images, by the same kinds of stress at similar points, by certain favourite words. From all of these, one can quite soon make a rough cut-out of the shape of one's mind; and one will probably be surprised at its simplicity, at the way a few words are used like incantations or like flags to be saluted. Which shows that our thought is not pliant enough.

— Richard Hoggart, *On Culture and Communication*

Style involves the repeated ways in which one achieves a distinctive *rhythm* in the use of language; rhythm is itself a function of repetition, and we identify style in those elements that recur frequently enough to be observed. Unlike "tone" and "voice," which alter from subject to subject and audience to audience, the comprehensive language rhythm called style remains relatively consistent. One's sense of rhythm in the use of language may be linked with many other rhythms in the universe:

All living things may get information about their orientation in space and time from the interaction of their body cells with electromagnetic fields and cosmic ray activity in the external environment. These interactions of energy could be used by the central nervous system in ways that we have barely begun to understand. It is possible that heartbeat is related to universal rhythms, perhaps even rhythms outside our solar system. The sensitive magnetic fields which man knows exist within each living cell certainly cannot help but be influenced by the energies of the universe.

— Dr. M. Samuels and Hal Bennett, *The Well Body Book*

On a more immediate level, rhythm may be that which regulates the responses we make to our world and directs the relationships among these responses. Rhythm encompasses all aspects of our lives, including such seemingly diverse activities as dance and work. According to anthropologist Havelock Ellis:

All human work, under natural conditions, is a kind of dance. Karl Bucher has argued that work differs from the dance, not in kind, but only in degree, since they are both essentially rhythmic, for all great combined efforts, the efforts by which alone great constructions such as those of megalithic days could be carried out, must be harmonized. The dance rhythm of work has thus acted socialisingly in a parallel line with the dance rhythms of the arts, and indeed in part as their inspirer. . . . Insofar as they arose out of work, music and singing and dancing are naturally a single art. A poet must always write a tune, said Swinburne.

— Havelock Ellis, *The Dance of Life*

Most of our physical activities are regulated by a response to rhythm, and some biologists now believe that patterns of rhythms that regulate physical, emotional, and intellectual changes can be identified:

Biorhythmists believe that the moment a newborn takes his first breath, he does more than begin to feel, taste, and smell. He also initiates the three important rhythms that will pulsate through his body in a regular pattern until the moment of death. First is the 23-day physical rhythm, which seems to parallel strength, energy, endurance and resistance to disease. The second is the 28-day sensitivity (or emotional) rhythm, which parallels periods of elation, moodiness and creativity. The third is a 33-day intellectual rhythm, which corresponds to a person's mental alertness, memory and logical skills. These three continuous rhythms can be plotted in a serpentine series of curves drawn on a chart. Because of the differing frequencies of each biorhythm, no two days are exactly alike. Some days some of the cycles are on the up side, some days they're on the low side, and some days they're crossing the threshold from up to down.

— Carol Saline, "Blame It on Your Biorhythms"

The creation of rhythm in the use of language is a fundamental technique in the achievement of effective communication. If an individual's sense of speech rhythm is somehow impaired, the ability to communicate efficiently also will be impaired. The reason this problem may occur is partially explained by recent experiments. Our initial encounter with language is generally through the mother's voice, her humming, singing, and talking, and a child deprived of these early rhythmic forms of vocal activities has serious communication problems later on. According to studies out of the State University of New York at Albany, rhythm is mental rather than physical, subjective rather than objective; it exists in the nervous system of the perceiver as much as in the object perceived. This means that our audience will understand our language best if we cast it in a rhythmic form that is compatible with the audience's. Robert Frost went so far as to say that he could determine *what* was being said in another room merely by listening to and defining

---

People change. Haven't you, too, tried to find out who you were meant to be when you were a child? Suddenly you discover strange, forgotten feelings — you haven't seen them for 50 years. And this is exactly what happens when you live a calm, regular life on this island, surrounded by people you want to be with. It's a question of finding your own rhythm. I think your pulse, your heart's movements, the movements of your soul, all these things combined, create your own rhythm. This is not superstitious. It is part of my professional thinking. If you live calmly, or just sit down calmly every day for about an hour, gradually you discover your own rhythm. But most of us don't and that's unhealthy, spiritually and physically. The important thing is not to let other people, other situations or conditions or circumstances hurt this rhythm too much. Sometimes, of course, it's healthy to be stressed. Sometimes it is good for me to get away from the island and live a more hurried life. But only sometimes. If you can find your own rhythm, you find a lot of other things at the same time.

— Ingmar Bergman, "A Visit with Ingmar Bergman,"
New York Times Magazine, December 7, 1975

the speech rhythms. Though we need to mesh our rhythm (style) with that of our audience, there is no need to give up our individuality. We probably have developed from many of the same sources, influences, and contexts as those of our audience, but we remain intact as persons. What we need to do, instead of relinquishing our identity, is to achieve a rhythm (style) close to the center of our whole psychobiological self, as opposed to the merely psychological or physiological or social self.

Our approach to style, then, will emphasize those repeated uses of language, as opposed to larger structural elements (paragraphs, sequences of paragraphs, devices for organization and addition), that contribute to rhythm. The greater the range of techniques for repetition a writer commands, the more likelihood that he or she will achieve effective communication. Lincoln's "Gettysburg Address" provides a good example of the uses of structure to build up a message and the uses of stylistic rhythm to give emphasis. As we have seen, it is built on a three-part structure (past-present-future), has a three-part theme (birth-death-rebirth), and features a style that employs frequent three-part repetitions ("of the people, by the people, for the people"). Varied repetitions of substance, structure, and language give the speech a highly rhythmic quality, and that quality allows it to communicate on physical or somatic levels deeper than the intellectual alone. That is why we can speak of the "music" of such a style, for it can communicate in ways beyond the semantic texture of the words.

SENTENCES

It is the role of style in rhetoric to emphasize the sentences, words, and sounds we want to put into relief. The sentence is the key to style. Paragraphs and their interrelationships are concerned with structure, with increment or addition; sentences manipulate the patterns of sounds, words, and phrases that create the rhythms of a writer's style. A sentence has two aspects, one grammatical and the other rhetorical. The grammar of the sentence creates clarity; the rhetoric of the sentence creates emphasis. Not every sentence in a paragraph needs to carry rhetorical weight, but those that do need to stand out from all the others. The choices of rhetorical devices we make constitute a part of our style. In John Kennedy's speech "Poetry and Power" (discussed in Chapter 2), an essential rhetorical feature that generates an identifiable prose rhythm is balance, as in these examples (the parts of the sentences that call attention to balancing are bracketed and italicized):

A nation reveals itself [not only] *by the men it produces* [but also] *by the men it honors, the men it remembers.*

*   *   *

But today this college and country honor a man whose contribution was [not] *to our size* [but] *to our spirit;* [not] *to our political beliefs* [but] *to our insight;* [not] *to our self-esteem* [but] *to our self-comprehension.*

*   *   *

We must never forget that art is not *a form of propaganda;* it is *a form of truth.*

The rhetorical stylistic balance, you will remember, mirrors the balance of poetry and power in a democratic society: that is the message Kennedy presents. Balance is one rhetorical characteristic, perhaps the central one, of Kennedy's style, and by repeating this technique in various ways he achieves an intense rhythmic quality in his sentence patterns. Balance, however, is just one way to achieve emphasis.

The English sentence can be ordered in several ways to achieve stylistic emphasis, variety, rhythm, and harmony of sound (euphony). The standard structure of the English sentence is *subject, predicate, object,* with modification added appropriately. Schematically, it looks like this:

(modifier)	*Subject*	*Predicate*	(modifiers)	*Direct Object*
Slugging	Henry Aaron	hit	a low outside	fastball.

There are times when clarity or emphasis can be better achieved through variations on this structure. You may want to draw attention to a particular idea within a sentence, so you organize the sentence in a way that will make that idea stand out. The beginning and ending positions

---

Good writers know that the spoken language is the life-giving source of the written language and that it is therefore perilous to stray far from speech. They also know that they are the inheritors of a long tradition of written language equally vital. If they disregard many of the rituals of prescriptive grammar, they also reject the carelessness and license of the spoken language. Between the Tower of Ivory and the Tower of Babel, the writers of recognized excellence have long pursued their own course.

— John Halverson and Mason Cooley, *Principles of Writing* (1965)

in the sentence, as in the essay and the paragraph, are positions of importance. Because key ideas sometimes get lost in the middle of a sentence, you may want to put important ideas in the initial or closing parts of the sentence structure. Two types of sentences concentrate on the opening and closing positions, the *loose* and the *periodic*.

The *loose* rhetorical pattern is the most characteristic sentence of our culture; it fulfills the psychological need to get the first things done first. In the *loose* sentence, the clause containing the main idea appears first in the sentence, leaving everything else to follow in a series of subordinate phrases or clauses. Following are examples of *loose* sentence structure (the main clause is italicized):

> *I used to park my car on a hill and sit silently observant,* listening to the talk ringing out from neighbor to neighbor, seeing the inhabitants drowsing in their doorways, taking it all in with nostalgia — the sage smell on the wind, the sunlight without time, the village without destiny.
>
> — Loren Eiseley, *The Immense Journey*

> *I had come over the hills and on foot in serene summer days,* plucking raspberries by the wayside, and occasionally buying a loaf of bread at a farmer's house, with a knapsack on my back, which held a few traveler's books and a change of clothing, and a staff in my hand.
>
> — David Thoreau, *A Week on the Concord and Merrimac Rivers*

> *Now they could see the Square,* empty too — the amphitheatric lightless stores, the slender white pencil of the Confederate monument against the mass of the courthouse looming in columned upsoar to the dim quadruple face of the clock lighted each by a single faint bulb with a quality as intransigent against their four fixed mechanical shouts of adjuration and warning as the glow of a firefly.
>
> — William Faulkner, *Intruder in the Dust*

Bear in mind that "loose" is not a negative term here, for though the results are sentences that are grammatically loose, each has a discernible rhythm created by the patterning of the additions, the "listening," "seeing," "taking . . . in" and "smell," "sunlight," and "village" structural repetitions of Eiseley's sentence; created by the repeated structures of "plucking" and "buying," and "books" and "change" sandwiched between "with a knapsack . . . and a staff" of Thoreau's; and created by the even more complicated structures of Faulkner's sentence. The loose sentence obviously is close to common speech patterns, which qualify and expand by addition more than by other forms of modification.

Perhaps that is what gives it its strength, for, as these examples suggest, the loose sentence can gather almost limitless power by the addition of selected but potentially infinite details.

Another way to achieve emphasis is to break up the traditional sentence pattern and thereby call attention to the "displaced" grammatical portion. Occasionally, we may want to alter the sentence in order to place the emphasis on an idea at the end. In this case the sentence is called *periodic*. The following sentence gets its rhetorical effectiveness from the interruptive phrase that shifts emphasis to the end of the sentence:

> It comes as a great shock to discover that the country which is your birthplace and to which you owe your life and identity has *not*, in its whole system of reality, *evolved any place for you.*
>
> — James Baldwin, "The American Dream and
> the American Negro"

A periodic sentence such as Baldwin's is especially effective when the final prediction comes as a shock, the solution of a mystery, or the conclusion of a paradox.

A more subtle displacement, such as a shift in the position of a modifier, can be equally effective in achieving emphasis. A case in point is the opening sentence to a story in *Dubliners:*

> North Richmond Street, being blind, was a quiet street except at the hour when the Christian Brothers' School set the boys free.
>
> — James Joyce, "Araby"

By placing a modifier ("being blind") after the subject rather than before it and by setting it off by commas, Joyce emphasizes the fact that the street is a blind alley. That fact gets preferred stylistic treatment here because it turns out to be significant in the development of the story, which concerns moral blindness and cultural initiation. Anytime, therefore, that we deliberately disrupt the conventional form of the sentence, we ought to have a clear rhetorical purpose; otherwise the emphasis may be disturbing. Use this technique selectively, and it can be one of the more effective means of generating rhythm in style. See how many different sentences, using Joyce's model, you can create just for the fun of it. Can you make some of them comic by using incongruous modifiers?

Another way to achieve emphasis in a sentence is by the use of balanced and parallel structures (the terms *balance* and *parallel* can be used interchangeably). If we have two or more ideas of equal importance, we might connect them in a form that suggests their equality, as in the Emerson example below. The form of such a sentence is often the compound grammatical sentence that consists of two or more independent clauses, as in Macauley's sentence:

> He prostrated himself in the dust before his Maker; but he set his foot on the neck of his King.
>
> — Thomas Macauley, *The Life of John Milton*

Whoso would be a man, must be a nonconformist.

> — R. W. Emerson

The rhythm of the balance can be heightened by beginning the parallel structures with the same words (the technical name is *anaphora*) and making the structures of equal length (called *isocolon*). For example, the sentence by Thomas Macauley cited above begins the parallel parts with *he* and each part contains about the same number of words (not counting, of course, the coordinating conjunction *but*). We can also achieve balance in sentences by reversing the grammatical patterns on either side of the conjunction. This rhythm, formed by crossing, is called *chiasmus*:

A   B   C   C   B   A

Mankind must put an end to war or war will put an end to mankind.

> — John Kennedy

And so my fellow Americans, ask not what your country can do for you; ask what you can do for your country.

> — John Kennedy

You like it, it likes you!®

> — Seven-Up Advertisement

The use of balanced and parallel sentences can dramatically accentuate the rhythmic quality of an essay or speech. Many oral presentations rely heavily on the use of balance, for when the elements involved remain relatively few, balance makes them more easily controlled and remembered. Like most devices, balance can get tiresome quickly, and the careful writer should avoid its overuse, however.

True style displays itself in elaboration, rhythm, and distance, which demand activity of the imagination and play of the spirit. Elaboration means going beyond what is useful to produce what is engaging to contemplation. Rhythm is a marking of beginnings and endings. In place of a meaningless continuum, rhythm provides intelligibility and the sense that the material has been handled in a subjective interest. It is human to dislike mere lapse. When one sees things in rhythmical configuration, he feels that they have been brought into the realm of the spirit. Rhythm is thus a way of breaking up nihilistic monotony and of proclaiming that there is a world of value. Distance is what preserves us from the vulgarity of immediacy. Extension and proportion in space, as in architecture, and extension in time, as in manners and deportment, help to give gratifying form to these creations. All style has in it an element of ritual, which signifies steps which cannot be passed over.

— Richard M. Weaver, *Visions of Order* (1964).

There are other qualities of sentences to consider in order to maintain rhythm and vitality in style. First of all, the lengths of sentences should be varied. If we use only short sentences, we may generate monotony. It is generally a good idea to save short sentences for moments of emphasis. Second, a variety of sentence openers should be used. Repetition of the same opening grammatical structures can create further monotony. The following paragraph provides a good example of sentence variety:

[1]For nations, as for families, the level may vary at which a solvent balance is struck. [2]If its expenditures are safely within its assured means, a family is solvent when it is poor, or is well-to-do, or is rich. [3]The same principle holds true of nations. [4]The statesman of a strong country may balance its commitments at a high level or at a low. [5]But whether he is conducting the affairs of Germany, which has dynamic ambitions, or the affairs of Switzerland, which seeks only to hold what it already has, or of the United States, he must still bring his ends and means into balance. [6]If he does not, he will follow a course that leads to disaster.

— Walter Lippmann, *U. S. Foreign Policy*

Lippmann alternates long and short, balanced, loose, and periodic sentences and uses a variety of sentence openers to produce a rhythmic vitality that keeps a reader's mind occupied. The first sentence, beginning with a prepositional phrase, inverts the usual order of the sentence (periodic), balances *nations* with *families,* and introduces a key word — *solvent* — all while remaining relatively brief. The second sentence follows an *if-then* pattern (with *then* understood) to suggest balance, but ends in a rhythmic three-part sequence — *poor, well-to-do, rich.* The third sentence, a crucial one in making an argument by analogy, is short and pointed. The next two sentences increase in length and open out the rhythm, sentence 4 being a simple, direct statement, and sentence 5 being an elaborated periodic sentence that includes three examples of countries to parallel the three types of families named in sentence 2 and that concludes with the paragraph's main theme of balance. The sixth and final sentence returns to a balanced *if-then* structure (like sentence 2), the rhythm of which is tight and which ends with a climactic word — *disaster.* Such variation offers one of the "musical" dimensions available to good prose, a dimension that makes us *feel* as well as *understand* meanings.

Remember that rhythm in sentences occurs when we employ a variety of sentence openers, sentence lengths, and types of rhetorical structures. But remember, too, that most sentences are simply what we call *mandated* sentences, sentences whose order is predetermined by subject and occasion, so do not get pretentious in sentence structuring any more than you would in choice of words. Use unusual rhetorical structures selectively and only at those times when variation is desirable for harmony or necessary for emphasis or clarity. Do not say, "On the horizon there is a ship" when a plain, "A ship is on the horizon" is mandated. The repetition of sentence structures in a variety of contexts throughout an essay will create a rhythm and identify personal style. Whether Hemingway with his extensive use of the simple sentence (which in Hemingway is often very *long*) or William Faulkner with his long, compound-complex sentences, all writers use forms that mirror their rhetorical stances. Hemingway saw humanity as a stripped, naked object facing an indifferent universe; when he strips his sentences to a bare minimum, they seem to come out of his understanding of the human condition. For Faulkner, humanity as a subject experiences the world as a flow of events: past, present, and future all are colored by the mind of the person experiencing them. Thus, Faulkner's sentences attempt to render the subjective stream of experience by filling sentences to the bursting point, loading them with an often unbearable weight of details, allusions, figures, and digressions, even breaking their bounds grammatically and semantically (the meaning).

EXERCISES

1. Point out the rhetorical characteristics that identify each of the following sentences as structurally *loose, periodic,* or *balanced:*

   a. And finally, stammering a crude farewell, he departed.

   — Thomas Wolfe

   b. In every free country, great or small, the spirit of patriotism and nationality grew steadily; and in every country, bond or free, the organisation and structure into which men were fitted by the laws, gathered and armed this sentiment.

   — Winston Churchill

   c. It was a big, squarish frame house that had once been white, decorated with cupolas and spires and scrolled balconies in the heavily lightsome style of the seventies, set on what had once been our most select street.

   — William Faulkner

   d. Some books are to be tasted, others to be swallowed, and some few to be chewed and digested.

   — Francis Bacon

   e. The concrete highway was edged with a mat of tangled, broken dry grass, and the grass heads were heavy with oat beards to catch on a dog's coat, and foxtails to tangle in a horse's fetlocks, and clove burrs to fasten to sheep's wool; sleeping life waiting to be spread and dispersed, every seed armed with an appliance of dispersal, twisting darts and parachutes for the wind, little spears and balls of tiny thorns, and all waiting for animals and for the wind, for a man's trouser cuff or the hem of a woman's skirt, all passive but armed with the appliances of activity, still, but each possessed of the anlage of movement.

   — John Steinbeck

   f. What our time needs is mystery: what our time needs is magic.

   — Norman O. Brown

   g.   To see a World in a Grain of Sand
               And a Heaven in a Wild Flower,
               Hold Infinity in the palm of your hand
               And Eternity in an hour.

   — William Blake

h. The men we met walked past, slow, unsmiling, with downcast eyes, as if the melancholy of an overburdened earth had weighted their feet, bowed their shoulders, borne down their glances.

— Joseph Conrad

i. The great question that has never been answered, and which I have not yet been able to answer despite my thirty years of research into the feminine soul, is this, "What does a woman want?"

— Sigmund Freud

j. Youth is a kind of delirium, which can only be cured, if it is ever to be cured at all, by years of painful treatment.

— Logan P. Smith

k. The thought was yet in his mind, when first one then another, with every variety of pace and voice — one deep as the bell from a cathedral turret, another ringing on its treble notes the prelude of a waltz — the clocks began to strike the hour of three in the afternoon.

— Robert Louis Stevenson

l. In the center of the great city of London lies a small neighborhood, consisting of a cluster of narrow streets and courts, of very venerable and debilitated houses, which goes by the name of Little Britain.

— Washington Irving

m. Swift pictures of himself, apart, yet in himself, came to him — a blue, desperate figure leading lurid charges with one knee forward and a broken blade high — a blue, determined figure standing before a crimson and steel assault, getting calmly killed on a high place before the eyes of all.

— Stephen Crane

2. Rewrite an essay you have previously written, concentrating on your sentence patterns. Try to experiment with different rhetorical forms (loose, periodic, balanced) to emphasize the ideas in the key sentences. In addition, work for a variety of sentence openers and sentence lengths. Hand in the original with the revision.

3. Compare and contrast the following two passages by Hemingway for their qualities of style. Define the kinds of sentences, the sentence openers, and sentence lengths. Explain how the stylistic qualities are in harmony with the subject matter.

They shot the six cabinet ministers at half-past six in the morning against the wall of a hospital. There were pools of water in the courtyard.

There were wet dead leaves on the paving of the courtyard. It rained hard. All the shutters of the hospital were nailed shut. One of the ministers was sick with typhoid. Two soldiers carried him down stairs and out into the rain. They tried to hold him up against the wall but he sat down in a puddle of water. The other five stood very quietly against the wall. Finally the officer told the soldiers it was no good trying to make him stand up. When they fired the first volley he was sitting down in the water with his head on his knees.

— Ernest Hemingway, *In Our Time*

Sometimes in the dark we heard the troops marching under the window and the guns going past pulled by motor-tractors. There was much traffic at night and many mules on the road with boxes of ammunition on each side of their packsaddles and gray motor-trucks that carried men, and other trucks with loads covered with canvas that moved slower in the traffic. There were big guns too that passed in the day drawn by tractors, the long barrels of the guns covered with green branches and green leafy branches and vines laid over the tractors. To the north we could look across a valley and see a forest of chestnut trees and behind it another mountain on this side of the river. There was fighting for that mountain too, but it was not successful, and in the fall when the rains came the leaves all fell from the chestnut trees and the branches were bare and the trunks black with rain. The vineyards were thin and bare-branched too and all the country wet and brown and dead with the autumn. There were mists over the river and clouds on the mountain and trucks splashed mud on the road and the troops were muddy and wet in their capes; their rifles were wet and under their capes the two leather cartridge-boxes on the front of the belts, gray leather boxes heavy with the packs of clips of thin, long 6.5 mm. cartridges, bulged forward under the capes so that the men, passing on the road, marched as though they were six months gone with child.

— Ernest Hemingway, *A Farewell to Arms*

WORDS

Word choice is the very center of the communication process. Our choice of words enables us to express meaning and feeling precisely in the ways best suited to our often complex purposes. Structure and rhythm, abstracted from our words, become empty qualities. Everything we have studied thus far functions to support the role of the word, for the word *is* the substance itself. Words and the ways you use them contribute significantly to the creation of style. In what follows we will treat words in several aspects: voice and tone, levels of usage, denotation and connotation, abstractness and concreteness, image, metaphor, and symbol. Taken together, these verbal elements or qualities may contribute more to your style than any other stylistic aspect of writing.

VOICE AND TONE

Probably the first thing we sense in a piece of writing after the sender's *voice* is his *tone*. We make a distinction between the *voice* directed toward the audience and the *tone* directed toward the subject matter, but the two, voice and tone, must ultimately be understood as one. No matter what the tone toward the subject matter — serious, half serious, detached, light, suspenseful, playful, ironical, or satirical — it must be adjusted to the voice with which we want to speak to our audience. If we engage in a dialogue about some scientific principle with an audience that expects us to use a voice of reason, then the tone we take toward the subject matter probably should be serious. Problems frequently occur when an audience cannot reconcile a speaker's voice and tone. Because the conflict often creates laughter or anger, a writer may want to exploit it precisely in order to attract an audience's interest. Humorist Don Knotts, doing, in his timid, embarrassed voice, an impression of Albert Einstein explaining the theory of relativity, creates humor deliberately. We do not want to unconsciously or inadvertently contradict voice and tone. In the following excerpt from *Trout Fishing in America,* Richard Brautigan deliberately generates a complex effect from the conflicts of voice and tone. We see the conflict in the disruption of expectations created by the words Brautigan uses:

> On this funky winter day in rainy San Francisco I've had a vision of Leonardo da Vinci. My woman's out slaving away, no day off, working on Sunday. She left here at eight o'clock this morning for Powell and California. I've been sitting here ever since like a toad on a log dreaming about Leonardo da Vinci.
>
> I saw him inventing a new spinning lure for trout fishing in America. I saw him first of all working with his imagination, then with metal and color and hooks, trying a little of this and a little of that, and then adding motion and then taking it away and then coming back again with a different motion, and in the end the lure was invented.

He called his bosses in. They looked at the lure and all fainted. Alone, standing over their bodies, he held the lure in his hand and gave it a name. He called it "The Last Supper." Then he went about waking up his bosses.

These three short paragraphs suggest how many elements can affect rhythm in writing. Rhythm is based on timing, timing on expectation. Because the human mind is capable of working on high levels of abstraction almost as easily as on low levels of fact, it can perceive rhythm (generate expectations or recognize even unexpected repetitions) in sounds (phonology, to the linguists), in grammar, and in meaning (semantics). Brautigan skillfully manipulates all these aspects of words in order to create his distinctive style. He bounces *funky* off *rainy*, both adjectives, but on different levels of usage: one is from soul, the other in this context from a popular Cole Porter tune. He gives us a lilting metrical pattern of sound, "funky winter day in" repeated in "rainy San Francisco" (note the sequence of accented, unaccented syllables). And he gives us, in this half-real, half-fantasy setting, "a vision of Leonardo da Vinci." Brautigan is "sitting here . . . like a toad on a log," but he's "dreaming about Leonardo da Vinci," the great painter of the Italian Renaissance, the creator of the *Mona Lisa* and designer of intricate devices and machines. Brautigan dreams of him inventing a spinning lure. You can pick up the analysis at this point (note the grammatical rhythms and repetitions of the second sentence of the second paragraph). What Brautigan has done is to weave an intricate verbal pattern,

---

A premise: within every human being there is the vatic voice. *Vates* was the Greek word for the inspired bard, speaking the words of a god. To most people, this voice speaks only in dream, and only in unremembered dream. The voice may shout messages into the sleeping ear, but a guard at the horned gate prevents the waking mind from remembering, listening, interpreting. It is the vatic voice (which is not necessarily able to write good poetry, or even passable grammar) which rushes forth the words of excited recognition, which supplies what we call inspiration. And inspiration, a breathing-into, is a perfectly expressive metaphor: "Not I, not I, but the wind blows through me!" as Lawrence says. Or Shelley's "Ode to the West Wind." We are passive to the vatic voice, as the cloud or the tree is passive to the wind.

— Donald Hall, "The Vatic Voice" (1968)

alternating low and high (levels of usage, seriousness, and meaning) in order to make us sense his warmth (towards us and his material).

In writing with more conventional purposes, both voice and tone are broadly labeled either formal or informal. But these two classifications encompass a wide range of choices. Word choices that relate to *voice*, representing our attitudes toward audience, might be called *colloquial, informal, formal,* or *pretentious;* these terms describe the range of speaker-audience relationships. The *colloquial* word suggests a more intimate relationship: I know you well if I speak to you of "my kids"; the *informal* also suggests intimacy, but we do not need to be close friends for me to refer to "my children"; the *formal* suggests we may not know each other at all, and I may use "offspring" instead of "children"; if I use "progeny" (in the same context), I am probably becoming just a little *pretentious* (or *ironic*), though in a very formal learned treatise I might use the word without pretense and not necessarily to refer to my own children.

Word choices that relate to *tone*, expressing our attitude toward subject matter, might be labeled *slang, informal, formal,* or *jargon.* At one extreme, *jargon* is to tone as *pretense* is to voice. Jargon elevates the material beyond its rightful level; names for objects or activities are especially subject to jargon. Calling a housewife a "household executive" is perhaps jargon, as calling "garbage men" "sanitation engineers" may be. The most likely uses of jargon occur when technicians in any field discuss their work, for they refer to their activities or the tools of their trade as if they were familiar to anyone — whether the activity is a zig-out, a fly pattern, a red-dog, or a counter; the tools a tachometer, a dynamometer, a spectrometer, or a monkey wrench. Jargon has a real and useful function among specialists, but it causes disfunctional communication when it is presented unexplained to nonspecialists. At the other extreme, *slang* is like colloquialism; one conveys extreme familiarity with the material, the other with audience. Given the nature of the *writing* context (audience, structure, style), we can see why we avoid an inappropriate colloquial voice or slang that demeans our material. We cannot be asked to back up to explain a term or to erase a violation of propriety when we write. Our most appropriate choices lie in the middle, for the two classes *informal* and *formal* give us range and flexibility without insulting either audience or material. Of the two, we usually prefer the *informal* wherever it is appropriate to our tone (we wish we *could* speak directly to you) and our subject (for the sake of clarity we sometimes must use formal terms). In the Introduction to *To A Dancing God,* Sam Keen, in explaining his attitude toward his audience, illustrates how *voice* can be direct and conversational, while *tone* (the level of usage relating to material) remains formal:

It takes considerable discipline to say "I" rather than to appeal to the authority of the anonymous "one," or the plural "we," or the mythical "modern man," or the venerable "Christian tradition," or the popular "common sense." And to refrain from excessive footnoting requires more than a little courage for one trained in the academy. In writing these essays I have had a growing need to write in the first-person singular, to refrain from hiding behind stylistic devices which are designed to give the reader the impression that an authority or an oracle rather than a person is speaking. My discipline and my courage have often failed. To write as a single person, to take responsibility for all the statements I make, requires greater vulnerability (that is humility) and self-assurance than I possess. However, my failure is an important part of the *process* which these essays exemplify and, therefore, I have not rewritten the earlier essays to eliminate the sentences and paragraphs that seem to have been produced by an anonymous and discarnate author.

To determine how formal Sam Keen's diction is, count the number of words for which there are readily available *informal* choices; for example, "avoid" instead of "refrain from," "university educated" instead of "trained in the academy," and for "discarnate," what? Still, we can feel that Keen speaks to us and even honors us by assuming that his words are also our words.

In contrast to the conversational, first-person, informal voice of Sam Keen is the third-person, formal "discarnate" voice of Richard Weaver in *Visions of Order:*

Not only the character but also the degree of a culture is responsive to the prevailing image of man. For what man tells himself he is manifests itself soon enough in what he does and may even predetermine what he can do. Historically speaking, man has been many things to himself, but the variation is only one side of the story. For if man has been many things, he is also one thing. Hovering over all the varieties is a harmonious ideal of man by which he must be judged if progression is to be at all possible. Even so empirical a thinker as John Stuart Mill, when he came to give his real or final reason justifying liberty, could not dispense with the imperative of this ideal. Now there are some images of man which impede this by holding people down to a low level of awareness and potentiality. The student of culture will be critical of all images that threaten true reaction — that is, reversion toward a poorer and less truthful concept of what it means to be a human being.

Of the two, the informal voice seems to be the one closer to our estimation of what reader-writer relationships ought to be. While Weaver's paragraph is clear, it makes us as much an object to be addressed as the material is an object to be understood, but in Keen's paragraph *I* seem to gain in identity along with Keen. We must remind you, then, to consider your audience *each* time you speak or write. It is often necessary — when writing exams, composition assignments, textbooks, scientific treatises, and the like — to address your audience and your material with objectivity and formality. In *mandated* situations, you do what is given to you to do. At those times, it is appropriate that you follow the mandate, the implied or explicit instructions. Regarding both attitude toward subject (tone) and attitude toward material, keep in mind what rhetorician Harold C. Martin says in *The Logic and Rhetoric of Expression:*

> There is something of make-believe in tone, just as there is in all art, no matter how deeply it is concerned to display the truth of things. A . . . manifestation of this make-believe, and a . . . means the writer has of making his identity felt in his work, is apparent in the stance he takes before his subject matter itself. No matter what the real situation is, he can appear to be detached or intimately concerned, actually in contact with the things he describes, or removed from them by thousands of miles or by centuries. He may proceed to see them as they appear to others or greatly distorted, as in the mirrors of an amusement arcade.

EXERCISES

1. Select any two of the quoted passages inserted throughout the text and analyze them for their qualities of *tone* and *voice*. Identify specific words within the passages that reflect either voice or tone, or both. For fun, you might also revise one of these passages in order to shift voice and tone either upward or downward on the scale.

2. Write a short essay (of perhaps 300 words) on a topic of your choice using word choices that relate to an *informal* voice and tone. Then write another essay (again about 300 words) on the same subject as the previous one, but this time use a *formal* voice and tone in your word choices.

DENOTATION AND CONNOTATION

Words have more than one dimension. They can function on a *denotative* level — the logical, direct, or specific meaning assigned in standard usage. The denotative is the core meaning, the meaning the dictionary can most readily identify. When words are used in a denotative way, they have a specific referent; they "name or indicate a specific object or concept or a definable class of objects and concepts." This is the denotative, dictionary definition of *denote.* A word such as *water,* perhaps harder to define than an abstraction such as *denotation,* nonetheless has a core meaning, a denotation, we can all understand. We use words denotatively because explicit meanings help prevent confusion in the mind of the audience. If all words we choose had only denotative meanings, however, there would be relatively little chance that the communication process could convey the complexity of our experience and thought. But very few words remain on the assigned, specific, and objective levels of meaning; many words we use also have subjective, indirect, and unassigned dimensions of meaning. These are the *connotations* of words that suggest a special, usually emotional quality in or attitude surrounding the object or idea for which the word stands.

Connotation occurs when a word picks up meaning as it is seen in association with other words. The word *water,* while it has its denotative meaning, can also, in one context, suggest fear, in another, a source of life, or, in another, coolness and calm and peace. Because contextual settings change, connotations of words often are contradictory; *water* may be the water of T. S. Eliot's line from *The Waste Land,* "Fear death by water," or it may be that of the old song sung by the Sons of the Pioneers, "Cool, clear, water." As writers or readers, we must recognize contexts in order to decide which set of connoted meanings to select.

Denotative usage is generally preferable in logical, objective forms of communication in which implicit meanings are neither appropriate nor relevant. In scientific studies, objective descriptions, and analyses of processes, words operate on a horizontal plane: meanings and words move directly, one-dimensionally, back and forth from one to the other. Connotative usage is associated with the more "literary," "artistic," sub-

---

One of the most important and effective uses of language is the emotional. It is also, of course, wholly legitimate. We do not talk only in order to reason or to inform. We have to make love and quarrel, to propitiate and pardon, to rebuke, console, intercede, and arouse. "He that complains," said Johnson, "acts like a man, like a social being." The real objection lies not against the language of emotion as such, but against language which, being in reality emotional, masquerades — whether by plain hypocrisy or subtler self-deceit — as being something else.

— C. S. Lewis, *Studies in Words* (1955)

jective purposes of language. We use the connotative meanings of words to provoke feelings and emotional responses; hence, connotation operates, we might say, vertically, multidimensionally, reaching out to pull in the halo of meanings that surround words. The way we use these two kinds of meaning depends on the subject matter and the audience for which they are intended. If we are writing an objective and logical essay, then we must be careful to employ words whose meanings have specific boundaries. To the scientist in a laboratory, *water* may be only "the liquid that descends from the clouds as rain, forms streams, lakes, and seas, and is a major constituent of all living matter and that is an odorless, tasteless, very slightly compressible liquid oxide of hydrogen H_2O which appears bluish in thick layers, freezes at 0°C and boils at 100°C, has a maximum density at 4°C and a high specific heat, is feebly ionized to hydrogen and hydroxyl ions, and is a poor conductor of electricity and a good solvent." To the farmer whose fields are parched from weeks of midsummer drought, water is that — and more — but can we even say just how much more? If we are writing an essay on what rainfall after drought means to a farmer, we may need to use words whose boundaries are limited, perhaps, only by the experience of the audience, which must participate in the material deeply and imaginatively. As writers, we constantly must test different words in different contexts, for only by experimentation can we get the right word for our purposes

EXERCISES

1. Explain in a few paragraphs an activity in which you regularly participate (such as driving to school, eating in the cafeteria, checking a book out of the library), using only words that are denotative. Then write about the same activity while selecting words that have a connotative quality: for example, in the first exercise, describe your drive to school as a "job," in the second, as an "adventure."

2. Analyze the connotative aspects that have associations and feelings attached to the words in the following passages. Note carefully how various words accumulate connotation because they appear in the context of other words that reinforce one set of meanings.

That day was but a thin solution of night. You know those November mornings with a low, corpse-white east where the sunrise should be, as though the day were still-born. Looking to the day-spring, there is what we have waited for, there the end of our hope, prone and shrouded. This morning of mine was such a morning. The world was very quiet, as though it were exhausted after tears. Beneath a broken gutterspout the rain (all night I had listened to its monody) had discovered a nest of pebbles in the path of my garden in a London suburb.

— H. M. Tomlinson, *The Sea and the Jungle*

Shall I compare thee to a summer's day?
Thou art more lovely and more temperate:
Rough winds do shake the darling buds of May,
And summer's lease hath all too short a date:
Sometimes too hot the eye of heaven shines,
And often is his gold complexion dimmed;
And every fair from fair sometimes declines,
By chance or nature's changing course untrimmed;
But thy eternal summer shall not fade,
Nor lose possession of that fair thou ownest
Nor shall Death brag thou wander'st in his shade,
When in eternal lines to time thou growest:
   So long as men can breathe or eyes can see,
   So long lives this, and this gives life to thee.

— William Shakespeare

A great many people seem to think that education is the answer to the problems of race in this country, but education as a means of breaking down racial barriers dies as an effective means of social change every day that black ghetto chiildren are taught that whiteness is rightness. The young slum dweller was told that poverty would be defeated, diminished, and finally removed from the United States. But by 1967 it had become obvious that the war in Vietnam had rendered that promise almost useless, if it ever was really meant. Violence has been the official policy of the United States Government in settling her disputes with other nations, and that belief has seeped into the police stations and slums across the land. War has brewed anger in the black community and has given birth to the belief that nonviolence is only a joke.

— Julian Bond, "A New Vision, A Better Tomorrow" (1969)

When I heard the learn'd astronomer,
When the proofs, the figures, were ranged in columns before me,
When I was shown the charts and diagrams, to add, divide, and measure
   them,
When I sitting heard the astronomer where he lectured with much
   applause in the lecture-room,
How soon unaccountable I became tired and sick,

> Till rising and gliding out I wander'd off by myself,
> In the mystical moist night-air, and from time to time,
> Look'd up in perfect silence at the stars.
>
> — Walt Whitman, *Leaves of Grass*

ABSTRACT AND CONCRETE

All words range between the *concrete* and the *abstract,* and the context in which the word is used is the difference that makes our message clear. The difference, in a given context, between abstract and concrete language can be described as the difference between generalization and specification. As a rule, the specific, concrete word is more vivid than the general, abstract one; the more we bring language down the "ladder of abstraction," the greater our chances of effective communication. This rule is not inflexible, but the reason it expresses a general truth is clear: abstract words do not appeal to our senses as readily as concrete words. We almost always grasp meanings more quickly through our senses than we do through abstract, conceptual thought.

In most contexts, if we see or hear the word *liberal,* it is probably unlikely that it will form a picture in the mind. A word such as *liberal* refers to qualities that an individual might have, but while we can visualize that person, we cannot separate the quality, *liberal,* from him.

One notion about style that needs to be erased at the outset is that style is simply "the dress of thought." It is difficult to determine just which school of rhetoric gave currency to the notion that style was ornament or embellishment, like the tinsel draped over the bare branches of a Christmas tree, but it is certain that none of the prominent classical rhetoricians — Isocrates, Aristotle, Demetrius, Longinus, Cicero, Quintilian — ever preached such a doctrine. All of these taught that there is an integral and reciprocal relationship between matter and form. "Thought and speech are inseparable from each other" — those words of John Henry Newman express the view of style that all the best rhetoricians held. According to this view, matter must be fitted to the form, and form to the matter.

— Edward P. J. Corbett, *Classical Rhetoric
for the Modern Student* (1965)

In order to understand the concept *liberal,* we must transform it, move it down from its airy abstractness and place its general meaning in the specific context of what "liberals" believe, say, or do.

The concrete word introduces meaning in specific detail. Hence, the words *wine* and *snow* create more sensuous images in our minds than *beverage* and *precipitation,* for in all likelihood we have tasted, smelled, felt, or seen wine and snow. Words such as *wine* and *snow* create, as by definition a concrete word must, sensory impressions, for they refer to objects that exist in the outside world beyond our minds. *Beverage* and *precipitation* are abstract words denoting classes of objects having certain qualities we could name, but those classes or categories are purely intellectual construction.

There are many times, however, when it is necessary to use abstract terms, times when abstractions lead to an economy of language that is practical and effective. Abstract words are often classifying words, and frequently it is necessary to talk about classes of things without defining specific objects in that class. But while words in a given context will be either abstract or concrete, there is also a continuum, a scale, a ladder, from abstraction to concreteness. *Wine* is more concrete than *beverage,* but it is less concretely specific than *burgundy,* which is less specific than "Gallo Hearty Burgundy." Concrete experience precedes abstract essence, and even a poet as much in love with the abstract as Wallace Stevens recognized that an abstraction like *beauty* begins in a concrete reality, material and sensuous:

> Beauty is momentary in the mind —
> The fitful tracing of a portal;
> But in the flesh it is immortal.

> — Wallace Stevens,
> "Peter Quince at the Clavier"

EXERCISES

Analyze the concrete qualities, those qualities that appeal to the senses, of the following passages.

1. We dare not forget today that we are the heirs of that first revolution. Let the word go forth from this time and place, to friend and foe alike, that the torch has been passed to a new generation of Americans, born in this century, tempered by war, disciplined by a hard and bitter peace,

proud of our ancient heritage, and unwilling to witness or permit the slow undoing of those human rights to which this nation has always been committed, and to which we are committed today at home and around the world.

— John F. Kennedy, *Inaugural Address*

2. I just spent two days with Edward T. Hall, an anthropologist, watching thousands of my fellow New Yorkers short-circuiting themselves into hot little twitching death balls with jolts of their own adrenalin. Dr. Hall says it is overcrowding that does it. Overcrowding gets the adrenalin going, and the adrenalin gets them queer, autistic, sadistic, barren, batty, sloppy, hot-in-the-pants, chancred-on-the-flanders, leering, puling, numb — the usual in New York, in other words, and God knows what else. Dr. Hall has the theory that overcrowding has already thrown New York into a state of behavioral sink. Behavioral sink is a term from ethology, which is the study of how animals relate to their environment. Among animals, the sink winds up with a "population collapse" or "massive die-off." O rotten Gotham.

— Tom Wolfe, *The Pump House Gang* (1968)

3.   **The Solitary Reaper**

Behold her, single in the field,
Yon solitary Highland Lass!
Reaping and singing by herself;
Stop here, or gently pass!
Alone she cuts and binds the grain,
And sings a melancholy strain;
O listen! for the Vale profound
Is overflowing with the sound.

No Nightingale did ever chaunt
More welcome notes to weary bands
Of travelers in some shady haunt,
Among Arabian sands:
A voice so thrilling ne'er was heard
In spring-time from the Cuckoo-bird,
Breaking the silence of the seas
Among the farthest Hebrides.

Will no one tell me what she sings? —
Perhaps the plaintive numbers flow

For old, unhappy, far-off things,
And battles long ago:
Or is it some more humble lay,
Familiar matter of today?
Some natural sorrow, loss, or pain,
That has been, and may be again?

Whate'er the theme, the Maiden sang
As if her song could have no ending;
I saw her singing at her work,
And o'er the sickle bending; —
I listened, motionless and still;
And, as I mounted up the hill,
The music in my heart I bore,
Long after it was heard no more.

— William Wordsworth

4. Write an essay in which you describe a particular person, place or thing using specific appeals to the various senses as part of your description.

IMAGERY, METAPHOR, AND SYMBOL

Use of concrete language produces *imagery*. Words that evoke sight are visual images; sounds, auditory images; smells, olfactory images; touch, tactile images; and words that evoke movement, pressure, and temperature are kinaesthetic images. We use concrete *imagery* in our writing because it appeals directly to the reader and because it creates the potential for *metaphor* and *symbol*, devices that bridge the gap between concrete object and abstract concept. Stevens' poem is concerned with the relationship between concrete being and abstract essence, the thing and its qualities. Such a subject seems more appropriate to philosophy than poetry, but Stevens enables us to grasp his abstract meaning, to connect it to a concrete image by use of metaphor. The word *metaphor* has a Latin root meaning "to transfer," and Stevens transfers his meaning this way: the quality of beauty is to any object as the frame is to a doorway ("portal"). The frame has an intrinsic association with the door, but it is not the door per se. Beauty may define or identify an object, but it is not the object itself nor can it exist without the object. Once we have experienced the door, the abstraction Stevens equates with *portal* can

> The man who understands a symbol not only "opens himself" to the objective world, but at the same time succeeds in emerging from his personal situation and reaching a comprehension of the universal. . . . Thanks to the symbol, the individual experience is "awoken," and transmuted into a spiritual act.
>
> — Mircea Eliade, *The Two and the One* (1969)

remain with us always. Stevens' metaphor allows us to understand what in philosophy would be most difficult to express and what Stevens expresses in a line: "The body dies; the body's beauty lives."

The use of symbolism is not normally thought an intricate part of expository and argumentative forms of rhetoric. But writers use it more often than is usually acknowledged; they use it and we fail to acknowledge it for the same reason: effective symbolism is almost invisible. In his highly influential philosophic study *Language and Myth,* Ernst Cassirer suggests that *words* are the key to controlling *things.* Words are our only means of knowing and understanding things, for it is only after we designate or name a thing that we control it. The primitive person tended not so much to *confuse* as to *fuse* the word with the thing, as a child might identify a doll as the person whom the doll represented; from this identification of word and object, both primitive person and child often attribute supernatural power to the word. For them the power of the actual thing resides in its designation, in its name; words are thus divine, not merely *symbols* standing for the thing — as the word is for civilized man, for whom it seems to have lost its magical force — but the thing itself. In a sense, however, any serious user of language shares the primitive view. This writer or speaker will employ words with a veneration not divorced from the supernatural, using them as a bridge of revelation to connect imagination and the world of external reality.

Many linguists insist that all language is symbolic, for reduced to its simplest terms a symbol is defined as something that stands for something else. The symbol in language, as we define it here, calls to mind *sensory images* of that "something else": if we are trying to explain *beauty,* for example, we may draw upon the image of the *rose,* for it conjures up *images* of the blooming flower and, through convention and inherent qualities, it suggests the *idea* of beauty. This need for symbolic indirection lies behind a good deal of literature. In the poem referred to previously, Stevens is trying to suggest a number of complex meanings — *beauty* is one, but life and death and their permanence-impermanence

> A sphere appears in my dream . . . and becomes a ball, a familiar childhood toy I had forgotten. At once the dream begins to heap up associations around this ball. It plays exuberantly with the word "ball" . . . with every possible rhyme, pun, slang connotation, homonym. . . . Out of this chaos of imagery and word-play, the dreaming mind rapidly improvises a strange dramatic coherence all its own, a totally original story in which everything echoes everything else and each thing rapidly slides off toward secondary and lateral associations. And perhaps, if this is one of those rare luminous dreams that can haunt the memory for years, there will be a ball that begins to glow and swell until it becomes a splendid, shimmering globe, bright as the sun, transparent as glass . . . a celestial orb . . . a crystalline sphere . . . The Hermetic world-egg. . . . By way of the dream, I am delving to the root meaning which has made the sphere "somehow" the uniquely right symbol of perfection for people everywhere.
>
> — Theodore Roszak, *Where the Wasteland Ends* (1973)

are also involved. One *symbol* Stevens uses to suggest some of these meanings is music; another symbol for these (and other) meanings is a young woman, the Susanna who figures in an apocryphal story of the Bible. Stevens uses these symbols (*music, girl*) because he simply cannot *explain* these meanings in ways the symbols can — nor can we in discussing the poem, so we suggest you look up and read the poem for all the meanings and dimensions — its "portals" we have left untraced.

There is another important school of thought concerning symbolism: attitudes associated with Jerome Bruner, Susanne Langer, Jean Piaget, and others suggest that reality itself is symbolic. That is why so much of our use of symbolism remains invisible to us: it *is* our reality, at least the only reality we know, so we do not easily notice any difference between symbol and "reality" symbolized. What Carlos Castenada and others suggest is that "alternate realities" exist. They exist because the human mind is capable of constructing them through intricate, interlocking systems of symbols. Uri Geller and Ceylonese fire walkers may be fakes or illusionists at best — though, in the case of the latter, there is no doubt that men and women have walked over beds of coals reaching a temperature of nearly 1500°C. But what phenomena such as parapsychology and firewalking suggest is that for us the world *is* only a set of symbols. If we change the symbols, we change our reality. Words *are* magic. Be careful with them.

> Man's efforts at creating a meaningful way of life in accord with the laws of nature have led to the view of himself as the microcosm. Through contemplating his very form and the nature of his existence, man has often found a correspondence or series of correspondences to the workings of the cosmos as a whole — the macrocosm. This perception is at the base of many symbolic systems. If man conceives of himself as a microcosm, his way of life and community also take on the character of a cosmic order. Inherent in this idea is an intuition of the basic harmony of the universe and of man's desire to realize himself accordingly. If nature is a harmony and man a part of nature, then man himself must be innately harmonic. The laws governing his mind and body reflect and partake of the functioning of greater nature.
>
> — José and Miriam Argüelles, *Mandala* (1972)

OTHER FIGURES OF SPEECH

Figures of speech provide alternative ways to clarify, intensify, and emphasize a particular point or idea. Aspects of imagery, metaphor, and symbol can be used for rhetorical and rhythmical purposes. The figures most closely associated with prose are *personification, allusion, paradox, irony, pun, synecdoche,* and *metonymy.*

Personification occurs when we attribute human or animate qualities to inanimate objects, as in the following:

> Then as the girls grew more sophisticated, as they acclimated themselves to the throbbing pulse of a cosmopolitan city, their attentions naturally switched to bus drivers.
>
> — Richard Brautigan

> Some lands are flat and grass-covered, and smile so evenly up at the sun that they seem forever youthful, untouched by man or time.
>
> — Loren Eiseley

> But words came halting forth, wanting Invention's stay;
> Invention, Nature's child, fled step-dame Study's blows.
>
> — Sir Philip Sidney

Allusion is the reference to a person, place, or thing either historical or literary that contributes to the understanding of the particular subject:

> The alternative to mind is certainly madness. Our greatest blessings, says Socrates in the *Phaedrus,* come to us by way of madness — provided, he adds, that the madness comes from a god.
>
> — Norman O. Brown

> I used to spend a lot of time worrying over word order, trying to create beautiful passages. I still believe in the value of a handsome style. I appreciate the sensibility which can produce a nice turn of phrase, like Scott Fitzgerald.
>
> — William Styron

> The novelist Henry James once remarked that "Americans are, as Americans, the most self-conscious people in the world." In this self-consciousness is imbedded the feeling that Americans are not only different as a peculiar people from Britons as peculiarly British, or from Russians as peculiarly Russian, but are superior. This belief is part of the special American attitude. We pride ourselves on our Americanism. We stigmatize attitudes we dislike, and values we condemn, by terming them "un-American." It would be easy to pick out of our past political history oratory and journalism expressions of Yankee boastfulness, of the Jefferson Brick braggadocio about being ready to whip universal natur' that Dickens satirized after his first visit to the United States. This belongs to our outgrown past. But the attitude persists.
>
> — Allan Nevins, *The Tradition of the Future*

Paradox is a statement that appears contradictory but may be really true:

> The longest way round is the shortest way home.

> Although we have the money and technology to send a man to the moon, we cannot solve the problems of our cities.

The following poem, written by a sixteenth-century poet, is built on a series of paradoxes:

Description on the Contrarious Passions

I find no peace, and all my war is done;
I fear and hope, I burn and freeze like ice;
I fly aloft yet can I nor arise;
And nought I have, and all the world I seize on,
That locks nor looseth, holdeth me in prison,
And holds me not, yet can I 'scape no wise:
Nor letteth me live, nor die at my devise,
And yet of death it giveth me occasion.
Without eye I see; without tongue I plain:
I wish to perish yet I ask for health;
I love another, and I hate myself;
I feed me in sorrow, and laugh in all my pain.
   Lo, thus displeaseth me both death and life;
   And my delight is causer of this strife.

— Sir Thomas Wyatt

Irony is saying one thing and implying something else, usually the opposite meaning of the word:

For Brutus is an *honorable* man;
So are they all, all *honorable* men.

— William Shakespeare

It is a very justifiable cause of war to invade a country after the people have been wasted by famine, destroyed by pestilence, or embroiled by factions among themselves. It is justifiable to enter into war against our nearest ally, when one of his towns lies convenient for us, or a territory of land, that would render our dominions round and complete. If a prince sends forces into a nation where the people are poor and ignorant, he may lawfully put half of them to death, and make slaves of the rest, in order to civilize and reduce them from their barbarous way of living.

— Jonathan Swift, *Gulliver's Travels*

A celebrated example of irony is Jonathan Swift's "A Modest Proposal," in which he ironically argues that Irish children should be fattened for the English meat trade.

Punning is a play on words. The device is found in a lot of contemporary advertising:

RCA — A *sound* tradition.

The medium is the *message*.

— Marshall McLuhan

The instance of the electric light may prove *illuminating* in this connection.

— Marshall McLuhan

Synecdoche is a figure of speech in which a part stands for a whole or a whole stands for a part:

Give us this day our daily *bread*.

The United States has the largest supply of *arms* (weapons) in the world.

It is the judgment of the *court* that the defendant is innocent.

Metonymy is an expression in which a word associated with another thing is substituted for that other word:

He addressed his remarks to the *chair*.

The Boston Red Sox have a good *bench* this year.

The military *brass* opposes the arms cutback.

These figures of speech, which do not always seem rational or logical, make writing more vivid in much the same way any concrete language will. Each provides a handle on the abstract from our experience. Personification, as in the sentence from Eiseley (page 158), gives a human image to the nonhuman and by doing so bridges a vast gap immediately. Allusion draws our attention to examples, details, or specific items about which we may know a great deal and which we can bring quickly into the circle of meaning. Puns at first lead our attention away from the real meaning, but after one false step they bring us quickly, sometimes abruptly, often humorously, back to it. We bring these figures of speech to your attention so that you can be aware of devices that go beyond logic and reason to achieve unexpected vividness and clarification.

SOUNDS

Sounds in writing are characteristically associated with the meter, rhyme, and alliteration of poetry, but there are times when sounds — the oral-aural elements of language — become important in prose as well. We have suggested several techniques that can affect the aural

> An artist organizes a whole work, with beginning, middle, and end, so it is usually possible to figure out what the various parts are accomplishing — whether the choice of words, the syntax, the metaphor, the connotations, the tone and rhythm, the narrative or dramatic manner. And of course a literary work is a concrete whole of speech that stands fixed, is repeatable, lets itself be examined closely.
>
> — Paul Goodman, *Speaking and Language* (1971)

character and rhythm of writing, including balanced and parallel sentence structures, coordinating conjunctions, imagery, and metaphor. To these can be added the sound patterns formed by alliteration, assonance, and occasionally even rhyme. The end result of using aural imagery and patterns of sound should be to make sound and sense combine to achieve the rhetorical purposes desired.

Alliteration (the repetition of similar consonant sounds) can help to achieve a particular rhythm, tying single words into manageable, memorable groups, usually of no more than two or three in a sequence. In Thoreau's "The mass of men lead lives of quiet desperation" the rhythm is achieved by clustering three groups of sound patterns:

> The mass of men
> lead lives
> of quiet desperation.

Thoreau's use of sound patterns helps to give the sentence its power and flow. Thoreau's alliteration, like that of the sports-writer and other writers for popular audiences, picks up the major pattern of aural emphasis found in Anglo-Saxon poetry, suggesting that there is something intrinsic to alliteration in English. "Poetry and Power" has an alliterative title, and in his speech John F. Kennedy also uses alliteration frequently. He heightens the rhythmic effect of language when he uses phrases such as "prized by politicians," "when power corrupts, poetry cleanses," "intrusive society and an officious state," and "pursuing his perceptions." On another sound level, that associated with the repetition of vowel sounds (assonance), Kennedy again is sensitive to the aural rhythms of the spoken word. Note the repetition of the long "e" sound in the following paragraph from the same speech:

He brought an unsparing instinct for reality to bear on the platitudes and pieties of society. His sense of the human tragedy fortified him against self-deception and easy consolation.

Not only does the repetition of a sound (either through alliteration or assonance) intensify the rhythm; it also subtly acts as a structural device to tie words and sentences and even paragraphs together.

A concern for sound in small and subtle ways certainly helps the rhythmic effect of our language and style. Even rhyming words at times can be an effective way to achieve an intense rhythm. The following sentence by Emerson was constructed as prose, not verse:

A foolish consistency is the hobgoblin of little minds,
adored by little statesmen and philosophers and divines.

Obviously, the more poetic you want to be with your language, as Emerson is, the more you must concern yourself with sound patterns. It can be overdone, however. Too much attention to sound can draw our attention away from the content. Sound can overwhelm sense, so we must be careful not to use alliteration, assonance, and rhyme simply for the sake of the sounds. The aural element must be used in an integral way to enhance the content of the writing.

EXERCISES

Analyze the relationship between sound and sense (meaning) in the following excerpts:

1.   And ever and anon with host to host
    Shocks, and the splintering spear, the hard mail hewn,
    Shield-breakings, and the clash of brands, the crash
    Of battle axes on shattered helms, and shrieks
    After the Christ, of those who falling down
    Looked up for heaven, and only saw the mist.

    — Tennyson, *Idyls of the King*

2. Everything was alive about them, flashing, splashing, and passing, ships moving, tugs panting, hawsers taut, barges going down with men toiling at the sweeps, the water all a-swirl with the wash of the shipping,

scaling into millions of little wavelets, curling and frothing under the whip of the unceasing wind.

— H. G. Wells

3. The first stanza of "Dover Beach" on page 91.

4. After all these years I can picture that old time to myself now, just as it was then: the white town drowsing in the sunshine of a summer's morning; the streets empty, or pretty nearly so; one or two clerks sitting in front of the Water Street stores, with their splint-bottomed chairs tilted back against the walls, chins on breasts, hats slouched over their faces, asleep — with shingle shavings enough around to show what broke them down; a sow and a litter of pigs loafing along the sidewalk, doing a good business in watermelon rinds and seeds; two or three lonely little freight piles scattered about the "levee"; a pile of "skids" on the slope of the stone-paved wharf, and the fragrant town drunkard asleep in the shadow of them; two or three wood flats at the head of the wharf, but nobody to listen to the peaceful lapping of the wavelets against them; the great Mississippi, the majestic, the magnificent Mississippi, rolling its mile-wide tide along, shining in the sun; the dense forests away on the other side; the "point" above the town, and the "point" below, bounding the river-glimpse and turning it into a sort of sea, and withal a very still and brilliant and lonely one.

— Mark Twain, *Life on the Mississippi*

5.   But oh! that deep romantic chasm which slanted
     Down the green hill athwart a cedarn cover!
     A savage place! as holy and enchanted
     As e'er beneath a waning moon was haunted
     By woman wailing for her demon lover!

— Coleridge, "Kubla Khan"

6. The passage by Steinbeck on page 163.

7. The passage by Joyce on page 133.

RHETORICAL ANALYSIS OF STYLE

*Whether we favor one tradition or another is finally irrelevant.
What does matter is the influential nature of our stylistic
heritage, for language is the basis of thought, and
it follows from this truth that inherited forms of expression
will inevitably perpetuate the forms of thought associated
with them. When we recognize that it can ultimately shape
our beliefs and the beliefs of other men, we assume
the responsibility of mastering style lest we be mastered by it.*

CARL KLAUS
Style in English Prose
(1968)

We have defined *style* as the way we achieve rhythm in language and *rhythm* as the variation of repetition achieved on all levels of structure. As it applies specifically to style, rhythm can be isolated and controlled by the writer. Perhaps the best way to get further acquainted with and thus to understand techniques of rhythm is through reading. If we can recognize the stylistic techniques used to achieve rhythm by other writers, we can use these techniques as models and experiment with them in our own writing. There are writers for whom we have an affinity and who can become our "teachers," much as we might imitate Henry Aaron's batting stance, the humor of W. C. Fields, or Liv Ullman's acting style. We turn to those writers who are trying to do the same things we want to do and who feel about things the way we do. These will be our models. It is not a matter of subjugating our style to that of another but of recognizing certain techniques that might be useful to our purposes and ideas.

We have treated matters of style primarily on the levels of *words* and *sentences,* for each of these levels has its own contributions to make toward stylistic rhythm. The stylistic effects of sentences and words can be examined in your own writing and the writings of others. The following outline may be helpful in your studies of the elements associated with each level:

I. Sentences
   A. Grammatical qualities (simple, compound, complex)
   B. Rhetorical qualities (loose, periodic, balance)

    C. Sentence openers
    D. Sentence lengths
 II. Words
    A. Tone
    B. Formal and informal voice
    C. Denotation and connotation
    D. Abstract and concrete
    E. Image, metaphor, symbol, and figures of speech
    F. Sounds — alliteration, assonance, and rhyme

Any sentence, paragraph, or complete essay or speech can be analyzed for its stylistic features; you discover for yourself how each level contributes to an overall effect. The rhetorical effectiveness of Thoreau's sentence cited earlier ("The mass of men lead lives of quiet desperation") is achieved primarily on the levels of word and sound, for it is not structure per se but sound patterning (*m*ass, *m*en; *l*ead *l*ives) and verbal counterpoint (*quiet* vs. *desperation*) that make the sentence effective. On the other hand, the following sentence by Jonathan Swift, from *Gulliver's Travels,* achieves its rhetorical effectiveness on the level of sentence structure, which sets up the sense of surprise that comes at sentence end: "She was very good-natured, and not above forty foot high, being little for her age."

   In the following paragraph by Thoreau, we can see how a writer's style integrates the different levels and effects:

[1]I have paid no poll-tax for six years. [2]I was put into a jail once on this account, for one night; and, as I stood considering the walls of solid stone, two or three feet thick, the door of wood and iron, a foot thick, and the iron grating which strained the light, I could not help being struck with the foolishness of that institution which treated me as if I were mere flesh and blood and bones, to be locked up. [3]I wondered that it should have concluded at length that this was the best use it could put me to, and had never thought to avail itself of my services in some way. [4]I saw that, if there was a wall of stone between me and my townsmen, there was a still more difficult one to climb or break through before they could get to be as free as I was. [5]I did not for a moment feel confined, and the walls seemed a great waste of stone and mortar. [6]I felt as if I alone of all my townsmen had paid my tax. [7]They plainly did not know how to treat me, but behaved like persons who are underbred. [8]In every threat and in every compliment there was a blunder; for they thought that my chief desire was to stand the other side of that stone wall. [9]I could not but smile to see how industriously they locked the door on my meditations, which followed them out again without let or hindrance, and *they* were really all that was dangerous. [10]As

they could not reach me, they had resolved to punish my body; just as boys, if they cannot come at some person against whom they have a spite, will abuse his dog. [11]I saw that the State was half-witted, that it was timid as a lone woman with her silver spoons, and that it did not know its friends from its foes, and I lost all my remaining respect for it, and pitied it.

— Henry David Thoreau, *Civil Disobedience*

Let us look at Thoreau's sentences first. Grammatically, the sentences range from the simple (and short) one that opens the paragraph to the intricate compound-complex concluding sentence. About half (five) of the eleven sentences are of the compound-complex type, accounting in large part for the varied rhythms created by the sound-unit lengths occurring within the clauses and phrases. For instance, the first sentence is balanced in its length and directness of syntax with the first clause of sentence 2, the trailing modifier "for one night" being set off from that opening rhythm and setting up the basic content of the remainder of the paragraph (a description of the sights, feelings, and thoughts of that one night). The second clause of this same sentence sets up an intricate verbal rhythm, which might be marked off this way:

and, as I stood considering
the walls of solid stone,
two or three feet thick,
the door of wood and iron,
a foot thick,
and the iron grating which strained the light,
I could not help being struck with the foolishness of that institution
which treated me as if I were mere flesh and blood and bones,
to be locked up.

This clause is by itself a complex sentence, periodic in its rhetorical structure, holding off the main idea ("I could not help . . .") behind a series of balanced sets of details that make Thoreau's tone more ironic when he gets to the word *foolishness* and the "mere flesh and blood and bones" (contrasted to *stone,* and *wood* and *iron*) the institution would lock up. These two sentences, with their three independent clauses, introduce the main content of the paragraph and lead to the series of parallel sentences that follow:

[3]I wondered . . . and had never thought . . .
[4]I saw that . . .
[5]I did not . . . and the walls seemed . . .
[6]I felt . . .

Sentence 6, concluding this sequence and leading into the shift of subject (from Thoreau to "townsmen") in sentences 7 and 8, is the exact middle of the paragraph; it very neatly returns to the *simple* structure of sentence 1 and seemingly contradicts its flat statement: *I paid no poll-tax* versus *I alone had paid my tax.* After sentence 6, the paragraph's sentences flatten out somewhat in rhythm, sentence 4 being *balanced* and *compound,* 8 again *compound,* 9 *compound* (and *loose* in its first clause), and 10 *compound-complex* (and *periodic* in its second clause). Only sentence 11, concluding the paragraph, comes close to matching the rhythmical intricacy of the first half of the paragraph, doing so no doubt because it is played off against sentence 2. Even so, the last sentence is only a compound of three independent clauses, the first of which happens to have three direct objects in parallel form. The sentence, schematized, looks like this:

> — I saw
>   that the State was half-witted,
>   that it was timid as a lone woman with her silver spoons,
>   and that it did not know its friends from its foes,
> — and I lost all my remaining respect for it,
> — and pitied it.

Words in Thoreau's paragraph can be looked at more quickly. The patterning of sentence 2 has already suggested that one use of words in the paragraph is to establish principles of contrast or counterpoint. So *stone, wood, iron,* and *mortar* are set against *flesh, blood, bones,* and *body.* Thoreau's words here might at first glance suggest his theme is the strength of one set of items versus the weakness of the other, but if one reads carefully one sees the crucial "*as if* I were *mere.* . . ." The contrast must work on some other principle, then, but what is it? What is stronger than the materials of the jail? What does the jail signify? That those inside are less free than those outside? Normally, but Thoreau's irony turns this premise upside down, so that his imprisonment means freedom and the townsmen's freedom means confinement. Thoreau's thoughts, his *meditations,* are what allow him to be free, and so we begin to realize that the crucial sets of words in the paragraph are those that identify *material* objects, considered potent or valuable, and immaterial or spiritual or mental conditions. Thoreau, of course, values the latter and makes the proper response to them a question of breeding, of human and humane dignity, leaving us with words such as *behaved, underbred, blunder, dangerous, punish, body, boys, spite, abuse, dog, half-witted, friends, foes, respect,* and *pitied.* Only three figures of speech contribute

The present writer, who has done some fieldwork in the mushy ground of the vast pampas of printed matter, can confirm that much that is daily written is of an almost intolerable dullness and ineptitude, and is socially very inefficient and wasteful, especially in the fields of science and technology. A very large amount of language-use has become institutionalized, so that much of its own conventions and styles needs some kind of documentation and description, if what is happening to our language is to be fully understood. Moreover, electronic aids to communication have speeded up, intensified and proliferated language-uses, both in the spoken and the written media, so that, again, some kind of disinterested documentation and, possibly, criticism are needed to make explicit, and give a means of assessing the value of, the kinds of cultural influences to which people are subjected. A study of style, in this sense, is an assistance to a rational statement of what society is doing with its language.

— A. E. Darbyshire, *A Grammar of Style* (1971)

much to this paragraph, and they contribute along the same lines: in sentence 2 the iron grating "strained the light," an image suggesting the effect of a material object upon an immaterial one; in sentence 10 there is the simile/analogy of the boys who would abuse a dog in the way the State would abuse a thinking rebel's body; and in sentence 11 there is the simile of the timid, lone woman locked up with her silver spoons, as if they were her most valuable possessions, more valuable than her life or her spirit. Go back and reread Thoreau. Note the irony, the rhythm, the wit of the paragraph, and the concrete and connotative use of language, and see if someday you can write a passage as fine as Thoreau's.

John F. Kennedy's "Inaugural Address" is a speech accessible to analysis in stylistic terms. Partly because it is a reading script and partly because it is subject to the conventions of modern printing, the address is broken into smaller, more manageable units than Thoreau's paragraph. Pick out a unit of Kennedy's prose and work with it as we have Thoreau's in order to see what is going on in it:

Inaugural Address

Vice President Johnson, Mr. Speaker, Mr. Chief Justice, President Eisenhower, Vice President Nixon, President Truman, Reverend Clergy, Fellow Citizens:

[1]We observe today not a victory of party but a celebration of freedom — symbolizing an end as well as a beginning — signifying renewal as well as change. For I have sworn before you and Almighty God the same solemn oath our forebears prescribed nearly a century and three quarters ago.

[2]The world is very different now. For man holds in his mortal hands the power to abolish all forms of human poverty and all forms of human life. And yet the same revolutionary beliefs for which our forebears fought are still at issue around the globe — the belief that the rights of man come not from the generosity of the state but from the hand of God.

[3]We dare not forget today that we are the heirs of that first revolution. Let the word go forth from this time and place, to friend and foe alike, that the torch has been passed to a new generation of Americans — born in this century, tempered by war, disciplined by a hard and bitter peace, proud of our ancient heritage — and unwilling to witness or permit the slow undoing of those human rights to which this Nation has always been committed, and to which we are committed today at home and around the world.

[4]Let every nation know, whether it wishes us well or ill, that we shall pay any price, bear any burden, meet any hardship, support any friend, oppose any foe to assure the survival and the success of liberty.

[5]This much we pledge — and more.

[6]To those old allies whose cultural and spiritual origins we share, we pledge the loyalty of faithful friends. United, there is little we cannot do in a host of cooperative ventures. Divided, there is little we can do — for we dare not meet a powerful challenge at odds and split asunder.

[7]To those new states whom we welcome to the ranks of the free, we pledge our word that one form of colonial control shall not have passed away merely to be replaced by a far more iron tyranny. We shall not always expect to find them supporting our view. But we shall always hope to find them strongly supporting their own freedom — and to remember that, in the past, those who foolishly sought power by riding the back of the tiger ended up inside.

[8]To those peoples in the huts and villages of half the globe struggling to break the bonds of mass misery, we pledge our best efforts to help them help themselves, for whatever period is required — not because the Communists may be doing it, not because we seek their votes, but because it is right. If a free society cannot help the many who are poor, it cannot save the few who are rich.

[9]To our sister republics south of our border, we offer a special pledge — to convert our good words into good deeds — in a new alliance for progress — to assist free men and free governments in casting off the

chains of poverty. But this peaceful revolution of hope cannot become the prey of hostile powers. Let all our neighbors know that we shall join with them to oppose aggression or subversion anywhere in the Americas. And let every other power know that this hemisphere intends to remain the master of its own house.

[10]To that world assembly of sovereign states, the United Nations, our last best hope in an age where the instruments of war have far outpaced the instruments of peace, we renew our pledge of support — to prevent it from becoming merely a forum for invective — to strengthen its shield of the new and the weak — and to enlarge the area in which its writ may run.

[11]Finally, to those nations who would make themselves our adversary, we offer not a pledge but a request: that both sides begin anew the quest for peace, before the dark powers of destruction unleashed by science engulf all humanity in planned or accidental self-destruction.

[12]We dare not tempt them with weakness. For only when our arms are sufficient beyond doubt can we be certain beyond doubt that they will never be employed.

[13]But neither can two great and powerful groups of nations take comfort from our present course — both sides overburdened by the cost of modern weapons, both rightly alarmed by the steady spread of the deadly atom, yet both racing to alter that uncertain balance of terror that stays the hand of mankind's final war.

[14]So let us begin anew — remembering on both sides that civility is not a sign of weakness, and sincerity is always subject to proof. Let us never negotiate out of fear. But let us never fear to negotiate.

[15]Let both sides explore what problems unite us instead of belaboring those problems which divide us.

[16]Let both sides, for the first time, formulate serious and precise proposals for the inspection and control of arms — and bring the absolute power to destroy other nations under the absolute control of all nations.

[17]Let both sides seek to invoke the wonders of science instead of its terrors. Together let us explore the stars, conquer the deserts, eradicate disease, tap the ocean depths, and encourage the arts and commerce.

[18]Let both sides unite to heed in all corners of the earth the command of Isaiah — to "undo the heavy burdens and to let the oppressed go free."

[19]And if a beachhead of cooperation may push back the jungle of suspicion, let both sides join in creating a new endeavor, not a new balance of power, but a new world of law, where the strong are just and the weak secure and the peace preserved.

[20]*All this will not be finished in the first 100 days. Nor will it be finished in the first 1,000 days, nor in the life of this administration, nor even perhaps in our lifetime on this planet. But let us begin.*

²¹ In your hands, my fellow citizens, more than in mine, will rest the final success or failure of our course. Since this country was founded, each generation of Americans has been summoned to give testimony to its national loyalty. The graves of young Americans who answered the call to service are found around the globe.

²²Now the trumpet summons us again — not as a call to bear arms, though arms we need; not as a call to battle, though embattled we are; but a call to bear the burden of a long twilight struggle, year in, and year out, "rejoicing in hope, patient in tribulation" — a struggle against the common enemies of man: tyranny, poverty, disease, and war itself.

²³Can we forge against these enemies a grand and global alliance, North and South, East and West, that can assure a more fruitful life for all mankind? Will you join in that historic effort?

²⁴In the long history of the world, only a few generations have been granted the role of defending freedom in its hour of maximum danger. I do not shrink from this responsibility — I welcome it. I do not believe that any of us would exchange places with any other people or any other generation. The energy, the faith, the devotion which we bring to this endeavor will light our country and all who serve it — and the glow from that fire can truly light the world.

²⁵ *And so, my fellow Americans, ask not what your country can do for you: Ask what you can do for your country.*

²⁶ *My fellow citizens of the world: Ask not what America will do for you, but what together we can do for the freedom of man.*

²⁷ Finally, whether you are citizens of America or citizens of the world, ask of us the same high standards of strength and sacrifice which we ask of you. With a good conscience our only sure reward, with history the final judge of our deeds, let us go forth to lead the land we love, asking His blessing and His help, but knowing that here on earth God's work must truly be our own.

— John F. Kennedy

Like "Poetry and Power," the address is a good example of the Kennedy style. The blending of a variety of grammatical sentence structures, the predominant rhetorical structure of balance and antithesis (see paragraphs 3, 6, 7, 8, 15, and 25 for good examples), the variety of sentence lengths (from 4 words to 80), the simplicity of diction, with a high proportion of monosyllabic words (71 per cent), the repetition of key terms ("pledge" and "peace"), the figures of speech, which create concreteness ("the torch," "chains of poverty," "corners of the earth," "the trumpet," "the glow from that fire," "iron tyranny"), and the sounds generated from alliterative patterns (see paragraphs 10 and 27) — all contribute to give the speech a harmonious, rhythmic quality which places it squarely in the tradition of commemorative oration with "The Gettysburg Address." Of these stylistic features, the one most characteristic of Kennedy's style (and perhaps also of commemorative oration) is the use of balance and antithesis. It gives him the opportunity to compare opposites (end-beginning, old-new, rich-poor, friend-enemy), but at the same time it indirectly indicates through the parallel and balanced structures that opposites can be reconciled. Kennedy establishes this stylistic feature in his first sentence, and brings it to a dramatic conclusion in the famous ". . . ask not what your country can do for you: Ask what you can do for your country." This latter sentence is a good index of the style of the address and that type of oration expected of statesmen and leaders of the people. Few of us will ever be called upon to compose such an address, but each of us can learn something of the power of language from the poetry of Kennedy's address. Before we consider imitating his style, we must consider Kennedy's purpose and his audience. He was speaking to *and* for a nation; he hoped to give expression to its noblest ideals and goals. In so doing he had to resort to the formality, the generality, the stateliness of the style of *eloquence*.

EXERCISES

1. Using the stylistic guidelines on page 187, write a stylistic analysis of a passage (several paragraphs) from a writer whose work you like. Indicate the relationship between the author's style and the substance of the piece. Hand in the passage with your analysis.

2. Write an essay on a topic of your choice in which you employ some of the key aspects of the writer's style you analyzed in the previous assignment.

5

⁓ SOUND AND SIGHT: ⁓
A NEW RHETORIC?

*Before the printing press,
the young learned by listening, watching, doing.
So, until recently, our own rural children
learned the language and skills of their elders.
Learning took place outside the classroom.
Only those aiming at professional careers went to school at all.
Today in our cities, most learning occurs outside the classroom.
The sheer quantity of information conveyed by press-
magazines-film-TV-radio far exceeds the quantity of information
conveyed by school instruction and texts. This challenge
has destroyed the monopoly of the book as a teaching aid
and cracked the very walls of the classroom
so suddenly that we're
confused, baffled.*

MARSHALL McLUHAN
"Classroom Without Walls"
(1960)

THE SPOKEN WORD

English is a mass medium.
All languages are mass media. The mass media — film,
radio, TV — are new languages,
their grammars as yet unknown. Each codifies
reality differently; each conceals
a unique metaphysics.

EDMUND CARPENTER
"The New Languages"
(1960)

One of the characteristics of language that we tend to neglect in our literate culture is the unique power of the *spoken* word. We often are such prisoners of literate culture that we find it difficult to accept the spoken word for what it is. If we think of speech at all, we see it as a poor substitute for writing, as something that would be better written down. We have come to this view as a result of grammars, dictionaries, the study of language history, the favored legal status of writing, and the pervasive sense of power conveyed by print. Grammars, while codifying what actually goes on in spoken language, give us the impression that patterns of language are set in concrete. Dictionaries, though recording both written and spoken language, have also made us believe that the meanings of words are unchanging, inflexible — if you can "look it up," you know *your* meaning is the only proper one. Histories of language lead one to the notion that language has no existence until written down. No history can be built upon spoken language before it has been translated into permanent, visual symbols. With the electronic equipment we have today we can record history, but that equipment is of no help to us in studying Indo-European language (see Appendix for a history of the English language). And yet the absence of writing in a culture does not mean that no spoken language exists.

Thus, certain indicators point to the supremacy of written language, but it is indisputable that for centuries before the written word we had only the spoken word. We would not suggest going back to a preliterate condition. We would suggest that one must understand something of the consequences of speech and literacy. The uses made of and the choices available in language communication create distinctive world views. Social scientists tend to separate societies into two broad categories. These are defined in part by language use. Howard Becker classified societies as either "sacred" or "secular," while Robert Redfield divided them into "folk" and "urban." One of the features of Becker's "sacred" and Redfield's "folk" societies is their almost total reliance on the spoken word. A classic study of a "folk" or "sacred" culture is Margaret Mead's *Sex and Temperament*, an analysis of the Arapesh society in New Guinea. Some characteristics of the Arapesh society, Mead noted, are the individual's concern for intimate and personal (primary) relationships, a willingness to express an emotional response, and a feeling for the sacred and the mysterious in life and nature. Interestingly enough, Theodore Roszak, in *The Making of a Counterculture* and *Where the Wasteland Ends*, and Charles Reich, in *The Greening of America*, both suggest that many of the same cultural characteristics found in the Arapesh and other oral societies can be found in an emerging counter-culture here in the United States. The emergence of these features in America could well be a result of the return of the spoken word. In our electronic media-oriented society, we have returned in some ways to a language orientation similar to that found in preliterate societies. The upshot is that the spoken word and *sound* itself have again gained a considerable prominence in our lives. We are no longer convinced that "reality" and "truth" come out of books, out of print only.

A THEORY OF THE SPOKEN WORD

The word is something that happens, an event in the world of sound through which the mind is enabled to relate actuality to itself.

WALTER ONG

The Presence of the Word

(1967)

In our culture, we move in a vast environment of electronically communicated language, and that language is oral in form and effect. This is not to say ours is primarily an oral culture, since it is apparent that there is a proliferation of the print media also. But what this means, according to Walter Ong, is that we are a culture with a "secondary" orality. Ong indicates that the "secondary" form imposed upon the primary visual form of print appears to be creating a total linguistic environment (i.e., language is all around us). That environment, Ong further indicates, is in the process of altering cultural and perceptual patterns. If this is so, then the question has to be asked, "What effect has the spoken word on a culture?"

Reliance on the spoken word affects our concepts of truth, history, mind, and language itself. In an oral culture, Ong says, the word is a unique happening; it is the only event that can put an individual into contact with actuality and truth. Because it is impossible in a nonliterate society to look up something, one can have no recourse to *history* as we understand it, based upon records and documents. Whatever "history" exists is a verbal fabric woven of the oral myths of the culture. These myths exist not in written texts but through the collective memory, the "re-collective" skills of a culture's members. Memory is therefore highly prized in oral cultures. There is little doubt that individuals in an oral culture have a far more sophisticated memory than we have in our technological society. When we forget something, we can probably retrieve it from the books in a library, but for an oral society the only information storehouse is the human mind. Because of the importance of memory, language too is affected. Language in an oral culture is often characterized by striking figures that function as much to assist recall as to evoke images. The substance of the language, moreover, generally reflects the life situation, and the working vocabulary of an individual offers a contact with actuality.

The spoken word — the word as *sound* — also affects a group's concept of itself, says Ong. There is, he says, a drive toward "group sense" and toward participatory activities in an oral environment. The reason for this phenomenon is found in the nature of sound itself.

Virtually everyone in a preliterate tribe is a specialist in the oral tradition. Eggan reports that in the remote islands of the Philippines messages are conveyed orally with an accuracy fabulous to us, aware as we are that a message or rumor need only pass through two or three persons before becoming unrecognizable. For these tribesmen, words are like buckets in a fire brigade, to be handled with full attention, while we feel we can afford to be careless with the spoken word, backstopped as we are by the written one.

— David Riesman, "The Oral and Written Traditions" (1960)

Sound is more real or existential, or perhaps only more insistent, than sight — the other main sense (reading) involved with language. A momentary sound, because it disappears as it is perceived, adheres specifically to one moment and, if we pay attention to it, absorbs us totally into a constantly evolving present. Something mysterious in the powers of sound captures us, in music or song or chants or spells. Words spoken become powerful tools for magic. Saying evil things of another, in most oral cultures, is thought to bring that person direct physical harm, in the same way as a voodoo man's sticking pins in a doll-like image of an enemy. One consequence of approaching words as having magic and mystery is a culture abounding in charms and magic formulas that create a religious aura in the community. Participation in patterned sound — music, recitation, cheers — lifts one outside oneself and creates a feeling of identity with others and the specific environment (often a temple, a stage, or a stadium). Above all, sound — as any good cheerleader or sound engineer at a rock concert knows — has the power to unite groups as nothing else can. It demands a response from others and thereby creates a shared awareness in the community. The spoken word as sound is reciprocal, for its very existence demands not one but two persons, a sender and a receiver, vibrations coded and vibrations recorded. Spoken words move from the interior of one person to the interior of another, from speaker to receiver, and under the best conditions create a sense of living exchange among persons, in much the same way that the noises of a forest often suggest life and, hence, animism — perhaps the most common "religion" of oral cultures.

What we appear to have today, Walter Ong says, is a language environment that has regained some of the characteristics of nonliterate oral cultures. These characteristics have manifested themselves in widely divergent ways. One of the most singular gatherings of our time is what has become known as the Woodstock phenomenon. In August of 1969 in Bethel, New York, the Woodstock Music and Art Fair occurred. Many words have been said and written describing the event, but most of them say something about it as "history's largest happening," with a "unique sense of community." Its expression as a communal event is characteristic of an oral culture. And no doubt it was the sounds themselves that brought over 400,000 people together. As the sounds of the words and music flowed over and into the audience, the reaction was simultaneous, instantaneous, all at once. This all-at-onceness, according to psychoanalyst Rollo May, created a bond, forged a chain of togetherness, fulfilled a yearning for community on the part of the participants. The same kind of experience, but at a great distance from the non-polemical music festival, can happen when an effective speaker com-

> A great many writers of fiction can trace the beginnings of their craft to their listening as children to family stories, to tangled yarns about their forebears, or to episodes of glamour or of farce or of dreadful tragedy involving living kinsmen and collateral branches still resident in County Clare or removed to Puget Sound. . . . Nearly everyone is told these tribal sagas and romances and parables; and everyone is in a sense a storyteller.
>
> — Jean Stafford, "Wordman, Spare That Tree!" (1974)

municates to a responsive audience. During the 1972 presidential election Shirley Chisholm's deep commitment to, and expert use of, oral language gave her effective control over her audiences. Frequently, as her speeches developed, her audiences would begin to sway to her verbal rhythms. Her effect — like that of the old-fashioned preacher — was achieved through the devices of sound; indeed, she was creating a kind of music.

In the emerging counter-culture, Roszak and Reich report there is a new level of consciousness, a new awareness. This awareness includes a concern for inner-directed values, a search for mystery and sacredness in everyday experience, a concern for people rather than things, a deep commitment to community, and a desire to embrace the imaginative and the emotional aspects of human experience. All of these goals or concerns or values are in a general way characteristic of an oral culture. The amplification of the spoken word necessary for it to compete with the written has been achieved by the development of electronic forms of communication. Communications theorists suggest that this new phase, this synthesis of old and new, and its accompanying psychological and societal reorientation are closely related — whether as *cause* or as *effect* may not be clear — to change in the ratio of our sensory perceptions. The change is from eye emphasis to ear emphasis.

We have suggested that, in the search for authenticity in your writing, you concentrate on language as a part of a historical, cultural, and individual development. Furthermore, in addition to the traditional forms of language associated with the spoken and written word, there is a special need for an understanding of the various languages of the media. If Walter Ong, Marshall McLuhan, and others are right, and we believe that language (all communication forms) shapes our world view and perceptual patterns, then it is important that we recognize the directions in which our language media are transporting us. One of the obvious and more significant characteristics of language today is its oral quality. This requires an understanding of the features of oral-aural language, the kind of language that is in harmony with the general tone of speech. This does not mean that the written word is dead or dying; on the contrary, it is being infused with a new life from oral sources of language in electronic media. With its concern for flow, balanced and parallel sentence structure, coordinating conjunctions as transitions (and, but, for), sound patterns of words (alliteration, assonance), and image and metaphor, oral language is making unusual and significant demands on the written word.

EXERCISES

1. Communicate your understanding of the oral-aural aspects of language using a subject, form, and audience of your choice. Do not write poetry or song lyrics; write lyrical prose. You might compose a speech or an editorial for a television or radio broadcast. You might consult with your instructor as to whether you can submit your assignment in the form of a cassette tape. *Or* write an essay analyzing a speech (such as Kennedy's "Poetry and Power" or Martin Luther King, Jr.'s "I Have a Dream") — or some other work you consider to be lyrical prose (Gibran's *The Prophet*, for example; select only a portion of a work of this length) — for the oral characteristics suggested above.

2. Write an essay in which you reconcile those characteristics associated with an oral culture suggested in this chapter (as well as your own observations of the counter-culture) with the following statement about writing and language by Richard Brautigan: "The time has come to mix sentences with the dirt and the sun with punctuation and the rain with verbs." Try to be as specific as possible by offering concrete experiences, details, and examples from your own observations and the text itself.

3. Write an essay in which you describe your feelings while attending a rock concert. From your experiences, do you believe that Rollo May's analysis (page 201) of the impact of sound at Woodstock essentially is correct? Try to relate his theories to your experiences.

A THEORY OF ELECTRONIC COMMUNICATION

All the news media, including the press, are art forms
that have the power of imposing, like poetry, their own assumptions.
The news media are not ways of relating us to the old "real" world;
they are the real world, and they reshape
what remains of the old world at will.

MARSHAL McLUHAN
"Media Log"
(1960)

With his book *The Mechanical Bride*, published in 1951, Marshall McLuhan established his definition of communication and art. He believes anything that creates an impression or communicates a message is part of the communications field, that any part of culture is art. In other words, it is communication and art that shapes society and not the other way around. That being the case, advertising, McLuhan argues, is one of the greatest influences for good or bad on our society. In a later book, *The Gutenberg Galaxy* (1962), he traces the ways in which the forms of experience both physical and psychological have been influenced by the alphabet and printing. Arguing that the change from "the mechanical technology of the wheel to the technology of electrical circuitry represents one of the major shifts of all time," he expounds one basic concept: the invention and development of the printing press, he says, provided the key to understanding recent Western civilization. We became what we are because print shifted the emphasis of man's acquisition and retention of information from a basically audial-oral-mnemonic method to a visual-print-physical storage method.

McLuhan's most widely known and controversial work, *Understanding Media*, appeared in 1964. The history of Western culture, McLuhan indicates in this book, developed in three stages: the first stage was the preliterate in which man lived interdependently and communicated orally; the second stage began with the invention of the printing press and was the stage in which man became generally independent, communicated by the printed word, and thought in a linear or sequential way; the third stage, the modern electric era of television, radio, film, and other electronic communications, has turned man back to the oral tribal stage. Some of the comparative qualities, for example, of McLuhan's three stages of history (as they relate to specific cultural areas and with McLuhan's biases showing) can be seen in the chart on pp. 205-206.

Some other ideas projected in *Understanding Media* are associated with technology and the media. Any medium, according to McLuhan, is a development that extends man's senses; the radio becomes an exten-

Preliterate Man (to 1500)	Literate Man (1500-1900)	Modern Man (1900 to present)
Communication Forms		
Speech	Reading, writing	Film, TV, radio, etc.
Ear	Eye	Electronic technology
		Central nervous system: BANG! (Everything happens at once)
"Acoustic space" (boundless, directionless, horizonless)	Time-space continuum (linear, limited, directed, working toward goals)	Circuitry: "You can't go home again."
Sung	Said	"Participation mystique"
Training of memory and tongue	Training in observation and study aimed at clarity, instruction	Opportunity for discovery
Knowledge		
Oral, poeticized product of collective psyche and mind	Classified and stored for "know nothings" (library)	Corporate participation in immediate experiences, involvement, responsibility
Encouragement of easy recall	Encouragement of disputation and argument: thinking on single, separate planes: detached patterns (emergence of science)	Encouragement of discovery through probing and exploration
Amateurism: intuition (dark of mind)	Professionalism: (light of the mind)	Awareness and total involvement
Meaning: through intuition, imagination, emotion	Meaning: prescribed through order (cause to effect)	Meaning: pattern recognition, active interplay
Teaching Methods		
Suggestion (poet), singing, oratory,	Saying with precision Visual and spatial	Entire human environment is a work of art:

Preliterate Man (to 1500)	*Literate Man* (1500-1900)	*Modern Man* (1900 to present)
memory and myth Wise: "blind"	Press, book, narrative line, plot, serial Packed education courses Wise: "seers"	"Everything we do is music." Dialogue (teach-in) and humor are our most appeal- ing environmental tools Wise: men of "inwardness"
Stress of attention: "hearing was believ- ing"	Stress of attention: "seeing was believ- ing" — "wait and see"	Stress of attention: NOW — reaction: suspended judgment
	General Characteristics	
World of mystery explained by myth and revelation (a voice)	Abolition of mystery through Newton's invention of clocklike machine as Supreme Being	Restoration of mystery: Newtonian "God is dead." Oriental mysticism: flowing, unified, fused, holistic, astrology, tarot cards, biorhythms, yoga, Taoism, etc.
Collective authorship	Individual authorship and copyright	Instant "steal" Xerox machines
Responses: primordial feeling, tribal emotion	Responses: brain- washed by propa- ganda	Responses: total engagement. "Be *with* it!"

sion of the ear since it allows man to hear speech from a great distance. Each medium, in addition, is either "hot" or "cold": a hot medium offers much detail in its transmittance and leaves the individual receiving the message with little to add from his own experiences; a cold medium offers little detail and requires involvement on the part of the individual receiving the message. Basically, the more senses used and the greater the participation in the communication process, the cooler the medium. Conventional printed prose is hotter than oral communication because it

> Wines have hard going in a literary society because their first appeals are sensory and direct. . . . A sip is very complex: as you raise the glass to your lips you take a slight breath, inhaling the smell of the wine as you taste it and feel it in the mouth. Three senses are reporting at once. Because wine is volatile and is a complex collection of tastes, the whole sensation is changing as the wine first touches your mouth, as it moves to your throat, as you swallow, and as the three senses recover from the action.
>
> — Marshall McLuhan, *Verbi-Voco-Visual Explorations* (1967)

supplies much information via one sense, the visual. It usually does not ask the recipient to participate through several senses. The oral form, by contrast, generally demands immediate involvement: an auditor must interpret words, intonations, gestures, and subtler forms of "body language." A lecture, therefore, would be hot; a class discussion would be cool; a realistic landscape by Constable is hot; a line drawing or a Charles Schultz cartoon is cool; a novel by Henry James, hot; one by Hemingway, cool.

McLuhan's books themselves frequently disturb people not by what he says so much as by how he says it. He demands a high degree of involvment from the reader; he is poetic and intuitive rather than logical and analytic. His basic unit is the sentence, but sentences which remain undeveloped topic sentences. His style is almost directly oral, but for readers accustomed to "hot" print, it is orchestrated so coolly it tends to be obscure. Nevertheless, McLuhan has a message that is important to us. Along with Walter Ong and others, he is pointing us to a new awareness of, and responsibility toward, the electronic communication forms. It is important for our psychic welfare that we learn the languages of the various media; and it is important for our cultural future that we understand the impact they have on our lives.

EXERCISES

1. Through an inductive reasoning process extend the preceding chart, comparing the three stages of history in the following areas: transportation, privacy, government, art and the artist, and jobs.
2. Using one of McLuhan's "picture" books (for example, *War and Peace*

in the Global Village or *The Medium Is the Message*), write an essay in which you paraphrase McLuhan's position. How effective are McLuhan's arguments based upon specific nonverbal presentations?

3. Analyze the following passage from McLuhan's *Understanding Media* for its stylistic features:

In accepting an honorary degree from the University of Notre Dame a few years ago, General David Sarnoff made this statement: "We are too prone to make technological instruments the scapegoats for the sins of those who wield them. The products of modern science are not in themselves good or bad; it is the way they are used that determines their value." That is the voice of the current somnambulism. Suppose we were to say, "Apple pie is in itself neither good nor bad; it is the way it is used that determines its value." Or, "The smallpox virus is in itself neither good nor bad; it is the way it is used that determines its value." Again, "Firearms are in themselves neither good nor bad; it is the way they are used that determines their value." That is, if the slugs reach the right people it is good. If the TV tube fires the right ammunition at the right people it is good. I am not being perverse. There is simply nothing in the Sarnoff statement that will bear scrutiny, for it ignores the nature of the medium, of any and all media, in the true Narcissus style of one hypnotized by the amputation and extension of his own being in a new technical form. General Sarnoff went on to explain his attitude to the technology of print, saying that it was true that print caused much trash to circulate, but it had also disseminated the Bible and the thoughts of seers and philosophers. It has never occurred to General Sarnoff that any technology could do anything but *add* itself on to what we already are.

4. Select ten advertisments from television or magazines and analyze them for their "logic" and consumer appeal. For example, a number of products are presented under the "logic" of testimony or endorsement (Joe Namath endorses hair conditioners, shaving creams, and popcorn machines), statistical or scientific claims, claims of uniqueness, comparisons with other products, ambiguous words ("virtually," "resists," "the look of," "fortified," "enriched," "can be," "tackles," "fights," etc.), and "complimenting" the consumer ("You've come a long way, baby"). Add your own classifications for the advertisements you have chosen.

THE MOVING IMAGE

The media are not toys; they should not be in the hands
of Mother Goose and Peter Pan executives. They can be entrusted
only to new artists, because they are art forms.
MARSHALL McLUHAN
"Media Log"
(1960)

More than 3,000 years ago the alphabet was invented. It facilitated systems of written communication, and, after speech, became the cornerstone in the attempt to establish and maintain the structure of society. In contrast to the long history of the written word, that of film and television as forms of communication is relatively brief. These media have existed only 1 per cent of the time humanity has been using some form of writing for communication purposes. Marshall McLuhan has made it clear that television and film have altered man's understanding and perception of self, people, society, and the universe. Since Gutenberg's invention of the printing press, we have in our culture traditionally associated "linear" print symbols with physical and psychological detachment. Reading a book by ourselves, however caught up in it we may be, we can still control the speed of the message. The electronic media do not permit us that control. Film and television are closer than a book to the flux of life itself, though in itself this immediacy may cause a paradoxical detachment in viewers. The closeness to life is especially evident with "live" television, for in a matter of seconds an electronic

On the day *Childe Harold's Pilgrimage* was published (1811), "I woke," said Lord Byron, "and found myself famous." The morning after the release of his first picture, the dog called "Lassie" was famous. Fame in Byron's time meant being spoken of by perhaps 2,000 people who read *Childe Harold* in the year after publication; fame for Lassie meant adoration on the part of ten million. Probably every literate person heard of Byron, just as everyone, including nonmoviegoers, heard of Lassie, but illiteracy in England in 1811 may have been 90 per cent; there's no illiteracy in films.

— Gilbert Seldes, "Communications Revolution" (1960)

signal from any place in the world can confront us with events in our own time — the present. In contrast to the experience of reading a book, though we have no control over the speed of the message of the moving image, we *can* control our emotional involvement. Many Americans literally or psychologically turned off scenes of Vietnam atrocities. We cannot leave the "live" image of television and film and hope to pick it up another day, but we can detach it from our personal feelings, turn it into something "out there," thereby controlling and dehumanizing our emotional response to the images of dying soldiers on the screen.

In short, the moving image leads to a new way of perceiving experience, one different from — not necessarily better or worse than — either speech alone or print. Stan Vanderbeek, a winner of many honors for his experimental films, attempts to define the nature of this new perception in an essay, "Culture-Intercom," that is constructed to look like a poem:

> I like to think that life is a dissolve . . .
> . . . and that seeing is the real illusion, that a sense
> of reality is a sense of the senses . . .
> that a sense of reality is a sense of non-sense . . .
> that movies should delight the eye and rearrange the senses . . .
> that movies are changing the art of seeing . . .
> that movies are an art of seeing . . .
> that movies are an illusion . . .
> that seeing is believing.
>
>   *   *   *
>
> Motion pictures are apparent motion . . .
> The film worker deals with "visual velocity" and "visual inertia."
> Laws of sight that seem similar to laws of physics —
> or at least no definitions of sight that contemporary
> artists are exploring.
> If movies and "vision" can assume the same meaning
> then visions take the path of least resistance, that is,
> intuitive logic, intuitive geometry, image-symbol making,
> that is just beginning in motion images.

Vanderbeek, as well as McLuhan and others, thinks that film and television have an immediacy, an instantaneousness, and an astonishing and total impact on the senses. Film and television are like the novel and poetry in their ability to compress and play with time, especially in the use of flashback and exploration of the subconscious and the dream world through the technique of metaphor and analogy. What poetry

> I am continually amazed by a society which allows the most extreme forms of violence to be shown in the mass media yet hesitates to permit the nude human form to be seen; a society in which it is permissible to watch people performing the most sadistic acts: robbery, torture, murder; but where you almost never see a couple sensitively making love or even touching intimately. . . .
>
> — Bernard Gunther, *How the West Is One* (1972)

and narrative project upon our inner eyes and ears, film and television project for our outer. As poet and reader "see feelingly," through the medium of words, so ideally filmmaker and viewer see feelingly through the medium of images. The relationship between these two forms is almost as close as concave is to convex. Consequently, an understanding of the language of film may help us with our understanding of language.

THE LANGUAGE OF FILM

There is an area in the human mind
(or heart) which can be reached only
through cinema, through that cinema which is
always awake, always changing. Only
such cinema can reveal, describe, make us
conscious, hint at what we really are
or what we aren't, or sing the true and changing
beauty of the world around us.

JONAS MEKAS
"Notes on the New American Cinema"
(1962)

The language of film is a combination of interrelated languages. The visual images that appear before the viewer may be accompanied by *music*, *dialogue*, *lighting*, *symbol*, and *narration*, elements we may identify with one or another of other media — opera, drama, and prose fiction, for example. It might seem, then, that film simply reconstitutes techniques from the several arts of music, theatre, painting, and literature. It is true that the painter's language is based on form and color, and the composer's language on sound; however, film has its own set of sensory involvements — basically visual and oral — that makes it different from any other form of communication. When truly effective, film is a combination of these languages — all in motion. What makes this combination possible is the invention of hardware or technology — the camera, celluloid film, and projector whose conjoined capabilities produce the illusion of movement film creates.

The creation of a film starts with the recording of subject matter into images and sounds on strips of film called *shots*. The *shot* is the elemental unit in the language of film. The way the filmmaker shapes and orders shots may reflect his or her feelings and thoughts as the technique creates its sense of narrative movement. Technically, the shot is defined by a change in camera position and is the smallest part of the film language out of which larger structures are composed. As far as substance or theme is concerned, the shot — unless it is made from a camera set in front of a staged play, in which case it is really not "film" — is an unfinished part of a meaning that depends on a sequence of other shots for intelligible significance. The shot therefore belongs to a larger unit of articulation. Several shots from the same location constitute a *scene*, which has a completed meaning. But that unit also belongs to a yet larger one. A series of scenes focused on a specific aspect of theme is called a *sequence*. Each of these units plays its part in a rhetorical pattern. The three aspects of film language — shot, scene, and sequence — function, then, much as the word, sentence, and paragraph function in the rhetoric of conventional written expression.

All aspects that are essential for a film's language must initially be

---

To say that someone *understands* a movie . . . often means very little because his understanding might involve only an awareness of the plot line, while he might lose the meaning or import of a story completely. To understand the plot of *A Clockwork Orange*, for example, requires little beyond following the acts of a young man who loves violence; but what is the director, Stanley Kubrick, trying to say about his "hero's" violence and about society's response? The process of understanding works on several levels, and the more a person notices various levels in a film, the more he understands.

— John Harrington, *The Rhetoric of Film* (1973)

expressed in the vocabulary of the shot. Like the writer who uses a variety of verbal patterns and rhythms in order to avoid monotony, the filmmaker avoids taking all shots from the same angle, height, distance, and with the same lighting and duration in time. Using a variety of these five elements creates a film language, like that of the best writers, that is dynamic and lively. In addition to tone and rhythm, subject matter in a film can take on a variety of appearances, depending on the way it is expressed, that is, depending on how it is shot and edited. Subjects need not be explicit and obvious in film any more than in literature, for each can be communicated through associations and connotations. To achieve the subtlest effects, the filmmaker, like the author, has besides his angles of vision certain other techniques that may go into giving the subject matter a personal value and meaning. These techniques — of movement, color, sound, and image — the filmmaker shares with other arts. What makes their combination unique to film as an art form is both the externalization of sound and image and the extreme range of focus available to the camera — in contrast to the internalization of print and the relatively narrow range of theatre.

These elements have been used effectively by the filmmaker Ingmar Bergman in *The Seventh Seal*. This early Bergman film (1956), set in fourteenth-century Sweden, studies the human condition through the quest of Antonious Block (a knight) to find some meaning in life and death. The film opens at sunrise with a series of shots (constituting a scene) focused on the knight, just returned from a ten years' crusade to the Holy Land, and on his surroundings. Visually, these shots concentrate on a beach, a rough sea, an ominous bird, and the knight at prayer. Movements in these shots are very slow — even the bird hangs in the air and creates a feeling of uneasiness. The black and white tones are muted, dark with heavy contrast, and sound is cacophonic, with the harsh grating of the sea on the rocks and the screaming of the bird. The organic combination of these related elements constitutes a sequence that prepares us for the knight's meeting with death. A scene later in the film contrasts with this initial one. Jof, a circus performer, is portrayed here in a series of shots that project a sense of life rather than death. The visual images are of trees, grass, wagon (home), horses, and insects; movement arises from a natural vitality in Jof, who awakens, juggles some balls, and stands on his head. Colors are lightened by the rays of the morning sun; and sounds are all harmonious, blending the neighing of a horse, the buzzing of a fly, the warbling of a bird, and the murmuring of the wind in the trees. The combination of these shots suggests naturalness, innocence, an interest in life. Contrasting these two scenes through the various structural elements of the shots — image, movement, color, and sound — Bergman establishes the film's theme of death versus life.

Each of us can profit from an understanding of the language of film. Since it is the smallest functional unit of film and combines to form a larger unit, the *shot* syntactically parallels the *word* of spoken and written communication, the *note* of musical composition, and the *brush stroke* of painting. Arrangement of shots determines the overall structure of a film, and cinematic meaning is established through the contexts of shots much as words achieve intelligibility through the contexts of language around them. Because of its appeal to our senses through use of detail to express and develop an essential idea, film and the study of film can contribute to the understanding of effective written and spoken forms of communication.

EXERCISES

1. Write a review of a film. In your preparation, take into consideration the following:

    a. The audience (we suggest you use the students in your class as your audience).

    b. In your presentation be sure to encourage the audience to see or avoid the film.

    c. Give a description (a plot summary) of the film and elaborate on those scenes that help support your interpretation of the film.

    d. Give a classification of the film somewhere in your introductory comments (for example, is it a "science fiction," "western," "disaster," "horror," etc.).

    e. Compare and contrast the film with other films done by the director or with other films of a similar theme and subject.

    f. Analyze aspects of the film such as acting, setting, sound, camera work, and special effects.

    g. Use a style that would amuse and entertain your audience.

    h. Be sure to argue for a particular meaning that you think the film projects.

2. Read several reviews (say three) of the same film and write an essay comparing and contrasting the various approaches of the writers. Do not limit the content of your essay to just the reviewer's statement

about the film, but also comment on the techniques the reviewers use (for example, some film reviewers are politically oriented while others seem to concentrate on the director while others concentrate on the actors).

The following are generally considered among the best of the contemporary film reviewers. We urge you to read their approaches to films.

John Simon (*Esquire*)
Pauline Kael (*The New Yorker*)
Andrew Sarris (*The Village Voice*)
Stanley Kauffmann (*The New Republic*)
Wanda Hale (*The New York Daily News*)
Gene Shalit (*The Ladies Home Journal*)

<hr />

APPENDIX
ঌ LANGUAGE IN HISTORICAL ও PERSPECTIVE

At a meeting of the American Anthropology Association in Toronto, Alexander Marshack delivered a paper explaining the significance of a bone unearthed by Francais Bordes in France. On the bone were symbols engraved by man at least 135,000 years ago. According to Marshack, the bone documents showed "a surprisingly high level of intentional image- and symbol-making thousands of years before Neanderthal man and before the full development of modern man." He went on to add that the inscribed bone provided "the first clue" to the origins of later writing symbolism and art and suggested the presence of a "high level of language usage even among early man." Beginning with such language symbols as those Marshack discusses, man has evolved that highly complex system of visual communication known as the written word. These complex systems demonstrate, as Ernst Cassirer suggests, that man is basically a symbol-using animal characterized by his intelligence and his ability to use symbols to communicate his thoughts. Words are invented to represent things or actions, emotions or concepts, and the alphabet we now use provides another among many ways to realize these representations.

There is little doubt that writing emerged from the graphic skills associated with early art. The systems for representing speech by visual means all have their origin in *pictography* (picture writing). Even the bone markings described by Marshack are representative of a fragment of speech; that is, they are presented in such a way that another individual looking at them can "read" their message. The early pictographs are generally stories without words and are usually associated with societies

> Writing . . . didn't record oral language; it was a new language, which the spoken word came to imitate. Writing encouraged an analytical mode of thinking with emphasis upon lineality. Oral languages tended to be polysynthetic, composed of great, tight conglomerates, like twisted knots, within which images were juxtaposed, inseparably fused; written communications consisted of little words chronologically ordered. Subject became distinct from verb, adjective from noun, thus separating actor from action, essence from form. Where preliterate man imposed form diffidently, temporarily — for such transitory forms lived but temporarily on the tip of his tongue, in the living situation — the printed word was inflexible, permanent, in touch with eternity: it embalmed truth for posterity.
>
> — Edmund Carpenter, "The New Languages" (1960)

of hunters and fishers and the primitive farming communities in Africa and America.

In its ideal use, the pictographic script requires that each word be symbolized by a recognizable sign. Pictures of animals would be represented by conventional drawings, while a circle with rays could mean "sun." Since there is no relationship between these "pictures" and the sounds of words, they are called *ideographs* or *hieroglyphs*, from the name given by the Greeks to the characters used by the ancient Egyptians in their writing. Writing as we know it, the breakdown of sentences into words positioned one after another, emerges only in advanced societies that have towns with a fairly complex system of trading for food supplies. Generally speaking, therefore, writing has a relatively short history, one of perhaps 6,000 years. Even today writing is not universally in use, inasmuch as about half of the world's population gets along without it. Eventually in the development of writing, sounds became represented and writing became a phonetic notation, though undoubtedly there was a long period of interpenetration of pictographs and phonetic notation in writing before the alphabet arose. The first case of the pure use of alphabetic symbolism is found on the tablets from the Ugarit library (Northern Phoenicia) bearing cuneiform (wedge-shaped) characters written from left to right; the date is estimated between 1600 and 1200 B.C., and the language used is a form of Western Semitic. It would appear that the alphabet arose out of an economic need, for of the thousands of Mesopotamian cuneiform clay tablets known today, most deal with economic transactions. The characters that were to develop into our alphabet appeared in Phoenicia about 1300 B.C. This alphabet had twenty-two letters, all consonants, from which it may be concluded — since there must at least have been interior vowels — that the letters represented syllables.

The first completion of an alphabetic system by the addition of letters denoting vowels was accomplished by the Greeks, who borrowed the consonantal alphabet from the Phoenicians around 1000 B.C. If the Greeks were to represent their language clearly, they could not avoid vowel signs, for in their language words often began with vowels. They found a reasonably simple solution to their needs by using letters representing Semitic consonants that had no parallels in Greek. The writing moved from left to right, and the form of the letters more or less resembled the rectangular shape of capital letters. Later, when speed of writing became necessary, quickly written small letters came into use.

The line of alphabetic development proceeded from Greece westward to Italy and the Italic speakers of the Indo-European language. Characters of the Latin capital letter script, like the Greek, were largely symmetrical in shape and very clear. The Latin script, with the aid of the Roman administration and later with the gradual extension of the Roman Church, spread throughout Europe. Thereafter, with European navigation and colonization, Latin script spread over much of the rest of the world, including the Americas. Today, it is the most dominant of the alphabetic forms.

Throughout history the use and influence of writing have been linked with the development of artifacts, of technology — the material used as the writing surface (wood, stone, clay, paper) and the writing

---

Until WRITING was invented, we lived in acoustic space, where the Eskimo now lives: boundless, directionless, horizonless, the dark of the mind, the world of emotion, primordial intuition, terror. Speech is a social chart of this dark bog. . . . A goose's quill put an end to talk, abolished mystery, gave architecture and towns, brought roads and armies, bureaucracies. It was the basic metaphor with which the cycle of CIVILIZATION began, the step from the dark into the light of the mind. The hand that filled a paper built a city.

— Marshall McLuhan, "Five Sovereign Fingers Taxed
the Breath" (1960)

instrument (stylus, chisel, quill, type). Harold A. Innis points out that frequently the material on which words have been written has counted more than the words themselves. Innis says, for instance, that the light-weight and easily stored papyrus used by the ancient Egyptians allowed their priests to control the calendar and the social memory; hence the writing medium became also the means for their influence on the dynasties and for their own power. For a long time the written word depended on the manual skill of carvers and other copyists. Their processes were slow and offered limited access to others. Few people could read and fewer still were able to gain access to the media as long as they remained clay tablets, stone, or laboriously copied, expensive manuscripts.

A turning-point in human history was reached when writing could be reproduced in large numbers of copies by a printing process that could use the cheaper products of a growing paper industry. The development of the printing process began in China, where multiple prints were achieved in the second century, wood-engraving in the sixth century, and movable type in the eleventh century. In Western Europe, after a limited use of wood-engraving, the manufacture of movable type and presses in the fifteenth century permitted the enormous multiplication of books and broadsheets; mass production of written messages permitted and made desirable a considerable extension of the skill of reading, even though education itself was not general for some centuries. Without print and paper, literacy on a broad scale would be neither desired by many nor physically possible; with them literacy has become a necessity. The appearance of the alphabet around 1500 B.C. and the development of the printing press in fifteenth-century Europe were vital to Western culture, and the implications of these two inventions are considerable.

Evidence suggests there is a definite relationship between the nature of a society and its primary form of communication. Since the invention of the alphabet and the printing press, Western civilization has based its primary form of communication on the written word. According to

---

The book, like the door, is an encouragement to isolation: the reader wants to be alone, away from the noise of others. This is true even of comic books for children, who associate comics with being alone, just as they associate TV with the family, and movies with friends of their own age.

— David Riesman, "The Oral and Written Traditions" (1960)

Walter Ong and Marshall McLuhan, there are vast differences in social orientation between a literate culture (one based on reading and writing) and an oral culture (one based on the spoken word). Both Ong and McLuhan have argued that the written word, among other things, has a permanence that the fleetingness of the spoken word, before the advent of sound recording devices, simply cannot have. One consequence of the written word, they say, is an overwhelming sense of order and control. It gives rise to an emphasis on the rational and the mathematical qualities that are at the center of Western civilization. With the invention of the printing press, the sense of fixity and control was further heightened, for the process of printing itself requires a rigid sequential series of actions that suggest the segmentations of reason, logic, and math. The result was that linear and sequential concepts became a significant part of Western man's reality, a reality based on the visual ("seeing is believing") and the rational.

With the stabilizing of words through alphabetic symbols and print came an interest in rules and laws to govern the use of the language. Grammar (derived from the stem of the Greek word meaning *to write*), as we know it, is the study of the structure of a language. As far as English is concerned, the rise of grammar in the eighteenth century established in book form a fixed way of analyzing the language that school children have learned for almost two hundred years. What the eighteenth-century grammarians did was to apply their "laws" to the written word, though the laws they applied came from Latin and poorly fitted the realities of English; it is only in recent years that this notion of grammar has been redefined to include the spoken language. Linguists — such as Otto Jespersen in his famous work *Philosophy of Grammar* (1924) — pointed out that grammar should not be considered a fixed body of laws but should be organic and "living." Jespersen stated that "language is a human activity" and therefore should address itself to understanding an individual's communication process. Since Jespersen's declaration, the study of grammar has shifted away from its "fixed" state toward areas of

---

An alphabetic culture . . . is likely to regard the literal meaning, in the sense of plain or definite meaning, as something altogether wholesome and altogether desirable, and to regard other remote, perhaps more profoundly symbolic, meanings with disfavor.

— Walter J. Ong, *The Presence of the Word* (1967)

---

modern linguistics such as *phonology* (sound), *morphology* (structure), and *syntax* (grammatical relationship), which are primarily concerned with the spoken word. Traditional grammar has been the province of historical linguistic studies, while modern language studies have become more and more descriptive and generative (that is, attempting to generate rules inductively from practice). The problem of the writer is neither solely one nor the other, neither only historical nor only generative. The writer must find a balance between the traditional, static, settled conventions of usage and structure and the often anticonventional, fluid, revolutionary expressions of the language he or she hears spoken daily.

✍ ENGLISH: ITS ORIGINS ✍ AND DEVELOPMENT

What is language, what attitudes toward it have people taken, what are its origins, why should a history of our language interest us? *Language* can be defined as a systematized combination of sounds that have meaning for persons in a given cultural community. Written languages have visual representations of these combinations of sounds. Some classical linguists such as Plato believed that language evolved naturally from, or perhaps supernaturally through, the mind of humanity. They believed that our immortal soul arrived in this world already equipped with an ideal language; the different particular languages spoken on earth developed as corruptions of this ideal form of speech. The most common attitude people take toward their own language is that it alone represents the ideal. Many people believed for centuries, for example, that the original language was Hebrew, so if a child were raised without any formal language direction, the Hebrews (and many later Christians) believed that the child would naturally speak humanity's original language, which, for them, would be Hebrew. The Hebraists are not alone in feeling this way about their language, for virtually all unsophisticated thinkers believe that their language has a connection with language's origins, or with reality itself, that precedes any other people's tongue.

In fact, the origin of language is not really known. There seems no foundation for Plato's notion of an ideal language pre-existing in the minds (or, we might say, the chromosomes) of humanity, but the modern linguist Noam Chomsky suggests that lanugage may have "biological properties." Language, as a means of communication, may have developed as a consequence of practical needs. Yet prior to need was the *capacity* for acquiring and using language. Such a capacity seems to be innate in man, for no evidence exists to suggest other animals have similar capacities, not even the higher primates such as the apes or chimpanzees. While the specific origin must remain lost in the dark corners of prehistory, many theories have been proposed concerning it. Some have been known jokingly as the *bow-bow* theory, the *pooh-pooh* theory, the *ding-dong* theory, and the *yo-he-ho* theory. The bow-wow theory is based on the idea of echo; that is, speech was simply an imitation of sounds that were heard. Onomatopoeia, the poetic device that weds sound and sense (bang, burp, tinkle, splash), is a good example of the theory. The pooh-pooh theory is based on the idea that language in its origin was ejaculatory rather than communicative. When confronting a situation that required an emotional response such as pain, sadness, or happiness, a person would likely respond with "ouch," "pooh," "oh," "ho," and "ha." The ding-dong theory is somewhat Platonic, since its advocates believe that language is derived from a pre-existing relationship between sound and sense. The basic idea is that an appropriate word — the sound or combination of sounds — will occur when a particular sensation or perception has been experienced; it is different from the bow-wow theory in that words are *not* considered merely arbitrary imitations of sounds, but in *essence* mean what they designate. Finally, the yo-he-ho theory is derived from the notion that words have communal origins; that is, the sounds, the grunts and groans uttered during a group action eventually come to be associated with the actions themselves: the sounds become the word for the actions.

The origin of language probably resides in the structure of the mind and nervous system. It lies in the capacity for symbolization. If this is the case, we began to develop language when we first realized that an object could symbolize meaning. Eventually, it was recognized that objects and gestures were limiting as forms of symbolic expression, and we therefore turned to the sound potential present in the respiratory system. We can assume that language existed long before history began to be recorded. Even the oldest Phoenician writings point to highly advanced linguistic systems suggesting that the words in these systems had been developed over thousands of years. Moreover, linguists have never found a simple, unsophisticated language. Our assumptions about language lead us to believe that the languages of modern, "civilized" cultures are more complex than those of primitive cultures. It simply is not so, for every known language can perform any function demanded of it. Even the language of the "Stone Age" Tasaday, a tribe recently found in the Philippines manifesting the most primitive culture ever observed, is an incredibly advanced symbolic system, one as sophisticated in its way as our English.

> The English language is not to be found in dictionaries and grammar books: it is to be found built into the brains of three hundred million native speakers. If they and the countless millions who have learned English as a second language were all to be wiped out, the English language would be as extinct as the dinosaur. Books would provide valuable fossil-like clues, permitting scholars to reconstruct many things about it. But the language itself is alive only so long as there are people who naturally and easily speak it when they need to communicate. Dictionaries and grammar books are nothing more than records of certain aspects of the language at given points in its ever-changing history.
>
> — W. Nelson Francis, *The English Language* (1963)

Whether all languages spoken on earth today have evolved from one language is not known. What we do know is that many of the languages existing today (there are more than 4,000) are alike in enough respects to be grouped into families. The family closest to us is called Indo-European. It includes the Celtic, Italic, Slavic, Hellenic, Iranic, Indic, and Germanic languages. Since English is part of the Germanic language branch, which in turn belongs to the Indo-European family tree, it is instructive to note some characteristics of its ancestor. Without written accounts scholars have found it difficult to trace the history of the Indo-European language, but conclusions based on cross-cultural comparisons suggest that it was spoken first by a group of agricultural peoples living in north-central Europe. Probably around 3000 B.C. these people split into smaller groups that eventually migrated as far west as the British Isles and as far east as China. The greatest evidence concerning these people and their language comes by inference. It can be inferred through comparative linguistics that their homeland was originally Central Europe since the words shared by the language descendants tend to identify north central European flora, fauna, and geographical conditions. Scholars have reconstructed names for trees that grow only in climates such as that of central Europe: names for birch, beech, aspen, oak, and the like, but not names for palm, olive, or cypress. Names that can be reconstructed for animals include wolf, bear, eagle, owl, thrush, and others, but not tiger, elephant, camel, and such others that could be found only in more southerly and moderate regions. A comparison of the Indo-European languages suggests that many of them have gone through extensive change (see diagram on p. 226). It would appear that modern Lithuanian, a stem of the Balto-Slavic branch, is closest to the original language. English, in a relatively short

Dutch
Danish
Norwegian Swedish
English German
Gothic
Russian
Polish
Scotch
West North East
Czech
Welsh
Slavic
Lettish
GERMANIC
Irish
Lithuanian
CELTIC
BALTO
SLAVIC Baltic
Old Prussian

**Derivatives of
INDO-EUROPEAN LANGUAGE**

ITALIC
INDO-
IRANIAN Indic
Sanskrit Hindu
HELLENIC
Latin
Iranic
Urdu
Portuguese
Classical
Greek
Old Iranian
Pustu
Spanish Italian
French
Modern
Greek
Persian

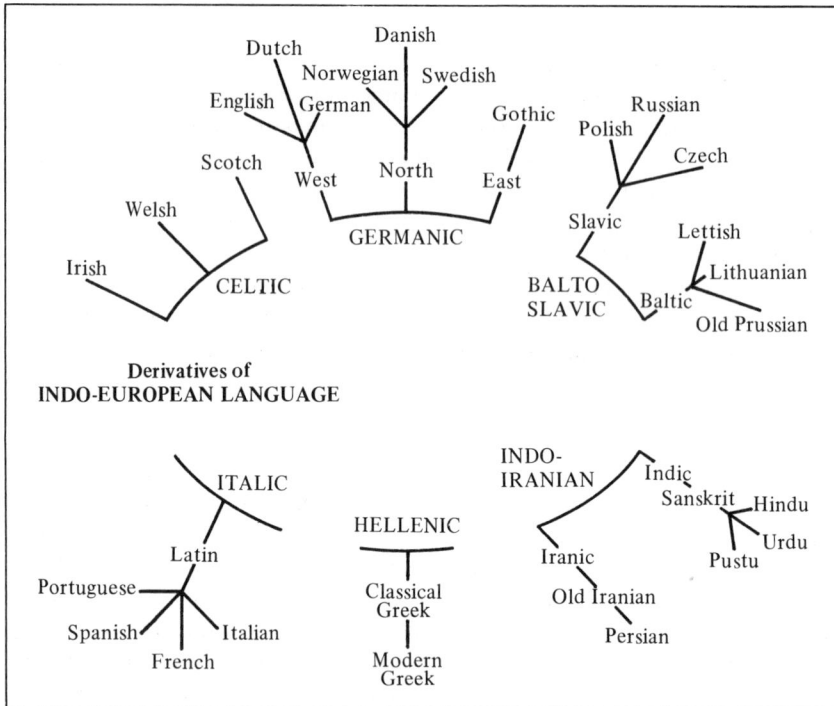

period of time, has undergone vast changes, largely through the main agent of linguistic change — borrowing from other languages.

The main line of development for English is from its Indo-European source through the subfamily known as the Germanic languages. At about the same time that the Greek language was in its cultural prime, our "English" ancestors — hunters and farmers located around the North Sea — were emerging as a different branch of the Indo-European tree. Unfortunately, except for a few *runes* — Finnish or Old Norse poems — the Germanic tribes left us no written record of their language development. All we know is that somehow a German offspring broke away from the Indo-European family. Probably the Germanic language was spoken just before the Christian era. Its historical impact, however, was not felt until the Germanic tribes began to spread across Europe. Their first significant confrontation with another language did not occur until Julius Caesar fought them in the Gallic Wars. The destruction of Rome in 410 A.D. by the Germanic tribes marked the end of the Roman Era and the beginning of the so-called Dark Ages. At about the same time as the collapse of the Roman Empire, the Germanic tribes known as the Jutes, Angles, and Saxons invaded

Britain and established the West German tongue that came to be known as English.

A Celtic people had been in Britain long before Julius Caesar invaded the island in 55 and 54 B.C. They felt little of the Roman occupation, however, until 43 A.D., when Emperor Claudius successfully claimed Britain as part of the Roman Empire. During the four centuries that the Romans controlled Great Britain, the Celtic tribes absorbed elements of the Roman civilization. But when the Roman armies were called back home to meet the Germanic invaders from the north, the untrained Celts had no chance against the rugged Anglo-Saxon invaders. Even so, the struggle was not easy, and about 200 years elapsed before the British Celts were defeated. For a while in the middle of the sixth century it looked as though the British would win when a great leader emerged whose legend was to grow into that of King Arthur. But in the end the Celtic tribes withdrew to the mountains of Wales and Scotland and across the sea to Ireland, leaving the field to the Anglo-Saxons and creating the minor Celtic languages of Wales, Ireland, and Scotland.

Our knowledge of the invasion that established English in Britain is derived primarily from a scholar known as the Venerable Bede. In 731 A.D. Bede wrote a history of the events in which he traced the roles of the various tribes in the conquest of England. Aside from Bede's bright light, the period immediately following the invasion is rather dark. The Anglo-Saxon influence was so great that inevitably most traces of the

---

English, like all other languages, is subject to that constant growth and decay which characterizes all forms of life. It is a convenient figure of speech to speak of languages as living and as dead. While we cannot think of language as something that possesses life apart from the people who speak it, as we can think of plants or of animals, we can observe in speech something like the process of change that characterizes the life of living things. When a language ceases to change, we call it a dead language. Classical Latin is a dead language because it has not changed for nearly two thousand years. The change that is constantly going on in living language can be most easily seen in vocabulary. Old words die out, new words are added, and existing words change their meaning.

— Albert C. Baugh, *A History of the English Language* (1957)

Celtic language spoken in Britain for centuries and almost all traces of the Latin language which had been in Britain for about 500 years were utterly destroyed in the areas that the Jutes, Saxons, and Angles settled. Out of the relocation of the Germanic tribes that inhabited various parts of England there emerged seven Germanic kingdoms. The different tribes that settled in the various parts of England left a specific language influence on the English people in a pattern of dialects. One tribe, the Angles, was responsible for the words *English* and *England.*

After the introduction of writing and the coming of Christianity, the centuries beginning with the seventh are illuminated with the brilliance of much literature both in Anglo-Saxon (or Old English) and Latin. One work, *Beowulf,* particularly emerges as an example of the sophistication of Old English culture. The only surviving complete epic in Old English (the tenth-century manuscript is now housed in the British Museum), *Beowulf* existed originally only in oral delivery and was probably composed not much later than 700. The epic clearly defines some of the characteristics of the Anglo-Saxon people and their language. From Old English, Modern English has inherited its sentence structure, its basic inflections used in tenses and plurals, and its vocabulary. The first eleven lines from *Beowulf* illustrate Old English and the sophistication of the poet in his use of alliteration, of a free form accentual line, his avoidance of rhyme, and the masculinity of his language:

HWÆT, WĒ GĀR-DEna   in gēardagum,
   Lo! we have listened to many a lay

þēodcyninga   þrym gefrūnon,
   Of the Spear-Danes' fame, their splendor of old,

hū ðā æþelingas   ellen fremedon!
   Their mighty princes, and martial deeds!

Oft Scyld Scēfing   sceaþena þrēatum,
   Many a mead-hall Scyld, son of Sceaf,

monegum mǣgþum   meodosetla oftēah,
   Snatched from the forces of savage foes.

egsode eorl[as],   syððan ǣrest wearð
   From a friendless foundling, feeble and wretched,

fēasceaft funden;   hē þæs frōfre gebād,
   He grew to a terror as time brought change.

wēox under wolcnum   weorðmyndum þāh,
   He throve under heaven in power and pride

oð þæt him æghwylc   ymbsittendra

Till alien peoples beyond the ocean

ofer hronrāde   hȳran scolde,

Paid toll and tribute. A good king he!

gomban gyldan;   þæt wæs gōd cyning!

Then his hour struck, and Scyld passed on to the peace of God.

What is considered the Old English period in the development of the language lasted until 1066. In that year England again was invaded, this time by William the Conqueror, the king of Normandy, a northern province of France. The language spoken in this province was Norman-French, a dialect of Latin. Hence, the Norman-French tongue that influenced English came from a non-Germanic branch of the Indo-European, so the subjugation of England by William, after his victory at Hastings, significantly changed the country and its language, inasmuch as French became the official language and the Church and educational programs emphasized Latin and French instead of English. The result was a great influx of French words into the English vocabulary, words such as *sermon, prayer, government, justice, court, chapter*, and *image*. Moreover, when English emerged from the French influence, it had become more dependent on word order (syntax) than upon word endings (inflections).

By the time of Geoffrey Chaucer (1340–1400) at the end of the Middle English period, previously incompatible French and Germanic words had been modified to the extent that they could function harmoniously in the English sentence structure as we know it today. Chaucer's *Canterbury Tales*, the greatest of the Middle English literary achievements, was written over a period of approximately ten years (1386–96), and manifests most of the significant language changes that took place after 1066 and before 1500. No doubt you had difficulty with the excerpt from *Beowulf*, for, aside from a few words you would recognize despite the spelling, there is little of English syntax that an untrained eye would detect. Indeed, the translation perhaps seemed incongruous, as one Anglo-Saxon word became several modern words. That happens because the inflections of the Anglo-Saxon word carry the word's articles and prepositions — the endings show gender and relationships provided in English by separate words. This seems strange to those of us who know only uninflected languages, but we must bear in mind that no one way is better than another: just different. The difference between Anglo-Saxon and Chaucer's Middle English will be clear at a glance, both because you begin to recognize individual words (regard-

less of whether they still have the same meanings) and begin to see that
syntax is similar to what you now speak and write:

Whan that Aprille with his shoures soote
The droghte of Marche hath perced to the roote,
And bathed every veyne in swich licour,
Of which vertu engendred is the flour;
Whan Zephirus eek with his swete breeth
In spired hath in every holt and heeth
The tendre croppes, and the yonge soone
Hath in the Ram his halfe cours y-ronne,
And smale fowles maken melodye,
That slepen al the night with open ye,
(So priketh hem nature in hir corages),
Than longen folk to goon on pilgrimages
(And palmers for to seken straunge strandes)
To ferne halwes, couthe in sondry londes;
And specially, from every shires ende
Of Engelond, to Caunterbury they wende,
The holy blisful martir for to seke,
That hem hath holpen, whan that they were seckc.
    Bifel that, in that sesoun on a day,
In Southwerk at the Tabard as I lay
Redy to wenden on my pilgrimage
To Caunterbury with ful devout corage,
At night was come in-to that hostelrye
Wel nyne and twenty in a companye,
Of sondry folk, by aventure y-falle
In felawshipe, and pilgrims were they alle,
That toward Caunterbury wolden ryde;
The chambres and the stables weren wyde,
And wel we weren esed atte beste.
And shortly, whan the soone was to reste,
So hadde I spoken with hem everichon,
That I was of hir felawshipe anon,
And made forward erly for to ryse,
To take our wey, ther as I you devyse.

Around the time that Columbus, searching for a passage to the East,
accidentally discovered America, the English language was finally established in the form we recognize today. Germanic and French elements
had been absorbed into a homogenous mixture. The Normans — cut off

from Normandy in the early 1200s — had begun to take on Anglo-Saxon speech and culture, and various dialects began to form in several regions of England; one of the several dialects, the London, emerged as standard English. Languages emerge triumphant for reasons that usually have little to do with the language per se. There were several nonlinguistic factors that led first to the ascendancy of the London dialect and then to its development into Modern English.

One factor was technological: the introduction of the printing press in England by William Caxton in 1476. The use of the printing press made it possible to mass produce and widely disseminate the written word. By choosing the London dialect as the standard for his printed books, Caxton halted the rapid language changes of the earlier years. While the pronunciation of English has changed significantly in the interim, the system of orthography (spelling) has altered relatively little since Caxton.

Another factor that influenced the development of Modern English was literary. Chaucer, Gower, and Lydgate had used the London dialect, and — as the major English writers of Middle English — helped to establish that dialect as the standard. During the English Renaissance of the sixteenth and seventeenth centuries, a similar process on a worldwide scale occurred. The works of several great writers, especially Edmund Spenser, William Shakespeare, and John Milton, won for English a high place in the world of learning and literature. Through their imaginative variations in making adjectives, nouns, and verbs work interchangeably in the English sentence, these writers demonstrated how flexible and dynamic the emergent language could be.

A third factor in the development of modern English was geopolitical, the rapid emergence of English as a world language as England became a world power about the beginning of the seventeenth century. Because of the mercantile and imperial contacts and the growing prestige of England, the English language frequently became the official language of governments in the New World. In the United States, the people who emigrated from Holland, Sweden, Germany, Poland, Russia, and many other countries hastened to learn the language of their new home, so that a generation later their descendants were added to the English-speaking list. But these same people contributed to the general expansion of the English language, for the overlapping of other languages with English, occurring especially in the United States, resulted in numerous loan words that were indiscriminately added to the earlier German and Norman-French vocabulary.

If a language is to triumph geographically and culturally, there must be forces other than those that provoke change, dissemination, and

> Languages constantly change, but there are certain conservative forces which obscure the process. Among them the influence of writing is perhaps the most important; written forms remain stable long after the spoken forms they represent have changed. If one considers the great gap between English speech and English spelling, for example, one can get a good idea of the conservatism of writing. In spite of the historical priority of speech, educated people who speak a language with a written form tend to think of the written form as prior to and more fundamental than their speech.
>
> — M. W. Bloomfield and L. Newmark, *A Linguistic Introduction to the History of English* (1965)

assimilation. There must also be forces for stabilization. Probably as a reaction against the freedom with which the language was used in the seventeenth century, the eighteenth century saw the development of prescriptive grammarians who tried to create a body of rules to stabilize the English language much as the earlier Latin grammarians had done with Anglo-Saxon. Another powerful agent for stability was the development of the English dictionary. Perhaps the most influential was that of Dr. Samuel Johnson, whose famous *A Dictionary of the English Language* appeared in 1755. In the American colonies the immediate impact of conservative reforms on speech was minimal, for by then typical American speech patterns had already been established. The tyranny of the grammatical laws was most dramatically felt in the relation of the spoken to the written word. The emergence of dictionaries and grammars has tended to distort the importance of writing, and only with recent linguistic studies has the written word been placed in its proper perspective, as something related, but not superior, to the spoken word.

EXERCISES

1. For other approaches to language history, read the introductory articles in a good dictionary such as *The American Heritage Dictionary of the English Language* or the *Webster's New Collegiate Dictionary.*

2. Trace the etymological sources of the following words: green, yellow, white, brown, goat, comma, paragraph, radical, history. Do

etymologies suggest how you can use a word in a new or unfamiliar way?

3. Look at the list of Indo-European words in the Appendix of *The American Heritage Dictionary*. Do many of our basic English words for concrete objects in, for example, our environment change radically throughout history? If not, why?

4. Get hold of a late eighteenth- or early nineteenth-century grammar (most college libraries have copies) and make some comparisons with a modern handbook. What are the major changes you can detect? How are these changes important to you?

5. One of the dynamic characteristics of the English language is its vocabulary "borrowing" capacity. Trace the ancestry of the following words in your dictionary to check on what foreign language they were "borrowed" from:

polo	bagel	banjo	nickel	vampire
tycoon	bamboo	toboggan	academy	plaid
ski	robot	sleigh	shampoo	canyon
swastika	tea	sauna	bankrupt	shamrock
flamingo	zero	taco	lilac	appendix

6. Another way a new word is added to a language is through combining two different words. A major source of new words occurs by adding a prefix, often from a foreign language, to a word. Using your dictionary, check the language source (Latin, Greek, etc.) of the following prefixes and the meaning of each:

anti-	para-	mis-	contra-
meta-	intra-	super-	juxta-
cata-	post-	ultra-	retro-

7. Write an essay in which you explore (analyze) the use of slang and jargon in your vocabulary and that of your friends. Break down the sources of the slang and jargon into specific areas (devote a paragraph to each) — for example, the words derived from the drug culture ("high," "upper," "downer," "bummer," etc.) or words related to sex, food, sports, politics, and so forth. If you are unsure of the meanings and sources of the slang words, consult a dictionary such as *The Dictionary of American Slang*. In your summary paragraph come to a conclusion about the source or sources that seem to be most frequently used by you and how these sources relate to your perception of self.

INDEX OF
⚜ RHETORICAL DEVICES ⚜

Example and Illustration

Metaphor

Narration

Testimony

INDEX OF
☙ SUBJECTS AND NAMES ❧

Piaget, Jean, 179
Pictography, 217–218
Pike, K., 31
Pirsig, Robert M., 116–117, 140–142
Plato, 28, 223
Poetry: and definition, 73; and figurative language, 107, 110–111; and moving images, 210; and sounds, 183, 184, 185
Point of view, 126, 133, 134, 135, 137, 138
Pooh-pooh theory, 224
Porter, Cole, 167
Pretentiousness, 168
Printing press, 204, 209, 220, 221, 231
Proposition, 48, 49
Prose, 64; figurative language, 110; and language of film, 211; rhythms, 156, 162, 185. *See also* Language
Psychology Today, 20
Punning, 182–183
Purpose: figures of speech, 180, 184; and sentence form, 159; of speech, 195; and structure, 57, 88, 89, 100, 101, 109, 117, 135; and word choice, 165, 172. *See also* Thesis

Quotation, 53, 57, 58, 78

Reality: and language, 4–6, 10, 223; and origin of writing, 221; and symbolism, 177–179
Redfield, Robert, 199
Refutation, 48, 50
Reich, Charles, 88, 99–100, 199, 202
Rhetoric: Aristotle's, 27, 28, 64–65; assumptions,

26–31; authentic writing, 4–5, 6–7, 51; methods, illustrated, 31–40
Rhyme, 184, 185, 188, 228
Rhythm: and figures of speech, 180; in film language, 213; language, 13–14, 153–156, 184, 187; and oral language, 202; in paragraphs, 53, 57; in sentences, 156–162, 189, 190; and sound patterns, 184, 185; and style, 187, 191; and voice and tone, 167; and words, 165
Rich, Adrienne, 7, 8, 17
Richards, I. A., 16
Riesman, David, 200, 220
Rockas, Leo, 67
Rogers, Carl, 51
Roosevelt, Franklin D., 112
Roszak, Theodore, 64, 179, 199, 202
Roughley, Theodore, 135–136

Saline, Carol, 154–155
Samuels, Dr. M., 153–154
Sarris, Andrew, 215
Scenes, film, 212, 213
Sears, Laurence, 72–73
Seldes, Gilbert, 209
Self: and authentic rhetoric, 26–31, 40; McLuhan on, 209; and metaphor, 111; reality and, 4–18; and style, 152, 156
Sentences: and example and illustration, 74, 77; and film language, 212; history of English, 228, 229; McLuhan's basic unit, 207; and origin of writing, 218; rhythm and style, 156–162, 187–188, 203; stylistic analysis, 189–190,

194. *See also* Balance; Loose sentences; Periodic sentences; Topic sentences
Sequences, film, 212, 213
Seven-Up advertisement, 160
Sexual roles, 7
Shakespeare, William, 114–115, 173, 182, 231
Shalit, Gene, 215
Shots, film, 212, 213, 214
Sidney, Sir Philip, 180
Sight, and language, 201
Significance, 55, 60, 70, 73, 81, 85, 142, 212
Simile, 92, 102, 103, 109, 191
Simon, John, 215
Simon, Paul, 3
Singer, Aubrey, 53, 56
Skinner, B. F., 11, 28
Slang, 168
Slater, Philip, 101
Smith, Logan P., 164
Smothers, Tommy, 111
Sounds, 188; and language of film, 212–214; origin of language, 224; and spoken word, 199–203, 222; and style, 167, 183–185, 188, 189, 194; writing, 218
Space, in description and narration, 132, 133, 135, 145
Speech, 40; and English language, 231, 323; oral language, 198–203; and origin of language, 223; patterns, 158; and writing, 209, 217–218
Speeches, 202; stylistic analysis of, 188, 191–195
Spenser, Edmund, 231
Stackpoole, E. V., 116

Stafford, Jean, 12–13, 202
Steinbeck, John, 138, 163
Stern, Paula, 52
Stevens, Wallace, 175, 177–179
Stevenson, Robert Louis, 164
Stream-of-consciousness, 15, 48, 55
Structure: analysis, 80–89; and authentic rhetorical method, 32; cause and effect, 115–128; choice of, 61–62, 101; and choice of words, 165, 168; classical pattern, 48–50; comparison and contrast, 92–101; concluding paragraphs, 56–59; definition, 62–74; description and narration, 132–145; of English, 228, 229; example and illustration, 74–79; of film, 212, 214; of "Gettysburg Address," 33–35, 40; and grammar, 221, 222; introductory paragraphs, 50–56; of Kennedy's "Poetry and Power," 38–39, 40; metaphor and analogy, 102–111; middles, 59–60; role of, 46–48, 60; of sentences, 157–158, 188, 189, 194, 203; and sound, 185; and style, 156, 187
Style, 32; defined, 152–153; figures of speech, 180–183; of "Gettysburg Address," 34–35, 40; imagery, 177–180; of Kennedy's "Inaugural Address," 195; of Kennedy's "Poetry and Power," 40; rhetorical analysis of, 187–195; and rhythm,

153–156; sentence rhythm, 156–162; and sound, 183–185; and words, 165–175
Styron, William, 143–145, 181
Subjectivity: and denotation and connotation, 171–172; and description and narration, 133, 135–138; and rhythm, 155, 162
Substance: and film shots, 212; in "Gettysburg Address," 33, 34–35; and rhythm, 156; and structure and style, 32, 40, 46; and words, 166
Summary, 50, 68, 72, 83, 87, 88, 98
Swift, Jonathan, 182, 188
Symbols, 177–180, 188, 198, 211, 217, 224
Synecdoche, 183
Synonym, 62–63
Syntax, 222, 229, 230

Television, 209, 210, 211
Tennyson, Alfred, Lord, 185
Testimony, 77–79
Thesis, 49, 50, 60–61, 62; and comparison and contrast, 101; and definition, 64, 73; and example, 74, 75, 76; statement, 55, 70, 81, 86, 97; and testimony, 77, 79
Thoreau, Henry David, 17, 21–22, 107–109, 111–112, 158, 184; stylistic analysis, 188–191
Time: in description and narration, 132, 133, 143–145; in television, 210
Time magazine, 52–53, 58

Toffler, Alvin, 76–77
Tomlinson, H. M., 173
Tone, 56; and balance, 189; of film language, 213; and rhythm, 153; and word choice, 166–170, 188
Topic sentences: and comparison and contrast, 95; in essays, 70, 71, 81, 82, 86, 87, 97; in example and illustration, 74, 76; in paragraphs, 67, 68, 69, 83, 119; and testimony, 78; undeveloped, 207
Transitions, 50, 55, 58, 68, 71, 84, 85, 89, 96, 97, 99, 101, 118, 120, 123, 124, 203
Twain, Mark, 12, 186

Unity, in description and narration, 132–133, 135, 137, 142
Untermeyer, Louis, 103–104

Van Doren, C., 43
Vanderbeek, Stan, 210
Vinci, Leonardo da, 167
Vocabularies, 6; in film shots, 213; and origin of English, 228
Voice: and rhythm, 153; and word choice, 166–170, 188

Warren, Robert Penn, 80, 103
Weaver, Richard M., 25, 161, 169–170
Wells, H. G., 186
Whitman, Walt, 173–174
Williams, William Carlos, 7
Winterowd, W. Ross, 60, 116
Wittgenstein, Ludwig, 104
Wolfe, Tom, 138–139, 176